Mazda
MX-5
Miata

© **Liz Turner 2009**

First published in 2002 as *You & Your Mazda MX-5/Miata*

This edition published in November 2009

British Library cataloguing-in-publication data:
A catalogue record for this book is available
from the British Library

ISBN 978 1 84425 698 3

Published by Haynes Publishing,
Sparkford, Yeovil, Somerset BA22 7JJ, UK

Tel: 01963 442030 Fax: 01963 440001
Int. tel: +44 1963 442030 Int. fax: +44 1963 440001
E-mail: sales@haynes.co.uk
Website: www.haynes.co.uk

Library of Congress catalog card no. 2009928030

Haynes North America, Inc.,
861 Lawrence Drive, Newbury Park,
California 91320, USA

Printed and bound by JF Print, Sparkford

Haynes Enthusiast Guide

Mazda
MX-5
Miata

H16 SJA

Liz Turner

MAZDA MX-5/Miata
CONTENTS

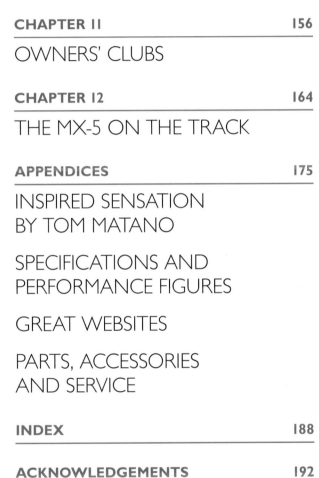

INTRODUCTION
RETURN OF THE ROADSTER

Driving enthusiasts all over the world should fall down on their knees and thank Mazda for the MX-5. If this cute, simple and brilliant roadster had not proved that there is a demand for a small, affordable sports car – and profit to be made from making one – there would have been no Lotus Elise, MGF, Honda S2000 or Pontiac Solstice. Even the TT and Z4 owe it thanks.

Back in the 1970s, in the years of BM-X ('before MX-5'), the roadster was almost dead. The once-teeming ranks had all but disappeared. The fear of ferocious safety regulations being introduced in the USA killed off all but the more expensive sports models, and new cars that might have been open-tops in previous times now sprouted metal rooflines.

By the end of the 1960s, Triumph and MG had become part of the same company, BMC, and Donald (later Lord) Stokes found himself in charge of a host of rundown factories and very little investment cash.

Based on the fact that the combined sales of the Triumph GT6 and TR6 had exceeded that of the MGB and MGB GT in 1968, it was decided that the next sports car would be a Triumph (even though MGBs had outsold Triumphs from 1964 to '67).

Given the flares, fat ties and triangular side-burns fashionable types chose to wear in the seventies, the awkward wedge of cheese known as the TR7 can perhaps be forgiven, but enthusiasts still yearned for the sheer abandoned joy of a roadster. That is perhaps the only explanation for the existence of, and the continued sales of, the Alfa Romeo Spider in 1988, which had been launched as the Duetto back in 1966.

Other choices for the enthusiast included the thrilling but thuggish TVR S with its attendant build-quality problems, and also in the UK the underrated Reliant Scimitar 1800 Ti, which went like the shine off a shovel thanks to its turbocharged Nissan engine but looked like a mouse and used Mini Metro instruments.

By the early 1980s, car magazines were constantly running wistful little pieces about the MGB replacement. (The MGF, of course, arrived about a decade late.) Nevertheless, despite the obvious gap

in the market, Mazda's decision to build the MX-5 can still only be described as brave.

In 1982, Ford US produced the two-seater Barchetta concept, designed by Ghia and received with delight at the Frankfurt Motor Show. The numbskulls who attended subsequent focus groups, however, panned its curvy body and diminutive size, so it was put on ice and, instead, six years later, Ford offered the American public the Mercury Capri.

To western enthusiasts, with their gaze fixed on MG and Lotus, it was almost impertinent of a Japanese company to try to fill the gap left by the great Brits, and beat the Italians at their own game. In fact, the MX-5 would be one of a clutch of cars to turn the image of Japanese cars upside down, along with the Toyota MR2 and the stunning Honda NSX, the Lexus LS400 and Nissan 300ZX, which all burst on to the scene at the end of the 1980s.

However, they were all battling against the early reputation of Japanese cars for rust, gauche looks and the liberal use of Eezee-bend metal trim. Even when their reputation for reliability and generous equipment had been laid down, Japanese cars were still easily dismissed in the West for their poor ride, uninspiring handling and characterless grey plastic interiors.

In the States during the early 1980s, the prejudice ran deeper. Japanese imports were kicking the corporate butts in Detroit and were now officially suspected of wearing 666 badges on their boots. There were also plenty of parents and grandparents of potential buyers who still hadn't come to terms with what had happened at Pearl Harbor.

It is therefore amazing – and gratifying – that a group of like-minded and determined individuals from Japan and America, with some inspiration and help from their allies in Britain, worked together to create a car that has captured hearts all around the world.

For this they should be congratulated, and we should give thanks again for a company brave enough to give people, not what they think they need, but what they really, really want.

← **The MX-5 brought back the kind of wind-in-the-hair thrill enjoyed by MG, Triumph and Lotus owners in the 1960s.**

CHAPTER I
EAST MEETS WEST COAST

From the privileged position of retrospect, it seems obvious that the Mazda MX-5 had to happen – of course there would be a market for a gorgeous, inexpensive sports car. The man who actually said this out loud to Mazda's MD, Kenichi Yamamoto in 1979, US journalist Bob Hall, says now: 'I'm no genius. The concept was a no-brainer. My biggest fear when we were working on the project was that someone else would do it first.'

However, no one did, and the seed Bob planted struggled like grass breaking its way through concrete before it finally saw daylight. Project chief Toshihiko Hirai has said: 'There were times when a small breeze from the wrong direction could have blown the project away.'

His right-hand man, Steve Kubo, adds: 'There was a lot of controversy inside Mazda, because many people did not understand the necessity of an LWS (lightweight sports car). They'd say: "But we have a lot of rain! It's cold! Room for just two people? But we have a family!"'

Design manager Tom Matano, says: 'When we were working on the initial concept and a theme, we felt that it was the right car that everyone had forgotten or abandoned due to safety and other regulatory reasons. We had a conviction. I found out later that MG and others had tried to bring them back without any success. Their proposals were killed on the basis of the scale of economy at many companies. I felt that we were so fortunate because we took a very narrow window of an opportunity at the right time with the right people. In retrospect, we couldn't have done it if one of the key people was not there, or we had tried at any other time.'

Bob Hall is more blunt, saying: 'This was not a well-liked project – there were those in the company who thought it was an utter waste of money. In fact, we had to avoid some people deliberately.'

Mazda looks West

As with so many of life's pleasures, timing was everything. Mazda had suffered greatly through the oil crisis of the 1970s, but good times were on their way. We may laugh or blush (depending on our age) at the memory of designer stubble, red braces and jackets with pushed-up sleeves, but the early 1980s was an economic boom time, and Mazda was forging an astonishing recovery. Its mainstays were the 323, 626, 929 and small commercial vehicles, plus the RX-7 sports car, which was selling well.

Layout engineer Norman Garrett says: 'I really don't think there was another company in the world that could have done this, who had the money, the engineering arrogance – and I mean that in a good way – who still used rear-wheel drive and happened to have a sports car which needed an entry-level smaller brother.'

The company's R&D budget at this time was bigger than that of Porsche, Mercedes and BMW combined, and since 70 per cent of its sales were in the US, the company decided to open design studios in America and Europe, to draw in some local talent and create cars to suit that market. The European office was established in Frankfurt; Mazda Automotive North America's Product Planning and Research Division, managed by Shigenori Fukuda, was founded in Irvine, California, opening fully in 1983.

The talent gathered there by the mid-1980s was astonishing. The design team brought with them

← The MX-5 had a long and tortuous development – it's actually incredible that it was launched. (Magic Car Pics)

> **DID YOU KNOW?**
> **Cultural differences**
> When the Japanese were researching what Americans wanted from a convertible, one frequent reply puzzled them. 'A lot of people said they wanted freedom,' says Steve Kubo. 'In Japan the word always has a political meaning. So we were wondering how exactly this car would improve human rights. Eventually I understood. It means freedom from daily life, duty, schedules, freedom at the weekend after all week at work.'

↑ Driving the dream: sun out, roof down and an open road. In the early 1980s the golden era of the roadster seemed over forever. (LAT)

→ Design genius Tsutomu 'Tom' Matano worked in Germany and Australia before joining the California team. (Mazda)

experience and ideas from around the world. The supremely talented senior designer, Mark Jordan, was lured away from GM where his father Charles 'Chuck' Jordan, was vice president of design. He was working for GM's German arm, Opel, in wet, cold northern Europe at the time so the decision to go to sunny California may not have been too hard. He

was joined by two more Opel men, Wu-Huang Chin and Matsao Yagi, with whom he'd established an excellent working relationship in Germany.

Another hero from the MX-5 hall of fame, Tsutomu (Tom) Matano, joined as manager of the design department at the end of 1983. Matano had worked in Germany for BMW and in Australia with

P508 (x508 ベ-2)

タイヤだL

↑ Bob Hall's hurried
sketch of 1979 planted a
seed in Mr Yamamoto's
mind. (Mazda)

GM-Holden as well as in Japan. His main inspirations from his days as a junior designer had been the Italian designers Giugiaro, Bertone and Pininfarina. He says: 'Today, I would add a few more people to my list. I admire Bill Mitchell [GM in the 1950s and '60s] and Tom Gale [vice-president of design at Chrysler who directed the Viper programme and a number of show cars] both for their design and organisational leadership.'

Jordan also puts the Italians, Giugiaro and Pininfarina, on his list of inspiring designers, and adds Jean and Ettore Bugatti and French cars from the 1930s until the modern day. He says: 'Inspiration can come from anywhere: architecture, products, organic forms, but most of all I look for an energy in something and try to translate that energy into a project. When I visit somewhere like the Pebble Beach Concours, I feel a passion and energy from the artistic expression of these historic cars.'

Norman Garrett III, who went on to found the Miata Owners' Club and write the extremely readable *Mazda Miata Performance Handbook*, joined the team in 1984 as layout engineer. He describes the international team he found as: 'a bunch of hot rodders who owned 76 different sports cars between them, ranging from Austin Healey Frogeye (or Bugeye in the USA) Sprites to Lamborghini Countachs.'

And they were based in the land not only of Deuce Coupes and lead-sleds, surf boards and movie stars but of dreams: California, with blue skies above, and the best test road in the world just outside the door, Highway One, the Pacific Coast Highway.

Bob Hall makes a suggestion

One of the first people to join the team was Bob Hall. When he arrived, however, he had no official title or a brief, and wasn't really sure what he was doing there. He says: 'I thought I'd be in PR, but no, when I arrived I found myself in product development.'

Hall is best known worldwide as a journalist and author who has worked for prestigious car titles in the USA and Australia. He has no formal engineering qualifications, but probably inherited some gasoline in his veins from his father, who owned around 300 classic cars including British sports cars. In fact, he learned to drive in a 1955 Austin Healey 100/4. ('A nice tractor with a walnut-grain dash.')

↑ **Shinzo 'Steve' Kubo, was MX-5 project chief Toshihiko Hirai's right-hand man. (Mazda)**

However, he went to high school in Japan, and can speak the language well enough to converse with Sydney restaurateurs and Japanese engineers alike. He says: 'I usually go back to Japan about twice a year to see friends. When I became a journalist, I built up quite a rapport with Kenichi Yamamoto and used to pop in to see him.'

One reason Hall gained favour at Mazda was that he was excited about the RX-7's Wankel rotary engine, rather than predicting its demise as an unreliable white elephant, like most of the scribblers at the time. Yamamoto would even occasionally run ideas for the RX-7 past Hall and, although any journalist would be itching to publish, Bob never betrayed his trust.

In 1979, he was West Coast editor of *Automotive News* and *Autoweek*, and in a now-famous conversation during his regular visit, in Spring 1979, Mr Yamamoto asked him what he thought Mazda should build next, now the RX-7 was finally on sale.

Hall says: 'The obvious idea was to build something using existing running gear. So we talked for a few minutes about what they could put together from the parts box. Then it came to me that Mazda could build a lightweight sports car based on the X508 323, because it was rear-wheel drive.'

If MG had been able to shift almost 40,000 vehicles a year during its last years, Hall was convinced a mass-produced modern and reliable equivalent could sell at least that many. He says: 'I even scribbled a quick drawing on the blackboard.

But I got the impression he wasn't very interested. That was why, when he left the room, I took a quick snap of it, because otherwise I thought I'd forget about it.'

However, Yamamoto-san didn't forget, either. In 1981, Hall found himself at MANA PP&R in California. As he says 'There I was, I wasn't a designer, I wasn't an engineer, working on design proposals.'

One of the first projects he got stuck into was the design of the tailgate for a B-series pick-up, but in February 1982, he felt a sharp tap on his shoulder and there was Mr Yamamoto. 'He asked what I was working on, and when I said a pick-up, he shook his head – they had plenty of people who could do pick-ups. He said: "That's a waste of time. You should do your sports car project."'

It was made clear that this pet project was something he should work on in his spare time, but he was joined for his Friday night homework by Mark Jordan, starting one night in March 1983. He says: 'Bob wanted me to do some sketches because he knew what he wanted to achieve, but couldn't visualise it. He started talking about the proportions and the low hood and I drew a very simple roadster with front-engined, rear-wheel-drive proportions, and it was just a little bit retro'.

LWS a-go-go

By 1983, Mr Yamamoto had been replaced as managing director by Michinori Yamanouchi who decided to set the new studios in America and Japan working on a series of stimulating offline projects, to see what they could come up with if freed from the restrictions of a production schedule. This was known as Offline Go-Go, an example of the Japanese love of English. So the project itself sounds like an echo of the 1960s.

A number of ideas were suggested, some were rejected, such as a series of modular engines and a three-wheeler, those to go ahead at MANA included an MPV, a 'kei' car (a high-tech mini car), a pick-up – and, of course, the roadster, known in the initial-crazy Mazda parlance as LWS (lightweight sports car).

The so-called Tokyo studio – actually in a rented office just outside Hiroshima – headed by Yoichi Sato, decided to make two coupés, one with a front

↑ The three models came together at Mazda's Hiroshima HQ in 1984, the MANA model's featured a removable hard-top, seen here on the ground to the left of the car. (Mazda)

engine and front-wheel-drive layout (FF) and a rear-wheel-drive, mid-engined model, that is the engine would be behind the driver, but ahead of the rear wheels (MR).

The FF would be popular with the company's accountants because it could possibly be based on the platform for the new 323. However, the resulting car would have faced all the criticisms levelled at the Punto-based Fiat Barchetta, that it looked great, but didn't drive like a proper roadster.

It would probably have suited less experienced or enthusiastic drivers, because front-wheel-drive cars tend to understeer. So, if you hammer too fast into a bend, the car will try to keep heading straight on rather than going round the bend. The natural reaction is to back off the throttle a bit, and then the nose tucks safely back in again.

Like the Mini, the FF concept provided a neat engineering solution because the engine runs across the engine bay (mounted transversely) and transfers its drive to the wheels either side. That means more cabin space, with no bulky transmission tunnel required to run down the centre of the car.

The disadvantage, however, is that the front wheels are trying to do two jobs at once – both putting the engine's power down and steering. The result can often be a tugging sensation at the wheel, or in a more powerful car, the wheels may simply spin as you try to turn out of a junction. Considering these problems, it was a real surprise when Lotus chose this route for its new Elan (see page 33).

The mid-engined, rear-wheel-drive structure is a classic sports car layout, which allows a perfect 50/50 weight split. It is favoured by Ferrari and Fiat's X1/9 and was very fashionable at the time, being used by several generations of the Toyota MR2. However, in practical terms, it usually means a small luggage bay at the back and room for a few odds and ends under a front bonnet, sharing space with the spare wheel. Rover opted for this layout for the MGF, and as an added consequence, the MG did not get a glass rear window until 2002. The MX-5 had one by 1998.

MANA's LWS would have a classic front-engined, rear-wheel-drive layout, still allowing a good front-to-rear balance, but also allowing each pair of wheels to get on with a single job – the rear wheels to drive the car and the front wheels to steer. This layout is recognised as a favourite for enthusiastic drivers, but in the early 1980s, it was regarded as old fashioned, and a backward step, because of the way the rear end can step out (much to the delight of those enthusiastic sideways drivers).

Tom Matano says: 'The mid-ship layout was developed for racing cars to get maximum cornering adhesion, it's designed for the track, but it feels artificial when compared to the FR (front-rear) layout.

'The lightweight sports car is like a pair of jogging shoes; the mid-ship layout is like a pair of spiked shoes. It should be better for much higher performance sports cars.

What happened to IAD

IAD appeared destined for great things in the 1980s. The company had branches all over the world, including the USA and Russia. It worked on concept cars such as the futuristic Lotus Venus (below) and the Lincoln Town car, as well as providing an essential subsidiary role for the Mazda design teams.

Tragically, its charismatic proprietor, John Shute, lost his fight with cancer, just as the MX-5 was being taken to people's hearts around the world. IAD was sold to Daewoo in 1994, and the acclaimed Matiz was produced at the Worthing studio, which had created the V705 prototype for Mazda. This facility was sold to TWR in 2001.

British design consultant, IAD, created some weird and wonderful show cars to advertise its expertise. Mazda called on the company's resources several times while its inhouse teams were over-stretched. (Simon Farnhell)

'The FF [front engine/front-wheel-drive] layout is like riding a chariot. It is not a natural movement when turning a corner.'

To describe why the LWS should be rear-wheel drive, Tom uses the example of a horse and rider – a theme that frequently recurs in the MX-5 story. He says: 'I asked everyone in the room to close their eyes to picture racehorses turning a last corner and heading for the finish line. They are kicking their hind legs to push forward, their fore legs are balancing and aiming towards the home stretch.

'Then, change the scene, where you are turning a last corner towards a goal on an oval track.

You are feeling the ground on your hips and your legs are kicking forward. Your hands are balancing and there's wind-on-your face. This is the most natural way of turning a corner. You watch the way animals run and turn. The idea of the lightweight sports car is to feel as close to this natural feeling in a four-wheeled vehicle.

'I am not sure whether my racehorse won the argument or not. But, from that day onward, this engine layout issue was not discussed. It may have been a pivotal moment for the MX-5 development. Mark Jordan agrees, saying: 'A mid-engined layout would have been totally wrong.'

→ MANA's roadster was a brave concept: its front-engined, rear-wheel-drive layout was considered old-fashioned. (Mazda)

Three cars go head to head

The first drawings for the MANA LWS, known as P729, were produced by Jordan and Yagi. Jordan has always been a Ferrari fan, and he admits there's a touch of the prancing horse about some of his early sketches.

However, he insists his strongest influence was the original Lotus Elan, saying: 'The Elan was the most ideal basis for this car.'

The first hurdle was a trip to Hiroshima in April 1984 where the two studios were to show their work. MANA's sketches were considered rather flat and Hall believes strongly that at this point, the LWS was pronounced clinically dead.

However, the Japanese management felt sorry for the American team, and did not want to crush their enthusiasm so early on with their very first project. So the team was allowed to take the project to clay model stage.

When the model arrived, however, the pendulum swung back towards the West. Sato has said: 'Maybe I was seeing a false image, or didn't see through the real value of the (first) MANA presentation. The roadster was neat and clean, but wasn't really animated. Little did I know that MANA would return with vengeance and such whack four months later.'

In September 1984, the two teams and their three models met again in Hiroshima. The Tokyo Studio's MR car was an angular vehicle, which looked very similar to Toyota's recently revealed concept MR2, (the production car was launched in March 1985). They had even built a running prototype similar in concept to mid-engined performance hot hatches such as the Renault 5 Turbo 2, but ran into problems with noise, vibration and harshness (NVH) because of the firm sporty suspension. Simply softening the suspension would have spoiled the whole effect, so this option was terminated.

The front-drive version looked surprisingly similar to its mid-ships brother, although with slimmer pillars and more of a coupé slope to its roof. It wouldn't turn heads, however. Even at this stage, MANA's model had the feminine curves, pop-up headlamps, open mouth of the production car. (Although perhaps its expression was closer to one of surprise than the now-familiar lovable smile.) It was parked between the two coupés wearing a hard-top with the gaps covered over by red tape and was

favourably received, but then the team whipped off the roof and brought the house down.

Bob Hall remembers: 'The leader of the other studio, Sato, leapt up and said: "We must build this!"'

At the end of the session, the coupés were wheeled away to the dustbin of history, but the FR roadster was still anything but Go Go. This was an offline project, and most people at Mazda still felt there was no market for it. Also, Mazda's PP&D department was swamped with projects considered to be more immediate and more important. These included the 1985 Tokyo Motor Show experimental GT, the MX-03 powered by a triple-rotor engine and featuring four-wheel drive and four-wheel steering. Then there was the idea of a 323 convertible and the MPV also developed from the offline work, with which the LWS was now competing for development cash.

IAD's prototype wows Santa Barbara

In Summer 1985, the British design agency IAD was commissioned to build a running prototype of the LWS. At the time, IAD was a hot new, cutting-edge design company, based in Worthing in the UK, but with offices in France, Germany, Japan, Moscow and California. It turned heads at every motor show with concepts such as the swoopy Lotus-based Venus sports car, which showed only an inch or so of tyre below its four enclosed pods, or a mini-MPV, almost a decade before the Renault Mégane Scenic.

No dimensions for the car to be known as the V705 had been laid down, but the designers at IAD were given the existing clay model and sketches, plus a list of parts from Mazda's existing products. They started with MacPherson struts from a 323 and an engine from a 929 wagon, and created a vehicle similar in construction to the original Lotus Elan with a solid backbone chassis and a GRP body. The red and white interior featured a large console stretching down the centre of the cabin and a furry hand-rest on the two-spoke steering wheel.

← Tokyo's front-engined, front-wheel-drive coupé would have pleased the accountants, but not the enthusiasts. (Mazda)

→ Mid-engined, rear-wheel-drive layout used by Tokyo's MR Coupé was popular at the time; it was used by the MR2 and, later, the MGF. (Mazda)

It looked the part, but it was big and underpowered, or as Bob Hall put it: 'On a hot day it wouldn't have got out of the depressions it made in the tarmac.'

In September 1985, a number of members of the MANA team flew to Britain and tried it out at the grey, cheerless Ministry of Defence test track facility known simply to British automotive journalists as 'Chobham'. (This facility can be spotted in hundreds of UK magazine and TV shoots simply because it is a safe and convenient place for action photography. However, as Mark Jordan remembers, those using it have to watch out for army tanks.)

Jordan wrote in a memo: 'We conducted a test drive of the V705 with three competitor vehicles: a Fiat X1/9, a Reliant Scimitar and a Toyota MR2. We tested each car on a high-speed loop, a road course and a skid pan. The Mazda prototype was completely functional, even down to the cigarette lighter, and felt very realistic as a production model.'

Looking back he says: 'The guys at IAD did a great job, but when I look at that car now, it had the round mouth shape, but its doors and the back were so flat. Cars around us at the time were so tight and angular like the Honda CRX and the Pontiac Fiero, that rounded shape was completely out of the industry. We needed to get that timeless roadster shape, which would live through the trends and wear well in the long-term future. That meant it might not be the trendiest and most fashionable on the block, but it would be one of the most satisfying for the long term. Our next two models became more and more rounded as we went along. That was really quite radical at the time.'

The prototype's next stop was due to be Hiroshima, but the managing director in charge of Mazda's Testing and Research Division, Masataka Matsui, decided he wanted to drive the car in its natural habitat first. So, in October 1985, the V705 stopped off in California, escorted by John Shute, the charismatic proprietor of IAD, and Mr Matsui flew in to LA to take a test drive through Santa Barbara.

In retrospect, this was not a smart move if the company wanted to keep the project secret. Santa Barbara was full of car nuts who were not fooled by the phoney Toyota badge on the car's number plates.

Norman Garrett remembers: 'Swarms of people were chasing us. We passed a Porsche showroom with about half a dozen people in there looking at 911s, but as we stopped at the lights, one by one

they came across and had their noses up against the glass looking at us.'

As if by magic, cameras appeared, and Garrett almost drove over one determined individual, but there was worse to come. As the car crawled past a café in State Street, trapped in a tight traffic jam, Bob Hall's horrified eyes met those of an astonished group of journalists and a photographer from *Road & Track*, having lunch after a coast-to-coast drive for a feature in the magazine. Coffees and jaws were dropped, and Hall had to make a frantic trip to the office to plead with the editor, John Dinkel, to stifle the scoop of the decade.

He says: 'I said, if they wanted to see a car like this built, they mustn't write about it. It would have been so easy for it to be killed off. And they didn't publish a word.'

That night, an elated group including Matsui, Garrett, Hall, Tom Matano, chief engineer Toshihiko Hirai, Steve Kubo and Shigenori Fukuda had dinner, and talked for hours over several bottles of wine.

Discussions of thrilling and responsive transport led to a session of 'horse talk' and it was probably here that Mr Hirai came up with the slogan that would hang above the studio where the MX-5 was born: 'Oneness of horse and rider'.

At the meal, the Americans were lobbying hard. Matsui had enjoyed the car and was impressed by the response to it, but he was still cautious. Were people just excited because they didn't know what the prototype was? Was it just because it was red and sporty?

'We were walking back to the hotel,' says Garrett, 'and Mr Matsui looked up at the sky and just said: "Maybe we should build this car". And all of us wanted to punch the air and cheer. If it had the support of such an influential man, it was going to happen.'

The next stage in the long, slow process was a feasibility study, and finally some proper money was put into the project. At this stage, Tom Matano was design manager, with Mark Jordan as senior designer, working with the talented Wu-Huang Chin, who would continue to work on future generations of MX-5. The clay modellers from IAD now also decamped to the California studio to work on the project, adding some razor-sharp humour to the excitement in the studio. Mark Jordan says: 'IAD had a great programme of being able to contract out their people. We had a choice of a couple of companies, but we were impressed by their talent. They were great modellers, including Martin McCreath and Brian Innocent.'

One day the latter was outside helping Bob Hall work on his MGA, and mentioned casually that he had worked on the model of the original.

A test drive was also undertaken in Japan in which a convoy of lucky drivers took turns to exercise their right feet around mountain roads in a 911 Cabriolet, a Fiat X1/9, Fiat Spider 2000, a Lotus 7 and an Elan, and make notes. Typically, the Elan's shocks had gone and the electrics were playing up, but everyone agreed it was the most enjoyable and direct-feeling car. Norman Garrett comments: 'People say we copied the Elan. In fact there's not a single nut or bolt shared, but we wanted to capture its spirit.'

A second full-size model of the LWS was completed by December 1985 and a month later, serious studies into production feasibility began. It was still possible that the next car on the MANA list would have been the kei car, which was technically innovative, but probably suitable only for the Japanese market.

Instead, Fukuda was lobbying for the LWS. He said to Yamanouchi Michinori: 'There's something about this car. Everyone working on it feels something. Surely this passion must translate to the market.'

He got his wish. The LWS was presented to the board of Mazda's managing directors and Bob Hall's old friend, Kenichi Yamamoto, now president of the company, supported the project wholeheartedly. At last, the LWS was going into production.

MX-04 Concept 1987

Mazda gave a tempting taste of what was to come when it unveiled the MX-04 at the 1987 Tokyo Motor Show. The MX-02 and MX-03 had both been rather uninspiring family cars, but this car was a sporty two-seater. The chassis could be fitted with a choice of three glassfibre bodies, a wedge-shaped coupé, or two different roadsters, none of which shared the finished MX-5's curves.

There were major differences under the skin, too. The MX-04 was powered by a rotary engine and had electronically controlled four-wheel drive. However, it shared the backbone chassis developed for the new car and used a similar double-wishbone suspension set-up.

Suzuki displayed a mid-engined roadster concept at the same show, causing Mazda executives a few sleepless nights as they wondered whether another manufacturer might pip their LWS to the post.

The wedge-shaped MX-04 Coupé was shown at the 1987 Tokyo Motor Show. It had four-wheel drive and a choice of three bodies.

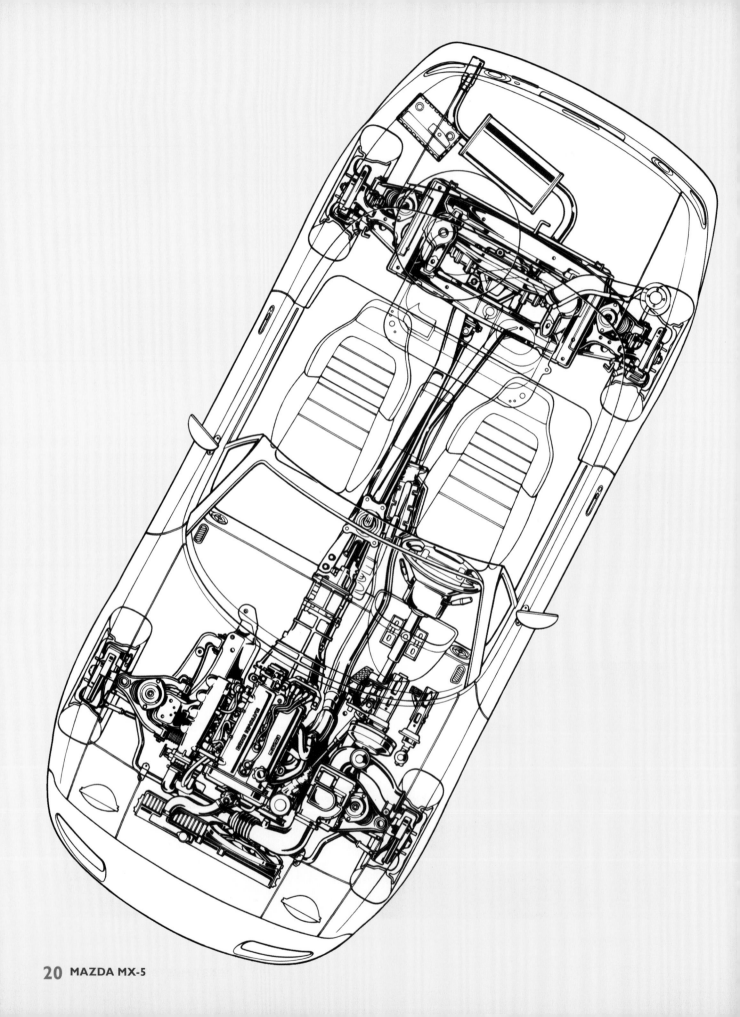

CHAPTER 2
CREATING THE PERFECT ROADSTER

Once the official go-ahead had been given for the lightweight sports car, in January 1986, a project manager was appointed. Step forward Toshihiko Hirai, chief engineer and to many the father of the MX-5. (Barbara Beach, ex-publisher of *Miata Magazine*, suggested this makes Bob Hall the biological father, while Hirai was the man who nurtured the Mazda to adulthood.)

The Japanese do not have the same history of building or driving small sports cars as the British and Americans, but Hirai understood exactly what the LWS should be and how to achieve it. Although he has now retired, members of the team still speak of him with a respect bordering on reverence.

A broad outline had already been established. The LWS should be a traditional sports car with an engine in the front and the power should be laid down by the rear wheels. The gearchange should be short and it should snick into place, the steering should be sharp and communicative. The engine should be a four-cylinder twin-cam; Mazda's famous rotary engine simply did not have the right personality. Marketing necessity also dictated it should be relatively low-powered. This was partly to separate it from the RX-7, but more importantly, having seen a whole generation of hot hatches killed off by huge insurance premiums, Mazda was keen to keep insurance costs low. Reasonable repair costs were a priority when choosing parts and designing body panels for the same reason.

The new car would be close in spirit to an MG Midget or a Sprite, cheap, cheerful but great fun at the weekend and capable of taking to the track.

Mark Jordan says: 'As enthusiastic car guys, we always want more power. But the balance was so good, that it was not just about the engine power, but the overall handling and the exhilaration of the car.'

Bob Hall christened it the KISS car, as in: Keep It Simple, Stupid. And yet creating such a car was anything but simple. As well as such technical considerations as judging the inevitable compromise

between flat cornering and ride comfort, performance versus economy, compact size and decent legroom, the team also had to take into consideration a raft of legislation covering emissions and crashworthiness. Then, of course, there was the high level of convenience and luxuries expected by drivers in the '90s compared with those in the glory days of the 1960s. In fact, in terms of equipment, the MX-5 would offer more electrical goodies as standard than most family models in the UK.

Mr Hirai approached this task by laying down the essentials for the LWS on what assistant Steve Kubo describes as his 'Fish skeleton' chart (see pages 22 and 24). Translated into English by Steve Kubo for this book, the chart has a central backbone running across the page with six lines, like ribs drawn at right angles to it.

This car needed kan sei, which in engineering terms translates roughly as 'feel'. So the ribs are labelled 'Seeing', 'Listening', 'Touch', 'Direct feel of brakes', 'Direct feel of performance' and 'Handling', the last two being linked by horizontal lines labelled 'Front engine/Rear-wheel drive' and 'Weight reduction'. More markers with notes along each rib note how the main objective set by that line can be achieved. For example, in 'Seeing', he notes that the open top must be stored below the deck line and that the fuel filler and dials should be round. Under 'Listening', he demands a strong and roaring exhaust note, yet the driver must be able to enjoy their radio at up to 80kph (50mph). Under 'Touch', he notes that

← The MX-5 has a very traditional sports car layout, and to achieve its supremely balanced handling, as much weight as possible is kept within the wheelbase. (Mazda)

DID YOU KNOW?
Porsches over the limit
Mazda's engineers 'totalled' three Porsche 944s, described by *Car & Driver* at the time as 'the best handling car in the world', while examining the on-the-limit handling. They knew that some of the most exciting cars tend to swap ends when pushed, and were keen to avoid this. As at least one British journalist spun the MX-5 on the first Japanese test drive, they may have been a little disappointed, but the Mk1 MX-5 was still one of the most forgiving and predictable sports cars on the market.

ONENESS BETWEEN HORSE AND RIDER

HANDLING

- High rigid body structure
- Minimise yaw moment of inertia (Shorter front/rear overhang)
- Low centre of gravity
- Minimise the camber-angle against the road surface (Adopting double wishbone suspension front/rear)
- Reduce steering gear ratio (Direct feel)
- Leave not uncomfortable kick-back through the steering mechanism
- Tight seat-holding
- Suspension/steering mechanism with linear and flat response
- Tyres

FRONT ENGINE/REAR-WHEEL DRIVE
- Develop exclusive matching tyres
- Pedal layout, suitable for heel-and-toe

WEIGHT REDUCTION
- Weight reduction of suspension parts (Control arm, tyres)
- Linear engine torque (From low to high speed range)
- Long travel of the accelerator pedal stroke
- Improve rigidity of whole steering mechanism
- PPF: Power Plant Frame (Direct connecting feel from the accelerator pedal through to the rear tyres)
- Improve horizontal rigidity in suspension system
- Waving hair in the wind
- Leave firmness which is not uncomfortable
- Appropriate location of foot rest
- Close gear ratio

DIRECT FEEL OF PERFORMANCE

TOUCH

- Rigidity in all operational functions (Brake, shift, clutch release, knobs etc.)
- Waving hair in the wind
- Thinner carpet
- Small shift lever knob possibly made of wood
- Being able to rest an arm on the top edge of the side door
- Short-stroked gear shift with knotchy feel
- Accelerator pedal travel (65mm)
- Uncovered (visible) rag-top link mechanism

DIRECT FEEL BRAKES

- Handbrakes (Realise high rigidity in the brake mechanism)
- Non spongy brakes
- Vehicle weight reduction
- Low centre of gravity
- 50/50 vehicle weight distribution
- Cooling
- As much possible to reduce leverage of the brake mechanism

LISTENING

- Being able to enjoy audio sound up to 80kph
- No seal (weather strip) separation up to 80kph
- Engine sound getting louder along with the engine speed
- Open top car (Contact outside world and nature)
- Strong and roaring exhaust note
- Eliminate mechanical engine noise (Metal clearance etc.)
- No booming noise at certain engine revolution/vehicle speed

SEEING

- Fuel filler lid location: (On rear fender, rounded-shape)
- Collapsible sun visor
- Tight interior space
- Responsive meters/gauges (Speed, oil pressure etc.)
- Making the car look light weight (Exterior styling, seats, aluminium road wheels etc.)
- Simple interior appearance (Design)
- Upright front window shield
- Round analogue meter
- Open top (Storing the rag top mechanism underneath the belt line)

you must be able to rest an arm on the top edge of the door. Under 'Direct feel of performance' he has added 'Waving hair in the wind'. All these things are essential to the roadster experience. It is also remarkable to realise that every note on the chart describes the MX-5 perfectly, and despite the difficulties, the team never deviated from it.

Elements noted along the more technical lines of the chart include 'Linear engine torque', 'Close gear ratios' and 'Weight reduction', including a note revealing that Mr Hirai had already decided that exclusive matching tyres would be needed to reduce unsprung weight.

At the end of the fish's backbone is the slogan that was hung above the studio: 'Oneness of horse and rider'. This phrase is known to riders all over the world and is commonly used to describe the pinnacle of achievement in dressage, but had also been used to describe the immaculate balance and trust between native Americans and their horses.

For Steve Kubo, it had a personal significance as he regularly enjoyed riding at the Serrano Creek Ranch in California. However, he says it also summoned up an image of a Samurai warrior and his horse. 'Everything is under control, he knows every move.'

Mark Jordan says: 'It was a key phrase we were to follow. We would say to ourselves that this was the type of car you wore. The feedback from any part of this car had to be beyond doubt.'

To achieve the goals on Mr Hirai's list, layout specialist Masaaki Watanabe and his team adhered to the principles so beloved by Colin Chapman: weight should be reduced, while the body should be as rigid as possible, allowing the suspension to do its job.

Engineer Norman Garrett comments: 'The Japanese are very philosophical and I think this project suited their way of thinking because we were

↓ **Balanced handling was to be the core value rather than power; the 1.6-litre MX-5 won *Autocar*'s handling day in July 1990. (LAT)**

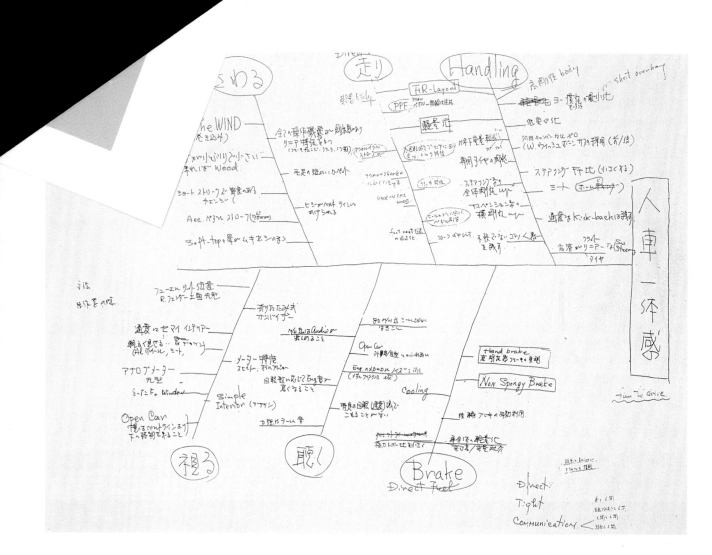

↑ **Toshihiko Hirai laid down every aspect of the LWS in this chart, and made certain that the team stuck to it. As a result, every phrase on this page describes the MX-5 perfectly. (Simon Farnhell, courtesy Mazda)**

searching for the pure essence. Like Colin Chapman, we wanted simplicity and efficiency, ideas which also fit in with the Japanese love of minimalism.'

In some ways, Mazda's lack of sports car heritage was a real advantage. It meant the team could start with a clean sheet and no preconceptions. However, the company's brilliant engineers had access to the most up-to-date technology.

Mazda was already committed to reducing the weight of all its vehicles, and had made great advances in the science of building lightweight vehicles. Plus, as Watanabe's engineers worked to create a strong rigid tub, to eliminate the evils of vibration and 'scuttle shake' the MX-5 became one of the first cars to use computer modelling for the entire design process.

The IAD prototype had used GRP for the body, but the real thing would be a steel structure, using aluminium and plastic where possible. One of the largest body panels on the car, the bonnet, has an aluminium skin – as many British sports cars did,

including the MGA. Strength was put into the front and rear bulkheads, door sills and the floorpan.

To achieve the required feeling of directness between the throttle and rear wheels, Hirai had laid down in his chart that the car would have a power plant frame (PPF), or a torque-tube structure. This featured a rigid beam of cast aluminium, offset to one side with the engine and gearbox assembly bolted on at one end and the rear differential at the other, and resembled the backbone chassis of the Lotus Elan. It was previously favoured by far more expensive machinery including the Ferrari Daytona, Porsche 928 and the C4 and C5 Corvettes. It reduces drivetrain wind-up and release (or shunt) as the throttle is opened up or closed, and as a bonus, assembly line time can be reduced.

From 1992, Mazda added a rear subframe brace which reduced the infamous 65mph vibration, and made the rear subframe more resistant to deflection under cornering loads, so the wheels and tyres stay in better alignment with the ground.

In 1994, when the 1.8 engine was introduced, the front and rear subframes were stiffened and braced, greatly improving rigidity and reducing flex in the platform.

For ultimate stability and grip, the team worked very hard on simply keeping as much of the footprint of the tyre flat on the tarmac for as much of the time as possible. To do so, they opted for a suspension set-up that was well tried and well proven.

The double-wishbone with coil-over shock absorbers will also be familiar to Ferrari fans. This arrangement is a favourite for sports cars because it provides optimum camber during cornering.

Another goal on Mr Hirai's fish skeleton was natural toe-in during cornering. This creates a stable suspension under neutral conditions and tends to damp out the forces of both engine and brake-induced deceleration. It was accomplished by locating the upper control arm ahead of the wheel centreline, creating a torque arm when side forces are introduced.

Weight distribution was also critical to the MX-5's delicately balanced handling. To keep the car flat on the road, a low centre of gravity was essential, and to achieve neutral handling on corners, Hirai noted a 50/50 front-to-back distribution to his chart (for the Mk1 it was actually 52/48 front-to-rear unladen).

Unsprung weight, another enemy of handling, had to be reduced. To explain: springs and shock absorbers support the car's body and chassis as the car moves, but they do not support the wheel, tyres and brake assemblies, so the suspension designer must keep these 'unsprung' pieces as light as possible, allowing them to react quickly to road inputs. A heavy wheel has more inertia when it is deflected upwards by a bump than a light one, so it will lose contact with the road longer, a lightweight wheel will also jar occupants less.

This explains why cost-conscious Mazda went to the expense of creating strong, but super-light, alloy wheels and commissioned special tyres from

↑ To create a feeling of instant response, a power plant frame (PPF) runs along the right-hand side of the propshaft connecting the engine and gearbox to the final drive assembly at the rear. (Mazda)

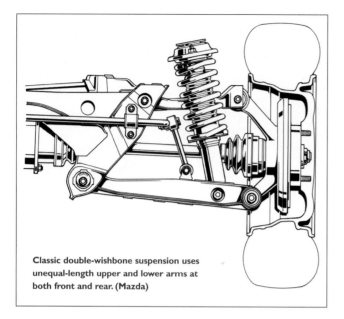

Classic double-wishbone suspension uses unequal-length upper and lower arms at both front and rear. (Mazda)

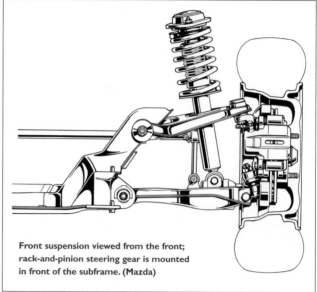

Front suspension viewed from the front; rack-and-pinion steering gear is mounted in front of the subframe. (Mazda)

→ Pressed, perforated aluminium PPF was designed with the help of Mazda's sophisticated computer design programs. (Mazda)

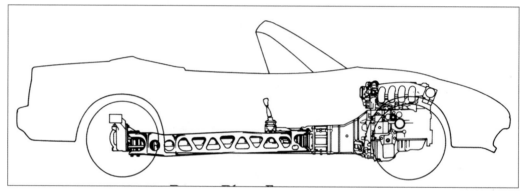

→ A rigid yet light structure was essential to the car's character; wheels and tyres were made specially to reduce the weight. (Mazda)

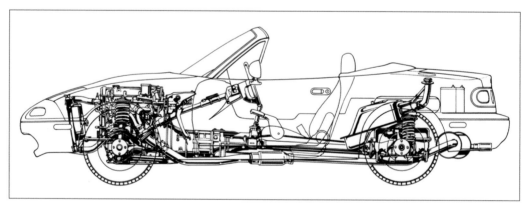

Dunlop. A press release issued at the time of the UK launch of the MX-5 in 1990 reads: 'The new lightweight Dunlop tyre allows full use to be made of the MX-5's roadholding ability and its tread pattern enhances the MX-5's elegant roadster appearance … Originally developed for use in the USA and Japan, subtle changes have been made to suit road conditions in the UK and Europe, with our need for enhanced wet grip.'

A Kevlar crossply 165/555-14in slick or treaded wet-weather form was made available for racing.

The original wheel resembles original 1960s Minilites, although it only has seven spokes as opposed to the classic eight, much to the disgust of some classic car fans. Norman Garrett claims the American team deliberately fitted the final model with a set of Panasport wheels on one side of the final model 'to give the corporate guys a hint'.

Powering up the Mk1

The engine began life as the 1.6-litre four-cylinder unit also used by the Mazda 323, with a cast-iron block and twin camshafts driving 16 valves. But before it settled beneath the MX's bonnet it was lovingly hot-rodded by the same brilliant engineers who had massaged the Wankel rotary engine into reliable life. The compression ratio was raised to 9.4:1 to increase power across the rev range. The cylinder head was ported for optimum horsepower and torque, and the camshafts were reshaped to maximise flow at high rpm. Precise amounts of fuel were delivered by a Multipoint fuel injection system. The crankshaft, rods and pistons were lightened to improve throttle response. A windage tray was added to the aluminium oil sump to reduce drag on the crankshaft from foaming oil.

Power was a modest 114bhp delivered at 6,500rpm and 100lb ft of torque was delivered at a sky-high 5,500rpm, but its response from 2,000rpm was excellent. Another impressive figure, thanks to its trim waistline, was 72.5bhp per litre.

The Mk1 likes to rev hard, and the engine tuning is designed to maximise power while giving an ever-increasing sense of acceleration (as noted on Hirai's chart) to subtly give the driver the impression there's more power than is actually there.

When it came to the exhaust system, the team had two vital and equally important goals. It not only had to let the engine breath efficiently (while meeting all the modern emissions regulations) it also had to make the right, satisfying noise. Hirai's aim was to create a powerful low-frequency sound while eliminating resonance or boom and he taped his favourite exhaust notes – including

↓ **Power came from Mazda's proven Type B6-ZE double-overhead camshaft 16-valve 1,597cc four-cylinder engine. It is mated to a development of Mazda's M-type five-speed transmission. (Mazda)**

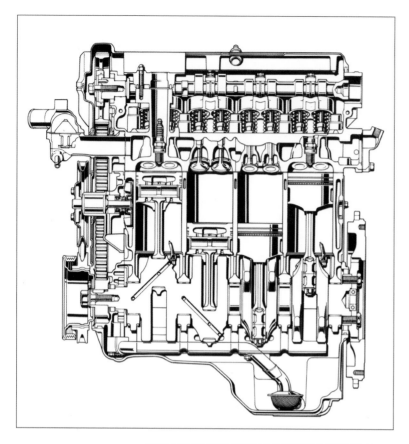

↑ Mazda's four-cylinder, inline engine produced 114bhp at 6,500rpm and 100lb ft of torque at 5,500rpm. (Mazda)

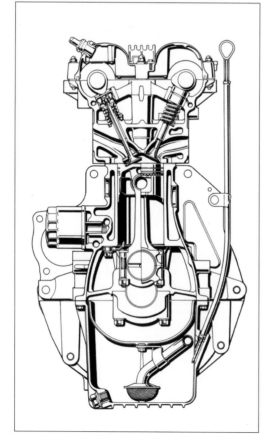

→ Twin overhead camshafts are driven by a single-stage cogged belt and operate four valves per cylinder via inverted bucket-type tappets. (Mazda)

those of the BMW M1 – and played them on his way to work.

In all, the team tried 25 different exhaust systems, before settling on the production stainless steel system. This has a tubular, low-restriction header (manifold), and well tuned muffler (silencer) which gives a crisp, throaty sound that tells anyone who's listening there's a sports car coming. In countries such as Japan and America, the system also featured a high-flow catalytic converter, but in the UK, this did not become standard until 1993.

The driver reaches out to grab the performance using one of the most satisfying gearchanges on the market. The lever is deliberately small and stubby, its action short, matched by that of the short clutch pedal which is precise and decisive. The thrill comes as the revs rise, the car shoots forward, then the lever snicks through the gate without hesitation or undue pressure, and you're off.

The steering, too, is quick and exact, feeding back exactly what the wheels are doing. Each of these actions was studied, considered and perfected long before the eager buyers got to experience the thrill of an MX-5.

Once again IAD were called in to assist by producing a series of test mules, and to help design the roof. Mr Hirai's specifications were that it had to be easily erected or stowed from the driving seat, and its latch had to be simple to use. It had to seal and keep the cabin snug and quiet at up to 80mph. Once folded, it had to stow completely below the car's rear deck line without taking up the entire boot.

The team also had to consider the comfort of those in the car when the roof was folded, but the idea of a windblocker was rejected outright (a decision which made a lot of money for accessory suppliers like Oris). The feeling of wind rushing through the follicles was too important to the roadster experience to be blocked out entirely. So the model went into a wind tunnel with a manikin head covered in long threads of yarn to make sure there was just enough – but not too much – breeze running through its imaginary follicles.

According to Steve Kubo, the inspiration for this came mainly from old Hollywood posters and films. He says: 'A beautiful actress gets into the car and her hair blows in the wind. We wanted to have some mild "wind squall". So we took a prototype to a wind tunnel and studied the windscreen angle and the door mirrors (which have a very important effect).'

← Mazda describes the interior as simple, like the Japanese tea ceremony. A more widely held opinion is that it's plain and rather disappointing, given the beauty of the exterior. (Mazda)

↓ Pop-up headlamps were common in the 1980s because large lamps were still necessary to achieve sufficient illumination. (LAT)

The pop-up headlamps, often assumed these days to have been a deliberately nostalgic touch, were actually forced by necessity. The new car needed good lights, and at the time, that meant a large lamp area, and the pop-up solution was used by a large number of cars at the time, from the MR2 to Porsches. By 1998, when the Mk2 was introduced, the large lamps – and therefore the pop-ups were no longer needed.

Anyone who has ever sat in a 1980s' Mazda, Nissan or Toyota could guess that the MX-5's interior was designed in Japan. To many owners it is the weakest area of the car, and it is a feature that has spawned an accessory market for those who want to brighten up the cheerless plastic with chrome vent rings, coloured dials and console inserts.

The seats and cabin were also clearly created using Japanese human resource data, and so Mazda drivers tend to be under six-foot tall. Large bottoms don't fit easily, either.

It constantly surprises this author that the Japanese have such a clear appreciation of textures when it comes to silk, water and stone, but somehow this never translates into the plastic surfaces within a car.

Tom Matano agrees that the interior is simple, and feels that part of the appeal of the Mazda is the opportunity to personalise it, as so many owners have done.

Mark Jordan comments 'Perhaps it is too plain; it didn't have the character it could have done. It would have benefited from a couple more inches of legroom, too.'

Hiroshima has the final word

Any project involving real passion is also guaranteed to see frayed nerves and bruised egos and hear plenty of raised voices. Despite the harmony of the MX-5's design, at times the atmosphere in the design and engineering studios was far from tranquil.

There were personality clashes, culture clashes and language barriers. Mr Hirai was often the arbiter, but in turn, he fought with Mr Tachibana, who wanted to make the engine more powerful and sophisticated. This would have taken the car closer to its big brother the RX-7, but it would also have added weight and cost to the affordable, lightweight sports car.

The teams in Hiroshima and Irvine also clashed violently as the project approached its conclusion. Starting from March 1986, the design team at MANA had begun work on their third clay model, based on a design by Tom Matano and chief designer Koichi Hayashi, supported by Mark Jordan and Wu-Huang Chin. However, the Americans were unhappy that the car had grown in length to meet some engineering requirements, and not everyone liked the pop-ups.

Brows were furrowed as the model was sent off to Hiroshima in the summer, into the hands of senior

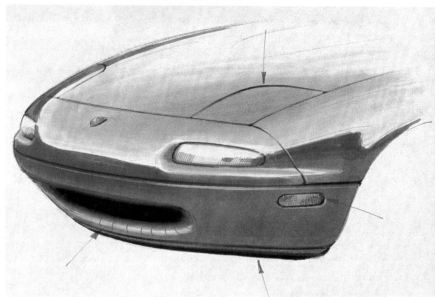

↑ Tanaka added arrows to Wu-Huang Chin's sketches indicating improvements to be made. The slightly drooping mouth was given a smile. (Mazda)

designer Shunji Tanaka. More fireworks followed as Tanaka joined those who felt the car had outgrown its looks, and he eventually persuaded Toshihiko Hirai to reduce the wheelbase by 13mm (half an inch).

He also felt the car needed to lose some girth, although whether this weight was fat or muscle is a matter of opinion.

Tom Matano says: 'After our proposal was approved to go to production, Mr Shunji Tanaka

↑ **MCL went for the obvious joke by getting topless model Linda Lusardi to pose with the MX-5 at the Earl's Court Motor Fair 1989. (LAT)**

was appointed to be the chief designer in charge of the MX-5 programme to take our theme to a realisation. During that period, he was inspired by the Noh expression as it was of true Japanese origin. He was a sculptor before taking up design, and he wanted the MX-5 to have a true Japanese origin.'

Tanaka was an enthusiast of Noh theatre, an ancient art form that makes Kabuki look like cutting-edge improvisation. On a stage empty but for a single pine tree, the actors wear lacquered masks, and their fixed expressions are transformed by slight tilts of the head to catch the light and shadow. Tanaka was a talented sculptor, and used to create Noh masks in his spare time.

Steve Kubo says: 'Tanaka wanted to brush up the design and give it more grammar. The curvature lacked sophistication, so he smoothed it down. The MX-5 has very delicate and sophisticated lines. I've heard it has 250 faces according to the light.'

Even though he was hurt at the time that his design was altered, Tom Matano is gracious about the result. He says: 'Mr Tajima, a well-known photographer, shot photos for the Miata book of development history prior to that historical introduction in Chicago in 1989. I heard that he mentioned to the staff that the MX-5 prototype was the first Japanese car he could photograph from any angle.

'I also heard at the launch, that it was definitely not Japanese, it couldn't be an American originated design. Therefore, it must have been designed in Europe and I was pleased. We wanted Mazda Design to have an identity of its own, and the MX-5 was the first. Cars that followed had similar characteristics. I felt that we were successful in achieving our goals.'

What they said

The reaction of the press and public alike was unadulterated joy, and the enthusiasm poured from keyboards all over the world.

'Its combination of communication, responsiveness, predictability and forgiveness make it the best-handling two-seater I've driven in recent memory – and my memory for such things is good.'
  Dennis Simanaitis,
  Road & Track, March 1989 (USA)
'Brilliant!'
  Autocar's single cover line,
  14 March 1990 (UK)

'Its quick steering, willing engine, short-throw gearbox, taut suspension and fits-like-a-glove driving position give it an instantaneous response that conjure up memories of the old Elan, only this time the headlights work and the water pump lasts a bit longer.'

Peter Egan, *Road & Track*,
November 1990 (USA)

'Its small, lithe, sexy, and best of all, it handles perfectly – factors that characterised Colin Chapman's two-seater and helped put it a generation ahead of contemporary British sports cars. It is perhaps ironic that it should be the Japanese who have recaptured the theme by providing an honest, relatively simple, rear-wheel-drive sports car at an affordable price (if you buy it in Europe or the US, that is) but then, times change.'

Car South Africa, December 1990

'Mazda's nouveau roadster has got it down pat. The MX-5 is an embodiment of the less-is-more philosophy. Its performance is moderate but honest, its styling simple yet significant, its dynamics understated but excellent.'

British journalist **Mike McCarthy** writing for *Wheels*, July 1992 (Australia)

The reaction both stunned and thrilled its creators:
'The best reward I get is when I see someone driving one with a big grin on their face.'

Bob Hall

'Nobody had any idea there would be so much interest, we thought it would be a niche vehicle, but it just exploded.'

Mark Jordan

'We all felt this would never happen again. My favourite thing is to sit at events and see smiling customers having a blast.'

Norman Garrett

'It is my pleasure and beyond my expectation on the success of the MX-5 from the time of its introduction to its sustained popularity today.'

Tom Matano

'We were surprised that the MX-5 sold so well. It is the car that people were waiting for for a long time.'

Steve Kubo

DID YOU KNOW?

Alternative-fuel MX-5

Mazda built three electric MX-5s and one hydrogen-powered car to investigate the potential of these alternative fuels (and, of course as a publicity stunt). As it was laden with 16 batteries, the electric car could only manage a top speed of 80mph (129kph), crawling to 60mph (96kph) in 21.5 seconds. The hydrogen car used a rotary engine from an RX-7 and gave much better performance figures – 13.0sec 0–60mph and a top speed of 93mph (150kph), compared with figures of 8.6sec and 119mph (191kph) for the original 1.6 MX-5.

Mazda produced three nickel-cadmium battery-powered prototypes in the early 1990s, developed jointly with the Chugohu Electric Power Company. (Andrew Fearon)

MX-5 v ELAN

Even now, those who don't know better will say 'The MX-5? They just copied the Lotus Elan, didn't they?'

It's true that Mazda bottled the essence spirit of Colin Chapman's original and that the new car shared a few of the engineering principles, but as the journalists writing back-to-back comparisons in the early days found, the two cars are quite different. They don't share a nut or a bolt and when parked side-by-side they don't even look similar. (Apart from having pop-up headlamps.)

The MX-5's real rival was not the old Elan, but the new one, launched in 1989. (Known as the M100.) The creators of this long-awaited car took an almost opposite approach to those at Mazda, and indicate what could have happened, had a different team taken charge of its development.

On paper, it looked as though the Lotus would win any contest. It had the badge, the history and a high-tech modern design. The body had been styled by Peter Stevens, designer of the McLaren F1 supercar with Gordon Murray, and it could would leave the underpowered Mazda behind on the first open stretch of road.

Westerners often observe with smug satisfaction, that the Japanese merely copy, whereas the British like to go out and invent something new (which may not work, of course). In the case of the MX-5, however, the use of proven technology shows common sense. The LWS had always been envisaged as a cheap car. Rear-wheel drive with wishbones all round might be old fashioned, but it delivered the fun.

Lotus, on the other hand, had too much to prove. Chapman had died in 1982 and the company was still struggling. A large part of the company's business was in research and development for external clients, so the new Elan had to be a showcase of modern technology.

The body was made of an advanced rigid composite. The standard engine was a 1,588cc, 16-valve 'Isuzu Lotus' unit delivering 130bhp at 7,200rpm and 105lb ft of torque; but the 165bhp Turbo SE delivered a storming drive and proved more popular.

There were squeals of disgust from the press when it was announced that the new Elan would be front-wheel drive. However, Lotus insisted this would be front-drive like no other. A new patented 'interactive wishbone' suspension was designed with the help of ex-F1 driver John Miles, in which each front suspension assembly was mounted on a separate raft made of heat-treated aluminium alloy.

On the face of it, they seemed to have succeeded. Most commentators were extremely impressed with the Elan's handling, although if anything, it was so well behaved, it was quite boring to drive.

When *Autocar* pitched it against the BBR Turbo MX-5 in 1991, the writer concluded: 'My vote goes to the Lotus … because it sets a higher overall standard in small sports cars that few of us believed possible. If, in so doing, the Lotus Elan loses some of the fun element, then that can only be put down to the price of progress.'

A less kind quote from *Autoweek* ran: 'The engineers at Lotus have done a wonderful job of teaching this pig to dance, but at the end of the day, you're still dancing with a pig.'

In the end, the main reason for the Elan's failure was its price. In 1990, the 130bhp Elan cost £17,850, the SE £21,620. The standard Mazda 1.6i simply offered far more fun per pound at £14,925 (or £20,220 for the BBR).

The Elan ceased production in 1992. After Bugatti took the company over from GM, a further run of 800 Series 2 cars was built from existing supplies of components in 1994. The licence was then sold to Kia, which produced its own version from 1996 to '97 powered by a naturally aspirated 1.8-litre engine. Just 1,000 were made and a handful of left-hookers made it to the UK.

PERFORMANCE

Elan
1.6-litre 16v dohc four-cylinder Isuzu Lotus
    130bhp @ 7,200rpm
    105lb @ 4,200rpm
    Max speed: 122mph (196kph)
    0–60mph: 7.6sec
    Urban/56mph/75mph:
        25.9/40.8/35.2mpg
    (Urban/90kph/121kph: 10.9/6.9/8.0
        litres/100km)

Elan SE
1.6-litre 16v dohc four-cylinder Isuzu Lotus, water-cooled turbocharger with air-to-air intercooler
    165bhp @ 6,600rpm
    148lb ft @ 4,200rpm
    Max speed: 137mph (220kph)
    0–60mph: 6.7sec
    Urban/56mph/75mph:
        26.2/42.2/31.8mpg
    (Urban/90kph/121kph: 10.8/6.7/8.9
        litres/100km)

The born-again Lotus Elan appeared to hold all the aces against the MX-5 when it was first launched. (LAT)

CHAPTER 3
MORE POWER

'Nice car, needs more power,' was a phrase that echoed from both sides of the Atlantic as soon as the motoring hacks got their hands on the MX-5. In America, a number of owners drove straight to Rod Millen Motorsport or other kindly power brokers willing to slip a turbo under the bonnet. Millen turbo kits were then shipped abroad and were popular as far away as Australia.

Mazda spokesmen must have had to bite their corporate tongues as the same questions came up at every press conference or interview. Would there be a 2.0-litre? Perhaps something bigger, such as a 2.5-litre V6? Would there be a turbocharged version, after all there was a turbocharged Mazda 323?

The answer was a firm no. Handling, not performance was to be the Mazda's core value, and the power had to be kept down to keep insurance premiums low. The Mazda Corporation made its intentions clear when the MX-5 was launched at the 1989 Chicago Auto Show alongside the Club Racer concept car – which had a standard 1.6 engine. The only upgrades for its imaginary weekend racing life were a big-bore exhaust and a set of Bilstein dampers. (See page 40.)

Interviewed on the stand by *Autocar*, Tom Matano commented: 'We wanted to bring back the feeling of weekend amateur racing as well as whetting the appetites of potential buyers by letting them see how the MX-5 can be personalised.'

The journalist also tracked down a spokesman who said firmly that there would not be a turbocharged version, explaining patiently, that a turbo was 'not suitable for this type of vehicle'.

Mr Hirai actually despised turbos, because they added weight and complication, and because they had a bad reputation for reliability in Japan at the time. Plus – a turbo would ruin the carefully tuned sound of the MX-5's exhaust.

Nevertheless, having seen the tuners getting to work in the USA, and with the possibility of Rod Millen Motorsport selling kits in the UK, the British importer MCL (Mazda Cars Ltd) in Tunbridge Wells, Kent, decided to get in first, even before the MX-5's UK launch in 1990. At the time, there were rumours of a 2.0-litre model to be launched in 1992, but in the meantime, the company decided to offer an 'official' turbo, then somehow managed to persuade the parent company to back its project.

Greed for speed and the BBR Turbo

Three British heavy hitters were approached: TWR (Tom Walkinshaw Racing), Turbo Technics and Brodie Brittain Racing with a brief to create an effective, affordable kit, simple enough to be fitted by technicians at Mazda dealerships after suitable training. It was a tall order, in particular because the essential bolt-on nature of the kit meant retaining the standard car's 9.4:1 compression ratio – sky-high for a turbocharged engine.

BBR's package, using a Garrett T25 turbocharger with integral wastegate and water cooling, was deemed the best solution. It boosted power to 150bhp at 6,500rpm and torque by more than 50 per cent to 154lb ft at 5,500rpm

The kit had 68 parts and was offered by 60 selected dealers. BBR made up a new exhaust manifold of high-temperature alloy and added a stainless steel exhaust downpipe and heat shield. A modified sump provided a return oil feed for the turbo lubrication. To cope with the extra heat under the bonnet, pipework for the power steering, oil system and cooling were all to competition spec.

BBR's revised engine management system consisted of an auxiliary electronic brain with three-dimensional mapping to control fuel injection, ignition and boost pressure. This conversion cost

← **Enthusiasts wanted more power from day one, but Mazda wanted to keep insurance premiums low. The 1.8 arrived in 1994. (Jonathan Elsey)**

£3,700 in 1990 and took 12 hours to achieve. To mark the car out visually, the proud owner drove off on special alloy wheels by Oz Racing with five flat spokes in a star pattern. The body wore a rear spoiler and BBR decals on the rear and on each wing beneath the side flashers.

Mr Hirai's reaction is not recorded, but was probably somewhere between bruised feelings and disgust when MCL persuaded the Mazda Corporation, not only to accept this conversion, but to offer Mazda's generous standard three-year or 60,000-mile warranty. It was the only conversion to receive this until the Australian MX-5 SP of 2001. The BBR conversion was also used again for the Le Mans limited edition of 1991.

The BBR Turbo went down well with British journalists. *Fast Lane* wrote: 'The new turbo package is, not to beat about the bush, staggeringly good, achieved without compromising any of the details that make the original MX-5 so appealing'. (December 1990)

Performance Car gushed: 'It's fun time! Snap the gear lever through its gate at 6,000rpm and in no time your hair will be standing on end. The engine delivers the goods in a superbly consistent rush and with no lag. You could be fooled into thinking there was a normally aspirated 2-litre engine under the bonnet.' (January 1991)

The more cautious *CCC (Cars and Car Conversions)* recorded: 'Correction is often great fun in this car, as the extra power helps you hold the tail out and power out of corners at most speeds. But it does get a bit tedious if you're doing it all the time, so one tends to drive the turbo with much more concentrated circumspection on how much boot you give it. You can't really throw it at lanes with abandon.' (1991)

The car did not prove massively popular considering the thousands of standard cars snapped up in the UK. Around 750 kits were supplied in the UK and a further 150 overseas between November 1990 and September 1991, but the number of actual conversions is unknown. It is estimated that only around 250 were made in the UK, and these cars are usually sprayed red,

↑ The Mazda's brilliant handling made it an instant hit, but some drivers yearned for more power. (LAT)

↗ The BBR kit had 68 parts, including a Garrett T25 turbo. It could be fitted by 60 selected Mazda dealers and was covered by a full warranty. (LAT)

→ British importer, MCL, got together with Brodie Brittain Racing to produce the 150bhp BBR Turbo. (LAT)

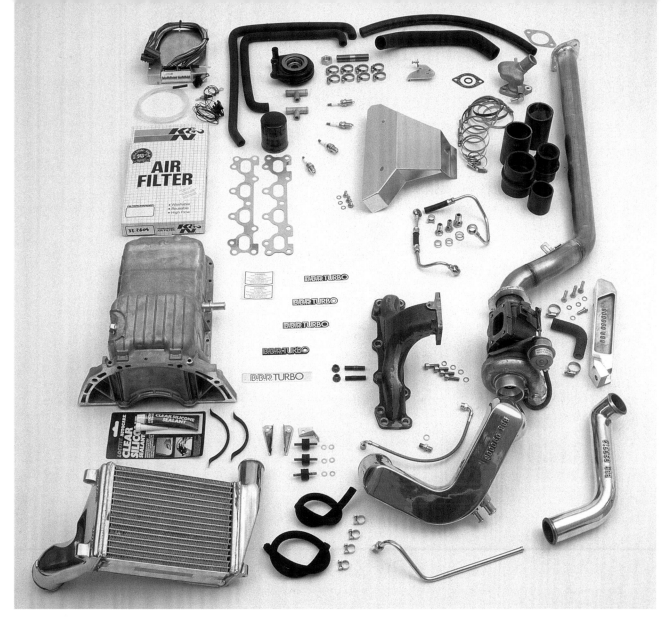

Rod Millen Motorsport Turbo

It was so obvious, whatever Mazda's beleaguered spokesmen said. The MX-5 shared the same basic engine as the 323 Turbo. It had the same 1,597cc capacity block, the same twin-cam 16-valve head and the same fuel-injection system. And it took Rod Millen less than six months to add the turbocharger.

California-based Kiwi, Millen, had been modifying Mazdas for close to 15 years. He'd competed in most classes of motorsport, from the Daytona 24 Hours to the terrifying Pike's Peak hillclimb and wowed the rallying world with his storming 4wd RX-7. Mazda itself had acknowledged the high quality of Millen's aftermarket work and even involved him in test programmes of new models.

Millen Motorsport set to work on one of the very first Miatas to arrive in the States, but the original aim was simply to create a running showcase for potential aftermarket items.

The engine was removed and stripped, the pistons and camshafts from the 323 GTX engine were fitted and the turbocharger bolted on, with the 626 turbo intercooler fitted right down in the nose of the car for maximum airflow and efficiency.

Larger injectors from the RX-7 were fitted. The ECU was reprogrammed and an additional computer added. Millen's workshop fabricated a unique 2.5in stainless steel exhaust system and manifold to let it breathe. The standard radiator had to be replaced with the slightly smaller 323 version to make room for the intercooler and its associated pipework.

The result was a power hike from 116bhp (USA) to a thumping 230bhp at 5,500rpm, all from the standard 1.6-litre engine.

As other modifiers have found since, the Mazda's chassis can cope remarkably well with more power, but it still needed to be tied down even more firmly to keep its nose and tail travelling in the right order. The Turbo was lowered an inch, with 25 per cent stiffer springs and thicker roll bars mounted on urethane bushes. Sterner brake discs from the RX-7 were added to give more stopping power.

If the car hadn't been painted a lurid shade of yellow, it wouldn't have announced its presence too loudly before disappearing over the horizon. It had 15 x 7in wheels produced for Rod Millen Motorsport by Panasport in Japan, wearing Bridgestone Potenza 205/50 RE 71 VR tyres (the wheels were also painted body colour). A small lip spoiler clamped neatly to the bootlid without any drilling, and a moulded glassfibre rear deck covered up the hood when it was stowed.

Nigel Fryatt from *CCC (Cars and Car Conversions)* drove the car in the US and fell in love with it. He wrote: 'Give it too much too soon, and the obvious happens. The combination of steering and chassis response does, however, mean that the resultant indiscretion can be corrected … This car deserves a fair amount of respect. Smooth is quickest for sure.'

The response to the showcase Turbo was so positive that Rod Millen Motorsport was soon offering a kit in the USA and abroad including the UK. The price was around $8,000 fitted for the USA. When it reached Australia, Greg Kable from *Modern Motor* got behind the wheel of an example wearing a more extravagant body kit including side skirts and a chin spoiler for the April 1991 issue. The tone of the feature was more measured than *CCC*, admiring the quality of the conversion, but complaining about the high price Down Under and bemoaning the loss of the standard car's friendly nature. He wrote: 'It doesn't have the nimbleness and agility that has endeared so many to the standard car.'

Nevertheless, the kits proved popular, particularly in the States, and Rod Millen Motorsport sold a large range of Miata tuning parts and accessories. The company's aftermarket parts were even evaluated for the 1991 UK One-Make Challenge (see Chapter 12). In answer to enquiries as to why this range had been dropped, a spokesman stated this was due to insufficient sales.

black or white. Some went to the USA, but did not sell well, probably because of cost.

Other options were available from BBR to improve grip, including a suspension conversion consisting of anti-roll bars front and rear with progressive-rate roll springs, a limited-slip differential plus wider, larger diameter alloys with Dunlop D40 M2 205/50ZR15 tyres.

For real speed freaks, BBR also offered a Phase II conversion, boosting power up to 240bhp, but this one was never sanctioned by Mazda or MCL.

The Phase II conversion involved a full engine rebuild with low-compression pistons, a gas-flowed and modified cylinder head, hi-flow injectors, a modified air-flow meter; fitting a larger-capacity intercooler, a full BBR 2.25in stainless steel exhaust system and extensive modifications to the engine management system. To keep these monsters on the road, BBR added a limited-slip differential, a full BBR suspension pack and a twin stainless steel 'targa bar'. Strangely, no mention is made of the brakes which had to cope with all this extra performance. (Brodie Brittain Racing does not offer support for these kits or the MX-5 BBR Turbo.)

Turbo performance

	Standard 1.6	BBR
Power	114bhp@6,500rpm	150bhp@6,500rpm
Torque	100lb ft@5,500rpm	154bhp@5,550rpm
0–60mph	8.76sec	6.8sec
Top speed	121mph (195kph)	130mph (209kph)

Despite these official figures, *Autocar* could only achieve 122mph (196kph) and 0–60mph (96kph) in 10.3 seconds. BBR claimed that the test car had had an incorrectly set ignition timing.

Enter the 1.8

It might appear that Mazda had finally given in and increased the MX-5's power in 1994 when the 1.8-litre replaced the first 1.6. The truth is that the bigger engine only compensated for the extra weight the car had gained, but things could have been different.

The MX-5 was a smash hit from launch, and local importers had kept up interest by producing their own limited editions, a process which has continued throughout the car's life. (See Chapter Seven.)

In Japan, however, the plans were more ambitious. In November 1990, Mazda set up its M2 division

↑ **The chassis was stiffened in 1992 to improve handling and reduce vibration. (LAT)**

Club Racer

The Club Racer Concept appeared on Mazda's 1989 Chicago Auto Show stand alongside the standard car. Painted glowing Sunburst Yellow, it gave a hint of all the weekend racing fun Miata/MX-5 owners would have. It was intended to bring back memories of low-powered, but fun and agile weekend racers such as the MG Midget and Austin Healey Sprite, which were often raced with very little modification.

Inside, it had a racing harness for the driver and a number of switches instead of a radio. Externally it lost the pop-up headlamps, using recessed lamps set back into the wings like those of the BMW Z1.

It used the stock 1.6-litre 16v engine, so show-goers were left to imagine how they might tune and tweak it for the track.

Tom Matano said: 'We wanted to bring back the feeling of weekend amateur racing as well as whetting the appetites of potential buyers by letting them see how the MX-5 can be personalised.' At the time, the company said it had no plans to race the car, but the UK importer MCL did set up a one-make challenge in 1991. (See Chapter 12.)

↗ Tom Matano's Club Racer concept car looked like a weekend racer, but it had a standard 1.6 engine. (Mazda)

→ The Club Racer's cabin had racing-style seats with four-point harnesses, inside, the stereo had been replaced by a row of switches. (Mazda)

↓ The striking Racer appeared alongside the brand-new Miata at the Chicago Auto Show 1989. (Mazda)

under Masakatsu Kato with Hirotaka Tachibana as his deputy. The division was to work on more offline projects and in December 1992 it produced the muscular MX-5 M2 1001 Roadster. The M wore a large front air dam incorporating two large round driving lamps, a rear spoiler, chromed door mirrors and a racing-style fuel filler. All were finished in a special dark blue paint and had leather seats and a leather-trimmed steering wheel. The standard 1.6-litre engine remained in place, but performance pistons raised the compression ratio to 10.57:1 and high-lift camshafts, polished ports and a less restrictive exhaust increased power to 130bhp at 6,000rpm (matching the MX-5 Challenge racers) and torque to 110lb ft at 5,500rpm. The bodyshell was stiffened and a more sporty drive was promised by its stiffer springs and tuned dampers. Its eight-spoke alloys, shod with special 195/50VR15 tyres are highly prized by hop-up merchants. The M2 was wildly popular. Only 300 were made, and after the first 200 had been sold, Mazda organised a lottery to find homes for the last 100.

This car was followed by the M2-1002 in February 1993, which had the looks, but a standard engine and no power steering. This one hardly deserved to be a success, but it also arrived just as the Japanese economy took a downturn into crisis, so the planned series of M2 cars was canned, only prototypes surviving. The programme has therefore been labelled a failure, but the M2-1002 previewed a number of important changes which soon reached the production car, including the stiffened body and Torsen differential.

The first change to the standard car came in 1992, when Mazda added a rear subframe member which reduced the infamous 65mph vibration. The modification made the rear subframe more resistant to deflection under cornering loads, so the wheels and tyres stay in better alignment with the ground.

Then in 1993, a catalytic converter was added to the UK car for the first time, blunting the 1.6 model's performance further.

The MX-5's first major change occurred first in Japan, then in the US and UK a year later, in a pattern that would be repeated for most major revisions. Starting from 1993 in the home market, and rippling through to the US, UK, Australia and other markets in 1994, the 1.8i and 1.8iS swept away the 1.6.

The new 1.8i's front and rear subframes were stiffened and braced. The increased structural rigidity

↑ The chassis was substantially stiffened again in 1994, and the 1.8 was fitted to compensate for extra weight, not to significantly improve performance; this car is a US Miata. (LAT)

reduced flexing in the platform and tidied up the handling, reducing nervousness on the limit, but it was at least partly deemed necessary to meet incoming side-impact regulations in the States. At the front, a transverse steel rod was installed between the lower double wishbone sub-assemblies, while two steel bars were added connecting the rear suspension to the body crossmember. In the cabin, another brace was added between the two seatbelt anchor towers.

The suspension was also fine tuned, with new dampers and bump stops, and a smaller-diameter anti-roll bar. Stopping power was improved with larger discs on each corner, 251mm in diameter at the back and 254mm at the front.

Needless to say, all this extra metal added weight, the 1.8 registering 1,040kg (2,293lb) on the scales, compared with 995kg (2,193lb) for the first 1.6. So the bigger engine was needed just to match the

The 'Lost' M2s

The poor state of the Japanese car market and the failure of the M2 1002 put paid to Mazda's plans to produce a series of top-spec M2 cars. These could have lifted the range in the manner of BMW M Sport cars or ST series Fords.

The M2 1003 would have had a special aero deck cover, echoed later by the M Speedster. It wore BBS alloy wheels, and the interior would have been specially trimmed to match the outer high quality.

The M2 1006 was nicknamed the 'Cobraster' by Mazda insiders. Two prototypes were built, powered by the 220bhp quad-cam 3.0-litre V6 engine from the 929. This mean-looking beast had a widened body and used RX-7 rear suspension.

The M2 1008 was a one-off coupé with a squared-off tail, Ferrari style. The coupé theme was explored further with the M Coupé of 1996, but that car's styling was not as radical. Just one more car was created with the M2 designation, the M2 1028 of 1994. This was described as a 'street competition' car and so featured a roll cage attached to the body at 10 points which considerably stiffened the structure. Its tuned 1.8-litre engine had a 10.6:1 compression ratio and produced 140bhp at 6,500rpm. It came with a detachable hard-top, but no soft-top.

Just 300 cars were offered for the Japanese market at a price of 2.8 million yen, and were snapped up within a couple of months. Of these, 115 were dark blue and 185 Chaste White – the national racing colour of Japan.

↓ The M2 cars were intended to offer a top-spec model in the manner of the BMW M-range, but the M2 1002 was more like one of Ford's Ghia models, offering a plush interior but a standard powerplant. (Andrew Fearon)

↑ The M2 1002's interior was lavishly trimmed in plush white leather, but it had no power steering. (Simon Farnhell)

← The M2 1028 had a tuned engine producing 140bhp, just 300 were made and these were snapped up in a couple of months.

↓ Described as a street competition car, the M2 1028 came with a roll-over bar as standard; it had a standard hard-top, but no soft-top. (Brochure lent by Andrew Fearon)

original's performance. The replacement was the 323F GT's 1.8-litre twin-cam, using hollow camshafts to reduce weight. Power was increased by 14bhp to 130bhp at 6,500rpm (128bhp in the USA), and torque was boosted by 10 per cent to 110lb ft, accessed 500rpm lower down the range at 5,000rpm. However, the new engine's rather coarse note encourages most drivers to change up well before that. At least the exhaust note remained as sweet as ever.

The snap-precision of the gearbox was also mercifully left well alone, as were the ratios, but the final-drive was changed from 4.3:1 to 4.1:1, so the 1.8's overall gearing was higher. The extra power was fed to the rear wheels via a new Gleason Torsen limited-slip differential, which replaced the previous viscous diff.

The ride had actually improved, so although still stiff, it was compliant enough for a long wind-in-the-hair trip without shrieking muscles the next day. The rack-and-pinion steering remained as sharp and communicative as ever, so the journey was still more important than the destination for an enthusiastic MX-5 driver.

The new car's reception was warm, if not as ecstatic as the reviews of the first car, and there were grumbles that more power had not meant more performance. Sideways-merchants were also disappointed that some of the car's previous oversteer had been tamed.

Norman Garrett comments: 'The car was heavier, so it needed more oomph. Power was up, so was weight, so net acceleration was the same, but the insurance issue stayed in the mindset. Again, the aftermarket solved the problem for the serious enthusiasts – thus Sebring Superchargers [the company Garrett set up after leaving Mazda] was born.'

Wheels writer Michael Stahl said: 'The 1.8 doesn't move the MX-5 forward so much as sideways'. (February 1994)

Autocar reported: 'The MX-5 turns into bends with the same legendary élan and soaks up mid-bend bumps as well as the old car. But where the first MX-5 would start to twitch its tail, especially in the wet, this one signals the limit more clearly and is more forgiving once you arrive there.'

At just £14,495 (close to £2,000 cheaper than the 1.6) the entry-level 1.8i wore plain 5.5J × 14in steel wheels and had pretty basic equipment, including manual windows. Its steering had no assistance, justified on the grounds that it gave a

↑ The interior of a 1.8 Miata shows simple control layout and every owner's favourite feature, the stubby gear lever, with its 'snick-snick' action. (LAT)

more pure, roadster experience and its steering wheel was a plain plastic hoop. The £17,395 1.8iS model offered power steering and a leather-clad wheel, airbags for driver and passenger, electric mirrors, a rheostat for the panel lights, a Clarion CRX87R detachable radio cassette unit with an electric aerial and anti-lock brakes. It was distinguished by super-light seven-spoke lighter alloy wheels, weighing in at just 10.3lb. These are highly prized by owners of other models seeking an attractive alloy wheel which actually improves handling, by reducing unsprung weight.

In both cars, the high-backed seats were replaced by new designs with an adjustable headrest, door pockets replaced the armrests and an immobiliser helped keep those vital insurance costs down.

Peter McSean wrote in *Autocar* of the base 1.8i: 'You don't need to be a purist to appreciate that this is the MX-5 getting back to where it belongs, which is as close to affordable as new two-seater, open-top sports cars get. After so many limited edition MX-5s puffed up with superfluous thises or thats, it's refreshing to see the car come back down to earth.'

It is worth noting here that most limited editions were based on the base car rather than the 1.8iS, and

so lacked its safety equipment, even if other desirable cosmetic items were added. (See Chapter Seven.)

The 1.6 returns in 1995

Halfway through the decade, rivals were beginning to spring up to cash in on the roadster market which Mazda had now proved, without any doubt, existed. By 1995, the MX-5 had seen off the new Lotus Elan, but another serious rival, wearing a prestige roadster badge was about to emerge, the MGF. The smart, mid-engined 1.8 wowed the press and public alike and would remain the MX-5's closest rival.

The new Fiat Barchetta looked the part, too, but was never popular in the vital UK market because it remained a left-hand driver. BMW had followed its quirky Z1 with the muscular Z3, which was an instant success, however, none of its many guises have been as involving as an MX-5, and with its higher price and slightly executive character, it has never appealed to the same buyers.

MCL in the UK retaliated against the MGF with more limited editions, including the popular California and classy Gleneagles in 1995, and the Merlot and Monaco in 1996, which boasted in their press releases of undercutting the MGF on price.

The razor-sharp marketing brains at Mazda Corporation decided to widen the range and slip a more affordable model beneath the 1.8-litre model and its new rivals. So the 1.6 was welcomed back, but it was a very different animal to the car its bigger-engined brother had replaced.

To maintain a gap between the two models, the new 1.6 was detuned to deliver just 88bhp, and its spec was spartan: steel wheels, no power steering, manual windows and no standard radio cassette. The body bracing and tweaked suspension of the 1.8 were omitted, which was just as well. With the weight these added, the 1.6 wouldn't have pulled the skin off a bowl of custard, let alone a rice pudding. The brake discs reverted to the original 235mm at the front and 231mm at the rear. The prices now stood at £17,395 for the 1.8iS, £14,495 for the 1.8i and just £12,995 for the 1.6i, so its appeal was obvious.

Final touches

Although there were no more major changes to the Mk1 after this, the MX-5 range underwent constant tweaks and tucks, and the limited editions kept rolling out in every market.

From 1995 in Japan and 1996 in the USA, a 133bhp Series II 1.8-litre engine was introduced,

featuring a 16-bit ECU and a lightened flywheel to allow the engine to rev more freely.

From 1996, UK cars lost their chrome rings, Laguna Blue was discontinued and armrests were reinstated, replacing the unpopular door pockets. The next year, a high-level brake light appeared on the bootlid.

In the USA, the Miata now had to meet tough Federal side-impact requirements and even tougher OBD 11 emissions rules.

However, the Mk2 was now well underway, the M Speedster and M Coupé cars shown in 1995 and 1996 just giving tantalising hints that the now dated-looking roadster was about to gain a new lease of life.

↓ **The 1.8i was a back-to-basics model featuring steel wheels, wind-up windows and no power steering. (LAT)**

CHAPTER 4

THOROUGHLY MODERN MAZDA

When writing about the Mk2, it is often mentioned that sales of the old model were falling off in Japan and starting to drift in the USA. In fact, the question should not be why was the Mk1 replaced, but why wasn't it remodelled far earlier? At the time, most Japanese cars including the Toyota MR2 and Honda Civic changed their image more often and more radically than Madonna. That the Mk1 lasted eight years is proof of its success and the reluctance of Mazda to mess with a formula that was bringing in hard cash during some very difficult times.

In the early 1990s, the company invested heavily in focus groups to look at the future of the MX-5, and consulted owners' clubs worldwide, whose members were understandably anxious about the future of 'their' car. The message that came back was clear: 'Don't change what you don't have to'.

As the company was quite strapped for cash, this was probably music to the accountants' ears. Unnecessary and expensive changes would be frowned upon, but for once the enthusiasts and the suits were in agreement.

When the sensitive project was kicked off in spring 1994, Martin Leach, managing director responsible for Product Planning, Design and Programmes asked all four of Mazda's technical centres, in the USA, Europe, Hiroshima and the Yokohama branch opened in 1987, to submit ideas, but insisted that changes should not be too radical.

Chief engineer for the Mk1 and the creator of its superb suspension, Takao Kijima, took over as programme manager from Toshihiko Hirai, who retired to become a lecturer at Japan's National Oh-ita University. Kijima's instructions to all four studios were that the new car must retain the front-engined, rear-wheel-drive configuration of the original. Also, the dimensions had to stay true to the principles of light weight and optimum distribution of that weight to aid outstanding handling.

Frankfurt

The various styling studios had actually been working on ideas for the new car since the early 1990s. The boss of the Frankfurt studio, Arnold 'Ginger' Ostlethwaite, and fellow-Brit Peter Birtwhistle, had produced some radical concepts, examining the idea of a stripped-down, back-to-basics roadster. Their concept cars, known as the Lean Machine and Two-for-One, were closer to a Caterham or a Lotus Elise than an MX-5. The more realistic Mark One of 1992 had a smooth and simple body closely resembling a Porsche Speedster minus its aerodynamic rear fin. A Mark One alternative featured twin projector lamps frenched into the front wings in the manner of an Alfa GTV.

Reminiscing in 2002, Birtwhistle observed a little sadly that: 'By then [1994] it was clear that we had to keep close to the original, but the pop-up headlamps had to go. They were too heavy.'

He and 'Ginger' would have liked to have given the MX-5 a more aggressive look. Their concept car of 1995 had smooth lines, also reminiscent of the Porsche Speedster – an area where they clearly agreed with Wu-Huang Chin, although their car was prettier than the wide-mouthed M Speedster.

They would also have preferred a more sophisticated interior, and suggested a curvy new centre panel using better quality plastics for the mouldings.

> ← The Mk2 had revised rear lights. This photograph was taken at the Chobham test track, where IAD first demonstrated the V705 for Mazda's US team. (LAT)

DID YOU KNOW?

A change of steering

The MX-5's rack-and-pinion steering was always quick and communicative, but there had been calls for improved high-speed stability and less on-centre twitchiness, so the steering ratio was switched on the S1 prototype from 15.0:1 to 17.0:1. Those who tried it, including the journalist Jack Yamaguchi, disliked the slower, more benign character and the ratio was swiftly switched back again.

The final sketches showed a roadster looking rather like a plump MGB with similar recessed round headlamps, and in some of them the alloy wheels gave the impression of classic wire wheels.

California

Tom Matano's team had also been putting in plenty of homework, exploring future possibilities for the Miata. The public and fun results of this were the Mi-

Ari featured at the 1994 Monterey Historic Races, the muscular M Speedster concept developed from it which appeared in 1995, and the M Coupé which followed them in 1996.

However, the most important model they produced was not seen in public. That was the so-called 'Trunk Model' produced in the early 1990s.

As might be clear from its name, this car was built to look at ways of increasing luggage space, and it had its spare wheel stowed in a well beneath the floor a feature which would follow through into the M Coupé and then the production Mk2. However, Matano's attention didn't stay with the rear of the car. The Trunk Model's Mk1 body had also sprouted a more pronounced sill line and the pop-up headlamps were replaced by oval headlamps. So, this car bore a very strong resemblance to the eventual Mk2.

Tom Matano says: 'On the second generation, we were faced with much more difficult tasks to get it right because the first generation was so successful in all markets.'

However, it is clear that he relished the task. He continues: 'When I saw the final model of the Mk1 after it left our hands for Japan, I was disappointed that all the careful tuning of the surfaces was lost. But in retrospect, that simplicity gave it a long life and the versatility for customising opportunities.

Now we had the opportunity to do the second generation the way we wanted.'

Nevertheless, Matano knew he had to work within very tight parameters. He says: 'I knew that the Japanese team wanted a bigger change, while North American customers didn't want any changes to their cars. So, I wanted to define the level of change from the first to the second for MRA

(MANA) team. I also made a list of key elements that should be carried over to the second.

'On the differentiation level; a car should be identified as an MX-5 from 100 yards away. At 50 yards away, people could not be sure whether it was the first or the second generation. Then, as a car got closer, you would know that it was the second generation. If, from 100 yards, people couldn't

↑ **MRA built the Trunk Model to investigate ways of creating more load space, but the resulting car looks very like the Mk2 MX-5. This car had a slightly extended rear end, but the trunk inside was far from a usable rectangle. (Mazda)**

→ Clay modellers working in MRA's California studio in Irvine. (Mazda)

↓ MRA's car had fixed headlamps and a low, wide mouth; the lines of its body were close to the Trunk Model. (Mazda)

↓↓ Hiroshima's model had surprised-looking upright circular headlamps; it was developed into Theme A. (Mazda)

have identified the new car as an MX-5, or if at the 50 yards mark, people identified it as the second generation, we would have gone too far.

'The reasons why I didn't want the second to be too far off from the first was to maintain the kinship as well as the club in one piece. We destroyed the RX-7 club once; we didn't want that to happen again. If you go to any MX-5 gathering in the world, now both cars are happily mingled as siblings.'

He was keen to retain the same simplicity front and rear as the first-generation car and what he describes as the 'MX-5's very special "No one can hate it" personality'.

He says: 'There were many cars in the marketplace that lots of people love. But, there are only a few that no one can hate. Mini and Beetle are two such cars. MX-5 is certainly right up there with them, and I felt that this was one of the key success factors of the first generation that stood out.'

Along with a clay model and sketches by ex-Chrysler man Ken Saward, the Irvine Studio (now known as MRA) submitted four pages of cartoons. These starred Professor Matano, who demonstrated essential elements of the new car: Inspired sensation, Affordable Fun and Symphony with Nature, and pointed out areas of the car which lacked interest and could be improved. The Prof claimed that the chubby and cute little Miata had been working out since 1989 and should now be more toned and muscular.

Yokohama

Sketches and a clay model presented by the Yokohama office gave the MX-5 a more tapered rear end and not only retained, but exaggerated the pop-up headlamps, giving them slightly domed lids. The first sketches were very radical, showing a grey and pink futuristic dash and enormous fantasy wheels wearing rubber so thin it would have had to be painted on. The more realistic model was a simpler shape than the eventual Mk2, but wore a black styling stripe down the side.

Hiroshima

Head of this team was Koichi Hayashi, now assistant programme manager, Design for Sports Cars. Having worked on the original car and loved it dearly, he found even thinking about a replacement difficult. However, he'd never liked the pop-up headlamps, and told Bob Hall with some glee that they had been dispatched. Instead, the car produced by Hiroshima (known as MC, for Mazda Corporation) had round headlamps, leaning backwards in the manner of Porsche 911 lamps. The body shape was less cuddly than a Mk1, but still very simple.

Choosing a theme

Leach and Kijima were spoiled for choice when faced with the entries. All four studios had captured the spirit required, and suggested interesting features, but this had to be narrowed down. Three were selected to be converted into full-sized models at their respective studios by January 1995. These were evaluated and two, Hiroshima's proposal, to be known as Theme A, and Irvine's design, Theme B, were selected for further development.

Theme A still had 911-style headlamps and as it was refined, it gained a Porsche-like nose and chin spoiler. Its door had a curved rear edge similar to that of the the M Speedster and M Coupé, which not only looked attractive but allowed more space for body strengthening.

Matano's Theme B strongly resembled the Trunk Model, and the production Mk2 can clearly be seen in its lines. Its headlamps were already the distinctive oval 'eyes' of the 1998 car housing auxiliary lamps within them. The sill line was also stronger and sculpted, although the line was to be refined further. The biggest difference was its lower and larger 'mouth', which is actually closer to the eventual 'five-point grille' opening of the Mk2.5.

California's Theme B was a clear winner, and

↓ **Yokohama's full-size clay model retained pop-up headlamps and the original chrome door handles. (Mazda)**

M Speedster 1995

The dramatic M Speedster, unveiled at the 1995 Chicago Auto Show, gave a glimpse of what the MX-5 could have become as a response to the much-anticipated BMW Z3, and other roadsters now roaring on to the MX-5's territory. At the Geneva Show just a month later, the MX-5 saw the debuts of the MGF, Fiat Barchetta and the bare-essentials Renault Spider.

Mazda's Speedster took its name from the 1950s Porsche so beloved by racers including James Dean – who sadly died in one. Its racing intent was evident from the twin racing headrests and solid racing bucket seats fitted with four-point harnesses. The seats, steering wheel and gearknob were leather-trimmed with red stitching. Beneath the headrests, which were cunningly hinged in the centre, were two racing helmets painted deep metallic red to match the body colour.

Its 1.8-litre engine delivered 200bhp with the help of a Lysholm compressor, usually the source of power and fuel efficiency in the Millenia S Miller-cycle engine, but in this application used as an ultra high-efficiency supercharger. Using a compression ratio of 9.0:1, its peak power was delivered at 6,500rpm, and it delivered 165lb ft of torque at 5,500rpm. The taut, muscular body was designed by Wu-Huang Chin, although his starting point was the already substantially modified Mi-ari.

A low, purposeful stance is given by a half-inch wider track, achieved by using more heavily offset wheels and modified suspension using 30 per cent stiffer springs, thicker anti-roll bars and adjustable Koni shock absorbers with a variable ride-height facility. The wheels themselves were attractive five-spoke alloys equipped with larger brakes;

250mm ventilated discs at the front and 225mm solid discs at the rear would provide ample stopping power.

The door has a graceful downward sweep, much like that of the RX-7, and flaring sills meet wider wings. At the front, four projector-beam headlamps peer from beneath lids which only need to pop-up halfway, but two over-sized driving lamps glare from either side of the grille 'mouth'. In an interview with *Autocar*, Tom Matano said that these give the impression that the car is breathing out hard during a work-out.

The twin headlamps have since become one of the MX-5 modifiers' favourite options, and several companies have offered a copy-cat aero-deck panel.

In the USA, the public was given a free-phone number to give their comments. The response may have persuaded Mazda that more power was not the way to go.

↑ The radical M Speedster has inspired many modifiers with its aero deck and twin lamps beneath half-closed 'eyes'. (Mazda)
↗ A pair of racing helmets in a matching colour are stashed beneath the headrests. (Mazda)
→ The monster engine delivers 200bhp at 6,500rpm thanks to a Lysholm compressor operating as a supercharger.
↓ Designed by Wu-Huang Chin, the Speedster was first shown in 1995; its door line reflects that of the RX-7. (Mazda)

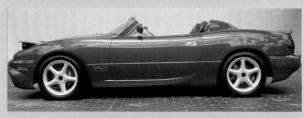

from there it was taken to Hiroshima for further refinement under Mr Hayashi.

As before, meshing design and engineering needs were difficult, and sometimes led to fireworks. Kijima and Hayashi were both happy about widening the track by 10mm at the front and 20mm at the rear. This would improve handling, and it would balance the look of the car now its 'shoulders' had developed. However, they then clashed violently because Hayashi wanted to make the wings 3mm wider – so adding size and weight. He won, and the car eventually grew by 5mm.

Interior design

It is interesting to note that when the first proposals were submitted in 1995, all four studios gave in much more colourful interiors, featuring two-tone seats and even two-tone dashboards.

Conservatism and costs won out, however. The quality of plastics and fabrics are much improved in the Mk2 and the dash has a few more curves, but the dials have no silver surrounds.

No more space was offered for tall drivers, either. The cabin remained as simple as before – and ripe for aftermarket accessories.

Practical choices

Kijima drove and assessed plenty of competitors, and consulted Mr Hirai at the beginning of the project. His aim was to keep all the best features of the original car, and improve on its weaknesses. He wrote in an essay: 'We must value and assert the MX-5's unborn soul and train, strengthen and refine the body'.

Because money was tight, around 40 per cent of the second-generation car's body was carried over from the original. Among the sections to be retained were the windscreen, its surround and most of the front bulkhead. That meant the old hard-top could be used, saving money for both development and production costs – it was also good news for owners looking for a cheap second-hand hard-top.

Some of the changes made to the Mk2 were forced by practicality. For example, new safety regulations insisted on better crash resistance and airbags, emissions controls were also getting tighter – and all these things added weight.

In response, the engineers had to reduce weight everywhere they could, shaving fractions of kilograms from engine components, a hollow steering shaft, brace bars and even a smaller horn. Just 2–3kg saved

↑ The Theme A final mock-up resembled an Alfa Duetto. It was very pretty, but its retro look didn't fit the brief for an updated MX-5. (Mazda)

← Hayashi tries the final seating buck for size. It's still a tight fit for European six-footers. (Mazda)

↘ Italian specialist nardi adapted an SRS airbag installation for its three-spoke design to be fitted in the MX-5. (Mazda)

↑ The full-size mock-up of Theme B looks very close to the finished product. (Mazda)

in the construction of the seats, tyres and hood were a major victory.

Kijima said: 'It's hard work to find the balance between strength and weight, but to make an all-aluminium chassis like the (Lotus) Elise would make the car too expensive'.

More luggage space was essential, and much of the work to achieve it had already been done in California with the Trunk Model project. The spare wheel and battery, previously inside the boot, where now housed below it, not only creating space, but also lowering the centre of gravity.

The pop-ups were no longer necessary because headlamp technology had moved on, and again, the

Irvine studio had studied the options and come up with a smart and modern solution. The oval lamps were one step further down the route from the paired headlamps beneath half-opened lids featured in the M Speedster and M Coupé and had already been featured in the Trunk Model.

There were howls of anguish from traditionalists when the car was first revealed, but to keep the pop-ups now would have been purely for effect, and because they were heavy and added the complication of more moving parts, they had to go.

Another much-mourned feature to disappear was the old car's cute, oval door handles inside and out, but the decision had been made to make the new car look more modern, so the shiny retro items were replaced by body-colour handles on the outside and plastic inside. These lacked the beauty of the old ones, but it has to be said, they are easier to use and break fewer fingernails.

A glass window with a heated element for chilly days was also clearly desirable but an electric hood would add cost, and went against the principle of simplicity. Instead, Mazda's team concentrated on making the manual action easier. So, unlike the plastic window, the glass item does not need to be zipped out before the roof is lowered, and the roof is actually lighter than the old one.

Because the windscreen surround remained the same, the new hood with its glass window can be fitted to a MkI with some conversion work. (See Chapter 10.)

Improving agility

The ability to eat corners for breakfast and plant a huge grin on the driver's face was, of course, paramount. To retain this ability and even improve on it was a remarkable achievement.

Every aspect of the car had to add up to a perfect 50/50 front-to-rear weight distribution, and the body was considerably stiffened, although this was another source of unwanted weight for Kijima to have to deal with.

Kato's PPF 'spine' was retained, along with the wishbone suspension set-up, but the suspension was further tuned. To optimise driving pleasure and increase stability, front suspension geometry changes focussed on lowering the roll centre of the car and increasing the caster trail by moving the upper control arms rearward and the lower ones forward. The planted-on-the-tarmac feel was also helped by the wider track.

A Torsen limited-slip differential became standard on the 1.8 model and the 1.6 Special Package offered on the Japanese 1.8 Mazda Roadster (the Eunos name was dropped, see Chapter Eight).

As a result of the many well-considered tweaks, the Mk2 was now able to string together a series of fast, sweeping corners far better than a MkI. The damping was much improved and coped

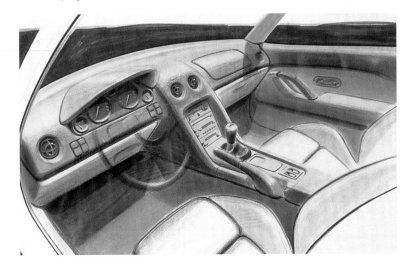

↓ Initial sketches explored some different ideas for the dashboard and centre console shapes. (Mazda)

better with bumps and rough surfaces when the
suspension was loaded up in a corner.

Some drivers felt the handling was not as much
raw fun as it had been, and enthusiasts missed
the power slides which were so easy to provoke
on the early Mk1. However, at the extreme, the
Mk2 was more forgiving, leaning gradually into an
understeering attitude, which is less likely to catch out
an inexperienced driver.

The steering remained as communicative as ever,
but thanks to a few minor tweaks, it felt a touch
lighter and more direct. The new Nardi steering
wheel for the 1.8 now housed an airbag.

Power

Once again, the option of a larger engine and its
associated costs were firmly resisted. The new car
was launched with the existing 1.8 and 1.6 engines, but
Mazda's hot rodders had been at work once again.

A new cylinder head was cast, featuring a more
upright intake port to improve breathing and
combustion. A lighter flywheel was fitted along with
new pistons to give a higher compression ratio and
the camshaft was given new profiles. A remapped
ECU ensured the engine made the most of its power.
Plus the breathing was improved, with improvements

including the use of Mazda's variable inertia charge
induction system (VICS).

The 1,839cc BP-2E (RS) unit now had 10 per
cent more power, 140bhp at 6,500rpm and 119lb ft
of torque at 4,500rpm. The 1,597cc BE-2E (RS)
unit delivered 108bhp at 6,500rpm and 99lb ft at
5,000rpm.

Neither engine was the smoothest nor the most
responsive around, however both were now punchier
and more flexible than before.

Six appeal

A number of manufacturers were working on six-
speed gearboxes at this time, but the upper echelons
at Mazda didn't seek one out.

Some of the younger engineers actually conspired,
instead, to make it happen. The gearbox manufacturer
Aisin-AI, based in Nagoya, Japan was known for its
work with Toyota. The company was interested
in developing a six-speed 'box for a front-engined,
rear-wheel-drive car, but Toyota didn't have anything
that fitted the bill. Needless to say, the company was
delighted to be given an MX-5 mule to work on, and
so the development of the Y16M-D gearbox began.

When a prototype six-speed gearbox was
delivered and fitted to a factory MX-5, the Mazda

M Coupé 1996

om Matano teased visitors to the 1996 New York Auto Show with a coupé concept for the MX-5 in the mould of the MGB GT, or Triumph GT6. This was, in fact, something BMW went on to do, when it added the hot-shoe M Coupé to its Z3 range.

The hard-top might not have made it into production, but this car revealed some features to be carried over into the Mk2 Roadster. The most important of these was a larger boot, with a spare wheel stowed beneath the floor, which had been developed for the secret experimental Trunk Model.

The Coupé borrowed its door line, sill moulding and twin-projector beam headlamps of the 1995 Speedster. It also had the same wider track, but wore different wide-rim five-spoke alloys shod with 205/45 R16 Dunlop SP8000 tyres.

Unlike the Speedster, it used a stock 133bhp 1.8-litre engine. Its overall shape was smoother and more elegant, too, in contrast to the previous car with its crouching stance and the cigar-chomping look given by the lower driving lamps.

As this was purely a show car, the roof was made of glassfibre, but featured a very large sloping rear window to achieve excellent visibility. Inside, a folding rack was provided behind the seats to hold some small items of luggage.

↑ GT6-style M Coupé of 1996 shares door, and extended sill line with the M Speedster, but it is a more elegant shape. (Mazda)

← Coupé shared the twin headlamps of the Speedster, but the nose was far closer to the production car. (Mazda)

team knew they had to grab it. Sadly, only Japanese buyers were able to have this transmission on a mainstream 1.8-litre model. The rest of the world only had the chance to try it in the 10th Anniversary Mk2.

Europeans could not order an automatic, either.

However, no one ever had any complaints about the five-speed box, and, thanks to reworked synchros, this felt slicker than ever.

Wheels and tyres

The standard wheel and tyre combination for the new car was a set of pressed steel four-bolt 14 × 6JJ wheels, except for the Japanese entry-level model, which had 14 × 5.5JJ wheels. Higher-spec models were given cast aluminium five-spoke, four-bolt 15 X 6JJ items. The tyres for both options were once again a lightweight design, weighing in at 0.6kg less for the 15in wheel and 0.5kg less for the 14in.

The brakes were 255mm diameter ventilated discs at the front and 251mm solid discs at the rear. Anti-lock brakes were standard on the 1.8-litre model in Europe and the higher-spec models for both engine sizes in Japan; it was optional in the States.

↓ **The Mk2 was launched at the Tokyo Motor Show in 1997 and the Eunos name was dropped. (LAT)**

Mk2 unveiled

The new car was unveiled at the 1997 Tokyo Motor Show, and went on sale in Japan and the USA that year, reaching the UK in 1998. It looked so similar to the original that some journalists referred to a mere 'face-lift' when, in fact, almost every element of the car had been studied and refined if not changed altogether.

Once enthusiasts got over the loss of the original and sat in the driving seat, however, the reaction was enthusiastic.

'It's an appreciation that creeps up on you slowly and then pulls into sharp focus when you come across an old model, which suddenly looks dated.'
John Barker, *Performance Car,* 1998 (UK)

'It really does feel more like a new car than anyone would imagine from looking at it … The biggest improvement, though is in the handling. When you cornered hard in its predecessor, understeer set in early and if you tried to slide the tail out, it could catch out the unwary by suddenly snapping into oversteer when the suspension bottomed out. The new MX-5 understeers less and … its easier and more controllable to drift.'
Yasushi Ishiwatari, *Top Gear,* 1998 (UK)

'There's nothing small or dainty about the driving experience any more. It's fast, focussed and fun'.
David Vivian, *Autocar,* 1998 (UK)

'It's behaviour was impressive, with a more taut feel that communicated the more seat-of-the-pants sensation of our old car…simply put, it's about the purest driving experience you can have in a modern production car.'
Douglas Knott, *Road & Track Special* 1998 (USA)

↙ **The MX-5 no longer had the stage to itself; the new model had to do battle with the Fiat Barchetta, BMW Z3 and MGF. (LAT)**

↓ **Brochure shows the ease of roof operation, plus the new standard windblocker. (Simon Farnhell)**

The optional detachable hard-top provides additional comfort and security.

The new hood features a glass heated rear window.

Protection against the elements

Rear visibility in the new Mazda MX-5 is always superb, thanks to the glass heated rear windscreen. Unlike all its rivals de-misting comes swiftly at the touch of a button.

The operation of the watertight hood is simplicity itself, and it can be lowered or raised in seconds. When it's down, it folds away from sight beneath a handy tonneau cover.

The folding wind deflector stows away behind the seats when not in use. (Standard on the Mazda MX-5 1.8i / 1.8iS models.)

When in place, the wind deflector provides protection against backdraughts. (Standard on the Mazda MX-5 1.8i and 1.8iS models.)

A bright, sunny day doesn't necessarily mean it's warm inside a convertible with its top down. And sometimes a drive in the cool of the evening would be ruined with the hood up. But on a long journey, the downside of this can be a stiff neck - which is where the Mazda MX-5's wind deflector comes in. (The wind deflector is standard on the Mazda MX-5 1.8i and 1.8iS models.)

Positioned behind the seats, the deflector prevents the airstream from flowing back into the cockpit. Annoying drafts are then diverted up and away from the driver and passenger.

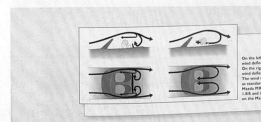
On the left: with the wind deflector in position On the right: without wind deflector. The wind deflector comes as standard on the Mazda MX-5 1.8i and 1.8iS and is an option on the Mazda MX-5 1.6i.

CHAPTER 5
THE Mk2 GETS A FACE-LIFT

The 2001 MX-5 quickly became known as the Mk2.5 because it looks so similar to the previous incarnation (officially it remains the Mk2 face-lift). This was a vital model for Mazda, however, having been substantially reworked under the skin to keep its nose ahead of marauding pretenders to its crown.

The biggest upcoming rival was the MG TF, given a face-lift by Peter Stevens (ironically designer of the MX-5's first rival, the Lotus Elan). Mazda knew the TF's mid-mounted engine would be more powerful than before and its hydragas suspension was to be dumped for a sharper set-up to deliver better handling (although, in the event, it turned out to be bone-jarring).

The new MX-5 was designed entirely in Japan, although the studios in Frankfurt and Irvine were consulted in advance on what their local customers would want. The views of the owners' clubs were also taken into consideration, and there was one clear message – we like it the way it is. Keep 'em coming, but don't spoil our car.

The company could have left the styling alone and slipped in a more powerful engine to take on its rivals, but Mazda stuck to the same principles laid down at the very beginning. The LWS would remain cheap to buy, run and insure, so the new car would stick with 1.6 and 1.8 engines.

However, the 1.8 would now benefit from sequential valve timing (S-VT), to deliver optimum performance and efficiency, taking its peak power up to 146bhp at 7,000rpm and 124lb ft of torque at 5,000rpm. The result is a claimed acceleration of 0–62mph in 8.5 seconds and a top speed of 127mph. The power is delivered to the road using the same stubby lever, but owners got a choice of five or six ratios, and UK buyers had the option of a four-speed automatic for the first time.

The biggest visual change was the 'mouth' which has given rise to the tag 'Sharknose'. The stretched opening echoed the new five-point grille seen on other new Mazda models, as Tom Matano says:

'We wanted to align the front design with other Mazda cars to strengthen the brand identity. We also intended to add a little stronger personality to meet a market request in Japan and USA.'

Peter Birtwhistle from the Frankfurt studio said: 'It has that same tension in space as the grille on other cars, but it doesn't need the grille itself. Brand recognition is important, but the sports car models (MX-5 and RX-8) can survive well enough without having Mazda stamped all over them.'

He explained that the new car's headlamps were given new reflectors and projector lamps beneath a clear glass cover 'to give it more interest at the front'. The rear lamp clusters were also revised.

Birtwhistle would have liked to have seen a brighter and more interesting cabin, but again the designers in Japan stuck to the traditional recipe. At least the dash was brightened by white dials and chrome surrounds – just like the accessory items fitted by many enthusiastic owners. New high-backed seats became standard, and buyers were promised a good level of equipment for the price, too, including good safety and security equipment. The 1.8 was also treated to some new 16-inch aluminium alloy wheels.

In the UK standard kit was upgraded to include power door locks, power windows, anti-lock brakes, an alarm and immobiliser. The 1.8i Sport came with leather trim, remote central locking with boot release plus power door mirrors and an electric aerial.

The most important differences were not so immediately obvious, however. The biggest change to the engine, as mentioned above, was sequential valve timing (S-VT), to deliver optimum performance. To give it a snappier throttle response and a wider, more usable power band, the engine was also given reshaped pistons and a higher compression ratio. An improved intake manifold and adjustments to reduce intake and

← The change was so subtle, this model became known as the Mk2.5; its new larger grille opening was designed to echo the then new five-point Mazda family grille. (Mazda)

MX-5 MPS

Mazda presented the promise of a high-performance and sporty future in 2000-01. The red-hot MPS Concept appeared first at the Tokyo Auto Salon December 2000 dressed in vibrant yellow paintwork. It stood beside RX-8 Concept at the 2001 Frankfurt Motor Show and the Tokyo Show, this time in red and wearing a hard top. A silver 'Clubman' version then appeared at the next Tokyo Auto Salon.

MPS stands for Mazda Performance Series, and the American version of the 323 MPS, known as the MP3, became a favourite with the 'import tuner' street-racing fanatics portrayed in the film *The Fast and the Furious*.

The MX-5 MPS was created to boost the sporting reputation of the newly launched MX-5 Mk2.5 and to help Mazda gauge the demand for a more powerful version of that car.

A Formula 4 1,930cc engine growled from beneath the bonnet, benefiting from Mazdaspeed racing technology to lift the power to 180bhp at 7,000rpm, and torque to 150lb ft at 6,000rpm. For quicker throttle response and higher output, four independent throttles and high-lift camshafts were adopted, yielding a piston speed of 19.8m/second. The power was fed to the wheels via a six-speed gearbox.

The suspension was modified with height-adjustable mono-tube dampers and springs to give even flatter cornering and increased grip. The front and rear suspension mountings points were reinforced with lightweight aluminium for enhanced rigidity. The Torsen limited-slip differential was also replaced by a prototype which tames the usual tailswing. Impressive 17 x 7J alloy wheels wore ultra-low-profile 215/40 R17 tyres while monster 314mm brake discs, ventilated at the front, hauled the MPS up sharp.

Road & Track drove the car in Japan, reporting: 'Turn-in is exceptionally crisp, with the car exhibiting flawless balance through all types of corners.'

A body kit not only gave an aggressive, lower and wider look, but also helped gravity keep the car glued to the road. Air outlets in the wings were designed to reduce air pressure inside and under the body to reduce rear-end lift, and a lip spoiler on the boot increased downforce at speed.

Inside, the lucky driver sat on

A hot MPS version of the MX-5 appeared alongside the new RX-8 at the Frankfurt Motor Show in 2001; Mazda was keen to hear whether owners wanted a performance flagship for the MX-5. (Mazda)

a combination black buckskin and Alcantara fabric seat and faced a sporty console featuring Alumite-finish metallic details.

Concerns about insurance costs and emissions regulations kept a production version of the MPS out of Europe, but Mazda in Australia answered the pleas of those craving for more power with the SP (see page 65), engineers at Ford in Detroit also toyed with the idea of a V6 Miata. A 210bhp version of Ford's 3.0-litre aluminium-block V6 was squeezed into an experimental monster called the Miata Detroit, also driven by *Road & Track*. Wearing a huge bonnet scoop like the muscle cars of old, the Detroit could reach 60mph in 5.8 seconds. Its peak power punched in at 6,500rpm, it produced 205lb ft of torque at 4,750rpm, and to handle it, the standard gearbox was replaced by the RX-7's five-speeder. *R&T* wrote: 'Once (the tyres) grab a bite of tarmac, hang on, because the car snaps forward like a hot rod, lifting the car's front end slightly in the process.'

Inspire? Stimulate? Soar? You ask for it, the Mazda MX-5 Miata delivers. Built as a pure sports car from the first pixel on an engineer's computer screen, this two-seat, drop-top roadster combines a DOHC engine that loves the redline with reflex-quick handling. And it's ready for action whenever you want some.

WHICH **VERB** WOULD YOU LIKE TO **EXPERIENCE** TODAY?

↑ **The MX-5 needed a face-lift to freshen up its image as its closest rival, the MGF was morphing into the more macho MG TF. (Simon Farnhell)**

exhaust resistance made its breathing a little easier. So, although the engine doesn't feel obviously more powerful, it revs with real verve.

To strengthen and stiffen the body, the side sills, tunnel gussets and other structural elements were enlarged and thickened. The sporty double-wishbone set-up was retained, but the suspension was fine-tuned, tweaks including modifications to the shock damping force and the option of Bilstein dampers for the 1.8 Sport. The brakes were also uprated, the master cylinder, vacuum booster and brake discs all growing in size on the 1.8. Anti-lock brakes with electronic brake-force distribution (EBD) help keep the car on the road in the most extreme situations.

As a result, it is as nimble and fluid on a series of curves as a greyhound with a rabbit in its sights, and its quick, communicative steering, precise gearchange and firm brakes make the driver feel as though the car is being operated by telepathy.

The six-speed gearbox allows quieter, more economical cruising on the motorway, but it is not universally loved. It needs plenty of stirring to keep within the power band, and it has a disconcerting dogleg when changing down from sixth to fifth.

However, as with all quirks, owners soon got used to it.

Safety was better than ever. Mazda's advanced impact-energy distribution and absorption system were introduced to protect occupants, along with standard twin airbags and three-point seatbelts with pretensioners on all models.

Opinions on whether the Mk2.5 could floor the MG TF and Toyota MR2 varied widely. The enthusiasts at *Autocar* forgave the MG TF its bouncy ride and put it on the top step of the podium. Steve Sutcliffe described the new MX-5 1.8i Sport as: 'The more grown up, purely because it is less frenetic. It rides exceptionally well, with no shimmy and a lot of control.'

The monthly magazine, *EVO*, put the MR2 at the top of its pyramid, followed by the MX-5. the TF's predecessor, the 160bhp MGF Trophy came third labelled as a 'softy' because of its hydragas suspension.

However, the monthly *What Car?*, felt that most people couldn't live happily with the MG TF's uncomfortable ride and planted the MX-5 firmly at the top, ahead of both the MG and Peugeot 206 CC, praising its pure fun and value for money.

Aussie MX-5 SP 2002

Just like MCL in 1991, Mazda Australia decided to quench the thirst of muscle-mad customers in its own market, by offering a locally developed, turbocharged MX-5 with a full Mazda warranty.

The 1.8-litre MX-5 SP went on sale in January 2002. Its 150kW (201bhp) and 280Nm (207lb ft) earn it the designation SP for Sports Performance, a badge previously worn by hot models of the RX-7 and Eunos 800.

It was developed by Sydney-based Mazda motorsport manager, Allan Horsley, who masterminded the company's many famous RX-7 wins in both touring cars and at the Bathurst 12-hour production car race. The cars were assembled for Mazda by Prodrive in Melbourne.

Mazda Australia's managing director, Malcolm Gough, announced that the six-speed manual MX-5 SP would go on sale priced at $55,540. Air-conditioning remained a $200 option, as some buyers were bound to head straight for the nearest race track.

Visual enhancements included a chrome fuel filler cap and scuff plates and an alloy gearknob and gear lever surround.

Gough said: 'This car will satisfy those MX-5 fans that have craved even more performance than that delivered by the standard model. However, the SP has been carefully developed to ensure that this MX-5 is as delightful to drive everyday as the non-turbo car.'

Allan Horsley added: 'From day one, our goal was to deliver a car with a progressive, lag-free, user-friendly power and torque curve. By employing a relatively low-boost system and with careful engine tuning, aided by a remapped ECU, we have been able to achieve our goal while delivering at least 33 per cent more power, Perhaps even more significant is the 55 per cent improvement in torque.'

The SP used the same S-VT 1.8-litre engine as the standard Mk2.5, but more than 215 parts are added or modified during the conversion. Boost came from a water-cooled Garrett turbocharger. New fuel injectors were fitted, and the ability to expel exhaust gases from the engine was improved by a free-flowing heavier-duty manifold.

Other changes included a larger radiator, oil-return line from the turbo to the sump, new spark plugs and a big-bore exhaust system with a deeper, sportier exhaust note.

Just 100 SPs were built. Mazda Australia had considered extending the numbers, but the price was too high to justify a bigger roll-out. Aussie buyers were very happy, however, when a version of the Japan-only Roadster Turbo appeared on their shores in 2003 (see Chapter 8). It was called the SE and cost around $10,000 less than the SP.

The Australian SP (Sports performance) was the first official MX-5 turbo to be offered since the BBR Turbo of 1991. (Mazda Australia)

The SP was developed by Mazda Australia's Motorsport Division. It developed 33 per cent more power and 55 per cent more torque than the standard car. (Mazda Australia)

MAZDA SP PERFORMANCE DATA

Engine: 1,839cc, inline 4-cyl, DOHC 16V, turbocharged and intercooled
Bore and stroke: 83.0 x 85.0mm
Compression ratio: 10.0:1
Max power: 201bhp (approx) @ 6,800rpm
Max torque: 207lb ft (approx) @ 4,600rpm
Brakes: front 270mm disc ventilated; rear 276mm
Kerb weight: 1,119kg (2,467lb)

↑ ↑ **Power was slightly up, and the body was stiffer than before; the six-speed gearbox was now offered in the UK. (LAT)**

↑ **The space-saver spare wheel is stowed beneath the floor as in the Mk2. (LAT)**

UK joins Europe

The Mk2 was introduced at a very difficult time for Mazda. By 2000, sales were falling worldwide and franchised dealers all over Britain were deserting the sinking ship, leaving large areas without a Mazda representative.

As a result, distribution was taken away from MCL to be dealt with directly from Europe. In 2002, Mazda was trying to revitalise the dealer network and promoting the brand relentlessly with TV advertisements and press events.

For a while it looked as if the change would bring the UK owners' club closer to the action, because its contact point became Mazda Europe in Frankfurt rather than an importing agent, and representatives were invited to a major party at Easter 2002 in order for their views to be heard. Sadly, however, such consultation events did not continue.

One major change was that Limited Editions would now be Europe-wide models created in Frankfurt. The first to appear was the Phoenix in March 2002 (see Chapter Seven). This used the same grey metallic paint and Saddle Brown leather colour scheme as the US SE Titanium Gray and the Australian Titanium.

All Change to save Mazda

Mazda freely admits it made a big mistake in the mid-1990s, by paying too much close attention to focus groups and trying to compete with volume manufacturers. The resulting products were conservative, bland, and – with the exception of the MX-5 – devoid of all passion.

'It was very frustrating for the design community,' said Frankfurt designer Peter Birtwhistle: 'The last 626 would have made a perfect surveillance car. No one saw you arrive, no one saw you leave and no one ever knew you were there.'

Abandoning this disastrous strategy, the company set about a radical return to its roots and successfully reinvented itself as the sporting arm of the Ford family. The first result was the Mazda6, a handsome family car with suspension tuned by Phillip Martens, who worked with chassis guru Richard Parry-Jones on the sharp-handling Ford Mondeo. This was followed by the wonderful Wankel-engined RX-8 and the sporty Mazda3 – a real hoot in MPS guise.

Mazda also considered hotting up the MX-5. The MPS concept was shown at Frankfurt in 2001 to canvas opinions about the idea of a hotter car, but the main response was once again: 'Leave it alone, we love the car as it is.'

Reaction in Australia was enthusiastic, however, and Mazda agreed to offer a warranty on the turbocharged MX-5 SP, created by the local distributor and Tickford in the manner of MCL and the BBR Turbo in 1991.

When interviewed for this book in 2002, Peter Birtwhistle said: 'Business sense says Mazda should refine it [the MX-5] and do a 911, allowing it to evolve through the generations.'

'Lots of customers – including an important number of female buyers like the car the way it is, they don't want anything too aggressive, and they like its compact dimensions and comfort. The MX-5 doesn't offend anyone. If a BMW Z3 driver sees a Porsche Boxster, there's a bit of a needle there, but they'd both wave happily at the MX-5 driver.'

Mazda designers, engineers and managers have always taken every opportunity to attend events, meet owners, chat and listen to their views.

Birtwhistle said: 'We need to understand what they want – it's very valuable information.'

↓ The Mk2.5 cabin took a small step upmarket and featured attractive white dials with chrome surrounds, just like the aftermarket versions many owners had fitted previously. (Mazda)

↓ ↓ The new car was stronger and stiffer, with fine-tuned suspension and improved brakes. (Mazda)

CHAPTER 6
Mk3: THE MACHO MX-5

Rumours about a new Mk3 flew around the world several times before its launch in 2005. When it finally arrived, the new car was bigger and more masculine in style than its predecessor – and it was capable of lapping the Nürburgring 15 seconds quicker. The lithe, lozenge-shaped body, with its bulging RX-8-style wheelarches, was first revealed at the 2005 Geneva Motor Show. However, in the UK, the first glimpse was reserved for the Owners' Club at its National Rally at Goodwood in August before production began in October.

The team developing this car had a task equivalent to revamping the recipe for Coca-Cola. Many American fans were furious that their car would now be known as an MX-5, and insist they will always call it a Miata. But what about the car? Could it be as good or better than its predecessors?

Even though the official title is Mk3, it was the first time the team had gone right back to the drawing board – not one single part is carried over. However, the MX-5 has one thing other long-lived cars do not: continuity. Team manager for the Mk3, Takao Kijima, was in charge of chassis development on the Mk1 and the Le Mans-winning Mazda 787B, taking over from Toshihiko Hirai for the Mk2.

The principle of Jinba Ittai, now translated as 'horse and rider as one', remains fundamental. Kijima quotes the example of the Shinto ritual of Yabusame, in which an archer must score a bull's eye as he rides past a target at full gallop.

Mr Hirai was invited back to teach the entire team about kansei engineering, and each department had to come up with ways to achieve Jinba Ittai. Team leaders then came together to create a new Fishbone Chart based on the original headings.

Chief Designer Yasushi Nakamuta also worked on the Mk2. As with the original, he challenged all three studios in Japan, California and Germany to come up with designs. Hundreds of sketches were whittled down to seven quarter-scale models, then three full-scale models, one from each studio. These were

lined up with a current car and viewed from 100m – a trick introduced by Tom Matano.

Although the American entry won praise, the Hiroshima model was the final choice because it was compact, simple and modern while tugging at the team's heart strings.

The German interior design team won a similar shoot-out and the cabin was developed at Oberursel.

Nakamuta speaks of keeping the car's 'MX-5-ness' while adding modernity. The previous car's slim waistline had to go to provide more space in the cabin, the larger arches sprouted to accommodate a wider track while keeping the overall shape slim. However, the rear lights are an MX-5 signature, so simple and beautiful that one sits in New York's Museum of Modern Art (Moma). Nakamuta says 'I didn't want to change them, so I found new interior components.'

Tom Matano was impressed by the new car's styling. He said: 'The key to a continued success as a legend is to maintain the heritage and lineage through the generations not only on its driving feel and styling, but also in spirit. From 100 metres away, you can see an MX-5 is approaching. From 50 metres away, it tells you that it is the Mk3, I did the same with the Mk2'.

Kijima admitted that starting afresh was a challenge, but he said: 'We had to meet new outside influences: emissions, crash worthiness and customers demanding more comfort.'

The third generation saw a change in the suspension for the first time. Wishbones are still used at the front, but a multilink set-up at the rear was designed to give longer travel over bumps. Some 473 sets of dampers were evaluated before Kijima made his choice. Technologies such as traction control and stability control were also added, because these days, customers expect them.

The lightweight aluminium 1.8 and 2.0 MZR engines used by the Mazda3, 5 and 6 were the

← The Mk3 declares its intent: the smiley mouth is gone and bulging muscles over the wheelarches echo the RX-8.

↙ Ingenious new design allows the driver to release a handle and drop the roof at a traffic light; tan roof was available on UK Sport.

The Mk3's Rivals at Launch

Like the Duracell bunny, the MX-5 has outlasted its original rivals. The Elan and no-luggage Toyota MR2 are gone and the MGF has been sold to a Chinese car manufacturer.

Of the survivors, the BMW Z4, the rev-happy Honda S2000 and the Audi TT (a 2+2, but definitely a rival in spirit) are way more expensive. Hot hatch coupé cabriolets simply cannot offer the same driving thrills.

Probably its closest rival, the Lotus Elise, is a hoot once you've wriggled into its driving seat, but its luggage space is even more limited, and you have to be supple to get out again.

When the Mk3 emerged, for the first time, however, two new American rivals were also heading out of the pitlane, offering roadster fun with convenience. The Pontiac Solstice and the Saturn Sky shared the same rear-wheel-drive Kappa platform, and 2.4-litre 170hp inline four-cylinder engine, linked to either a five-speed manual or optional automatic.

The sexy Solstice took on the new Mk3 MX-5 in USA and Canada. A European version was called the Opel GT.

The Saturn Sky was visually close to the Vauxhall VX Lightning concept, which was the car that GM built for the 100th anniversary of its British subsidiary in 2003. It was offered in Europe as the Opel GT.

The Pontiac Solstice was more voluptuous, and its face was close to that of the 2002 Solstice Concept, but it wore the Lightning's Batmobile-style flying buttresses on its shoulders.

The Sky joined GM's family brand at $23,690, the Solstice at $19,995. Both cars were fun to drive, but neither was as quite as sharp and alert as the MX-5. Other drawbacks were the fiddly roof systems and tiny boots (sorry, trunks).

Their biggest problem, however, was the 'credit crunch' starting in 2008. As this book goes to press both Saturn and Pontiac have been axed by struggling GM. The MX-5 Miata wins again.

← Jinba Ittai: the horse and rider as one, has become a new logo.

↓ The team chose the Japanese design (right), but took some features from the European full-sized clay model (left).

most suitable in the Mazda family. However, various auxiliary parts were repositioned in order to shorten the units and keep as much weight as possible towards the centre of gravity. The engine is also tilted 10 degrees to accommodate the intake manifold.

As before, overall weight was critical and Kijima's 'gram strategy' had every engineer hunched over a set of scales. The bonnet, boot, engine subframe and suspension control arms are aluminium; 84g was saved by simplifying the rear-view mirror. As a result, despite being 40mm longer, 40mm wider and 15mm taller, with much more safety kit, the car is only 10kg heavier than the Mk2.5.

The new z-fold manual roof is a triumph. You release one handle and push it down in six seconds without getting out – leaving enough time to change a CD before the lights change.

Testing took place in eight countries and, in the UK, former Formula One World Champion Jackie Stewart was asked for his comments.

The result? The new MX-5's simple lines evoke the first-generation car, but its flared trousers are not universally popular, and the car sits rather high, leaving a large gap between the tyres and wheelarches.

↑ **Takao Kijima developed the Mk1's brilliant suspension; he took over from Toshihiko Hirai for the Mk2 and Mk3.**

← **Mk3 retains the sturdy backbone of the original car with wishbones up front, but a new multi-link set-up at the rear. The 2.0-litre MZR engine is shared with the Mazda3, 5 and 6.**

↑ The new car was tested in eight countries for durability and handling in extreme conditions.

→ Cabin is more roomy and the German design studio added more bling.

← Both new engines are made of lightweight aluminium. The 2.0-litre has a variable air intake system.

As you slide into the bucket seat, everything feels familiar, but as you settle down, significant differences sink in. It's as if you've come home and gradually realised your partner has redecorated while you were out. The old cabin was cosy and deliberately simple. This new one is roomier, smarter and executive in feel. The dials are straightforward, but have attractive chrome highlights, and there's a strip of shiny plastic trim across the dash. Four cupholders are perhaps a little excessive in a two-seater car, but the luggage net in the passenger footwell is handy.

The engine sounds gruff as it fires up, and then the fun starts. Even at low speeds, this car feels alert and light on its feet. That MX-5 grin quickly creeps across your face and if there's a long route you're already thinking about taking it.

Once you're out on the open road, it remains true that the MX-5 experience is not about outright speed. The 2.0-litre is nippy enough, but you need to use the gears to get the best out of it. That's hardly a chore, though. The satisfying snick of the stubby lever through its short gate and the feel of the precise, communicative steering are at the heart of Jinba Ittai.

↑ Boot is larger than before; fitted luggage sets are available to make the most of it.

Reviews at launch were not 100 per cent favourable. The more enthusiastic road testers felt that the suspension set-up was biased too much towards predictable handling and a refined ride rather than exuberance and fun. A number of British enthusiasts opted for the Mazda Eibach lowering kit, which lowered the car by about

Ibuki Concept 2003–4

Enthusiasts began to salivate as the covers slid off the cute Ibuki Concept at the 2003 Tokyo Motor Show. Its name translates as 'breathing new energy into' or 'adding vigour', but to fans it meant a new MX-5 was on the way. Plus, its simple lozenge shape hinted at a return to the look and spirit of the Mk1.

Every concept is an opportunity to experiment with futuristic ideas, so the Ibuki came as a 1.6-litre petrol electric hybrid with a six-speed manual transmission. Lightweight material used throughout included carbonfibre and recyclable fibre-reinforced plant-based plastic, and it had a low, curved windscreen.

Reaction to the Ibuki was enthusiastic, and some elements were taken from it, but

← Ibuki's interior was ultra clean and high-tech; it featured recyclable plastic and a curved windscreen.

Yasuchi Nakamura says: 'It looked too industrial and artificial, when thinking of the MX-5, you need more warmth and humanity.'

↓ The Ibuki concept hinted at a return to a clean, simple shape. Power came from a 1.6-litre petrol/electric hybrid set-up.

30–35mm and greatly improved the handling (Mazda Part Number: Eibach Lowering Kit 4100-77-774A). The springs could also be purchased from specialist suppliers.

In the end, it seems the engineers took the hint and tweaked the Mk3.5 to give it more whoohoo. These things are a matter of personal taste and

driving style, however, and some drivers prefer the more executive feel of the Mk3. (See Road tester's Choice in Chapter 9.)

So, with the Mk3, the MX-5 has become a dynasty like the Porsche 911 or Corvette. Its third generation has MX-5ness by the bucketload – and that's all we asked for.

← Dual exhausts add nice burble to engine note; Sport model wears 10-spoke alloy wheels.

Mazdaspeed's Roadster M'z Tune Concept drew crowds at the Tokyo Auto Salon, tuner enthusiasts loved its 18in wheels.

DID YOU KNOW?

Mazdaspeed Roadster M'Z Tune Concept 2007

The Mazdaspeed M'z Tune Concept drew crowds to Mazda's booth at the 2007 Tokyo Auto Salon. In fact, reporters grumbled that photo opportunities were few and far between because so many people surrounded the concept throughout the show. The M'z featured a complete body kit with lower side skirts, plus a vented bonnet and front wings. Sporty 18in Mazdaspeed wheels with Advan rubber promised better performance as well as head-turning looks.

The M'z shared the booth with the Mazda Roadster Kurenai, a concept based on the new retractable coupé.

MK3 Upgrade – 'Lots of Fun'

When this car appeared, Mazda tried gamely to call it the Mk3 Upgrade. However, its fate was sealed by the April 2009 edition of the UK Mazda MX-5 Owners' Club magazine, *Soft-Top Hardtop*, and the headline '3.5 anyone?'

It was revealed at the MX-5's 20th anniversary celebrations at the Paris Motor Show in 2008 and the 2009 Chicago Auto Show in the US before being launched as both a soft-top and hard-top coupé from spring 2009.

The 3.5 had a bigger grin than its predecessor and its fog lamps sat in an organic leaf-shaped opening. Both features echo a series of wild concepts shown by Mazda in 2008 including the Furai, Taiki and Kiyora (for those with long memories: 'It's too orangey for crows').

The Mk3.5 had reason to grin, too, because at launch this model was as well equipped as its predecessor, but it focussed on fun. A lower front roll centre, retuned suspension and improved steering feel gave back the 'yee-hah' factor missing on the more executive Mk3.

The 2.0-litre engine had a higher rev limit and a sportier sound. On the inside, it benefited from a forged crankshaft, fully floating pistons and newly designed valve springs.

The six-speed manual transmission was slicker than ever thanks to carbon-coated surfaces on the first to fourth gear triple-cone synchronisers. The third to fourth synchroniser diameter was also increased.

The sporty six-speed automatic offered two clever new control technologies: Direct Activematic (DAM) and Active Adaptive Shift (AAS).

→ Japanese 2009 model looks wonderful in yellow. Sadly, the colours offered for the UK at launch all reflected our gloomy weather.

↑ The facelift models' complex rear lamp resembles a classic radio.

the MX-5 is – and will remain – more enjoyable than any competing car.'

Concluding a rave review in *EVO* magazine April 2009, John Barker wrote: 'The bottom line is that the MX-5 is back to being brilliant again. It's great to be able to say that, and to be able to suggest something other than a fast hatch to those looking for a satisfying drivers' car for less than £20K, new. There are plenty of hatches that are more powerful and quicker in a straight-line, but none is as entertaining or life affirming as this little rear-drive roadster. Thank you, Mazda.'

These sentiments were echoed across the world, not just for this model but every one, and we'll look forward to the next one, scheduled for 2012.

Detail Improvements

The description of the Mk3 Upgrade included a number of detail changes as well as the fresh face and mechanical tweaks. In the UK the model names were now SE, Sport Tech and PowerShift.

All models were now gifted the features of the previous Option Pack as standard. These were: alloy wheels, cloth soft-top, stainless steel scuff plates, leather steering wheel with audio controls, leather-wrapped gear knob and handbrake lever, additional speakers and a storage net.

The previous black dash became silver and

Measures to reduce cabin noise included reinforcement to one of the cross-members and stiffer door modules. In addition, the Coupé gained urethane filling in the front suspension cross-member and damping material in the front roof section.

Mazda played down the changes to the car's character. Programme Manager Takao Kijima said: 'Although the kind of driving experience that people find enjoyable in a lightweight sports car never really changes, maintaining it in a vehicle that must also meet the continually changing demands of society is a daily challenge for Mazda engineers, and a particularly vital mission with the MX-5. Speaking as the engineer in charge of MX-5 development, I'm convinced that

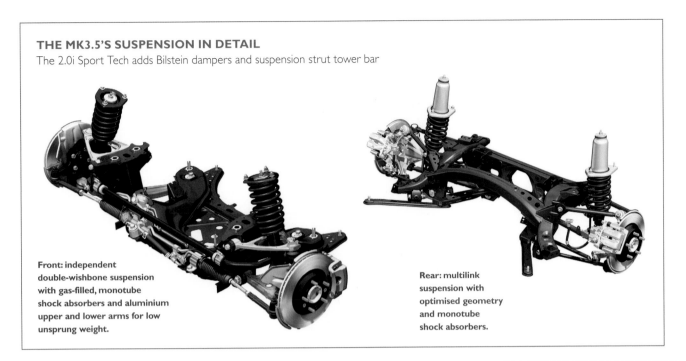

THE MK3.5'S SUSPENSION IN DETAIL
The 2.0i Sport Tech adds Bilstein dampers and suspension strut tower bar

Front: independent double-wishbone suspension with gas-filled, monotube shock absorbers and aluminium upper and lower arms for low unsprung weight.

Rear: multilink suspension with optimised geometry and monotube shock absorbers.

included a trip computer while leather seats now included a five-stage heating element. An auxiliary input jack for MP3 players became standard for all; Bose audio, Bluetooth, cruise control and climate control became standard for the Sport and PowerShift models (climate control was optional for the SE soft-top).

Upmarket Coupé

Mazda decided to give the retractable hard-top Coupé a more upmarket identity compared with the soft-top, and this was emphasised through a number of design features. The soft-top has a fin-type grille, but the Coupé has a mesh grille framed by a chrome ring; the headlamp inner bezels are painted silver on the soft-top but have a chrome finish on the Coupé; the fog lamp inner bezels are black on the soft-top but painted silver on the Coupé. The outer door handles are body coloured on the soft-top but have a chrome finish on the Coupé. The high-mounted stop light has a red lens on the soft-top but a clear lens on the Coupé.

Record-breaker

The MX-5 first entered the *Guinness Book of World Records* in 2000 as the best-selling sports car ever,

↑ **It's hard to recognise the MX-5 from this design sketch.**

with over 600,000 sold. As this book goes to press the number is close to 900,000 and still rising. As of February 2009 Mazda had recorded the following staggering figures:

Mk1 (1989–1998)	431,506 units
Mk2 (1998–2005)	290,123 units
Mk3 (since 2005)	138,559 units
Total	860,188 units

It has a long way to go to catch up with some other automotive favourites, though. More than 21 million old-style VW Beetles have been made, and 5.3 million original Minis were produced before it was replaced by the BMW version.

The MX-5 Retractable Hard-top

The first car to lift its entire lid and stow it in the boot was the Peugeot 402 Eclipse Decapotable back in 1935 (the roof mechanism was patented by Georges Pain in 1931). Perhaps the most dramatic example is the Ford Fairlane Skyliner of 1957–59. However, the car responsible for the current rash of retractables is the Mercedes SLK. Peugeot hit back to offer a disappearing roof to the masses with the 206CC.

If there was one car that didn't need an electric roof of any sort then it was the MX-5. From the very beginning its roof has folded with a minimum of muscle or fuss. When it appeared, however, the reaction was an instant 'gotta-have-it'.

At launch in the UK and Europe, the hard-top coupé was christened the MX-5 Roadster Coupé and was available on all trim levels, always with climate control as standard. In North America it was called the MX-5 Power Retractable Hard Top and was available on all but the lowest trim level. In Japan it was called the Mazda Roadster Power Retractable Hard Top.

Hood up, it's gorgeous. Hood down, the metal hood cover gives the car a long, sleek deck.

The Coupé looks stylish with the hood up, it's also quieter inside.

Pushing the button and watching the hood unfold is, of course, a pleasure. The action is as smooth, quick and elegant as you'd expect from an MX-5. The author of this book also discovered the truth about her core of inner laziness. When the Coupé was in the drive, its hood went down with every turn of the ignition key, whereas the resident 1995 Eunos Roadster's hood frequently stays up for short journeys.

Another advantage is a reduction in noise on the motorway, although the Mk3 and 3.5's soft tops are extremely snug and keep the cabin pretty civilised already. A hard-top will always give the body an extra degree of stiffness, too, to add an edge to the handling that only on-the-edge drivers will notice. Another, rather sad advantage, is that you can't slash a metal roof.

A special version of the Coupé was shown at the 2007 Tokyo Auto Salon (in December 2006), alongside the Mazdaspeed M'z Tune. The Kurenai Coupé Concept was glitzed up with extra chrome and purple paint with glass flakes, and the interior was trimmed with red Italian leather and Alcantara. Mazda described it as 'a chic open-style customized model perfect for passionate people'.

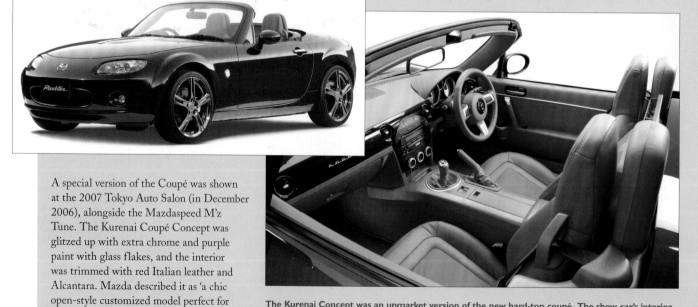

The Kurenai Concept was an upmarket version of the new hard-top coupé. The show car's interior was trimmed in soft red leather. It would have been hard on the eyes for a long trip, though.

The MX-5's retractable hood is poetry in motion.

CHAPTER 7
SPECIAL EDITIONS

Frequent limited editions were used in every market to boost sales, produced locally in the early years. As the Mazda factory turned out cars in batches of a particular colour, importers in each country would create their own specials. For example, the UK Merlot coincides with the US M edition, and the 1998 Berkeley and Eunos VR Limited both have Sparkle Green paintwork.

As well as their striking colours, limited editions frequently offer more equipment and nice touches such as a wooden steering wheel or splashes of chrome trim. So they tend to command higher prices than the standard cars, even if the buyer is not an aficionado. As a rule of thumb, those offering power steering, electric windows and other goodies will be in more demand than those offering little more than a nice colour and a badge.

UK models

In the UK, the importer MCL bought cars from Mazda and was then allowed to enhance the cars or even respray them as the sales department thought fit. Additional novelties such as the Gleneagles' flat hat were sourced and added to increase desirability.

The cars chosen to be limited editions were frequently base models because it was more profitable to buy a plain car in a good colour, dress it up with some alloy wheels and nice details then sell it for a higher price. This is a common sales tactic employed by most volume car manufacturers.

From 1990 until MCL lost the Mazda franchise in 2001, UK limited editions were built at its distribution centre at Sheerness. Mark Fryer worked at Sheerness, preparing new Kias. He remembered that he and his colleagues often threw in ideas to build a story or a character for a new special MX-5 based around a colour. The Monza was suggested after one employee had visited the

Italian Grand Prix. A batch of rich red wine-coloured cars became the Merlot. Bright sunny yellow cars, evoking sun and sea escaped becoming the MX-5 Bognor and were christened California.

One of the first UK specials, produced around the same time as the first limited edition was the Le Mans. Originally 24 were to be built, but a number of dealers recoiled in horror at the orange and green jester outfit, and after the first 10 had been slow to move the run was cut short. Only 22 were ever completed. The final pair, which had had their BBR turbos fitted, were sprayed a nice, safe black. Several more languished on dealer forecourts for a while before coming back for the same treatment. One, belonging to Clive Southern, had its green sprayed over orange by the dealer, and he bought it for a cut price. It is possible that only a handful still exist.

The most elaborate special was the Jasper Conran of 2000. Sadly, it missed the mark because it was selling for Mercedes money, and it is believed that MCL lost a great deal of money on the project. Again, some lucky owners got to snap up the most stubborn forecourt sitters for a song.

UK Special editions

BBR TURBO
Built: approx. 200
Strictly speaking, the BBR Turbo was not a limited edition. As detailed in Chapter Three, it was created for MCL in the UK by Brodie Brittain Racing of Northampton. Kits were sold to and fitted by Mazda dealers and the entire car including the conversion was covered by the manufacturer's warranty. They were usually red, black or white.

These cars are extremely rare – a number have been spotted in scrapyards, so fewer than the original 200 exist in the UK. Some kits were sold in the USA, but did not prove popular and were soon withdrawn.

← The US Special Edition was the equivalent of the Niseko, and used the same photos for its brochure.

↑ **The BBR Turbo kit included a rear spoiler, but** *Autocar's* **test car, driven against the Lotus Elan in 1991, did not have one. (LAT)**

→ **1991 Limited Edition had British Racing Green paint and its wire-lookalike alloys were painted green between the spokes. This immaculate car was stored for a decade. (Liz Turner)**

↗ **The Limited Edition had matching brass plaques displaying the car's individual number on the dash, and a leather wallet. (James Mann)**

They are generally reliable, although exhaust manifolds tend to crack and cost several hundred pounds to replace. If there are problems with the ECU, it is all-but impossible to replace with an original, but you can use an aftermarket ECU tuned to the turbo by a performance specialist. A record of regular servicing and, in particular, plenty of nice fresh oil is essential. There have also been cases of leaks from the oil take-off pipe from the sump (the turbo uses the same oil as the engine) so look out for any signs of oil patches where the car has been parked.

Because the BBR is not a limited edition, it doesn't come with a numbered plaque, certificate or gifts. The conversion was only suitable for the Mk1 1.6.

1991 MK1 LIMITED EDITION
Built: 250
Price new: £18,249

The Mk1 Limited Edition celebrated the first birthday of the MX-5 in the UK and was finished in BRG, with tan leather trim, leather-bound over mats, wood-rim wheel, gear knob and handbrake and deep pile carpet. Each car came with a numbered dash plaque, a leather wallet with matching plaque, a certificate of authenticity and an embossed leather key fob. Specification included central locking, a special console with distinctive clock, Clarion CRX111R radio-cassette with four speakers and polished treadplates. The unique BBS alloys, 6Jx15 painted green inside, haven't been repeated since, so make sure you buy a car with a good set.

1991 LE MANS
Built: 24
Price new: £20,499

Produced to celebrate Mazda's victory with the quad-rotor 787B at the Le Mans 24-hour race, and wearing the same green and orange paint scheme, plus plastic stick-on white tape (*Motor Sport* described it as looking like a cross between a slice of Battenburg and an Argyle sock). Underneath, the bonnet was the BBR turbo conversion, and it wore a ground-hugging body kit with a rear spoiler sourced from Finish Line.

It ran on OZ alloy wheels of 6J × 15 with a winner's laurel leaf and Le Mans 24 decals, and was well equipped, featuring power steering, electric windows, central locking and an alarm. The optional hard-top came in matching solid green. Each car came with a wallet including a card signed by the Le Mans-winning driver Johnny Herbert, who is perhaps better known in the UK for his long Formula One career.

The official number made was 24, but actually, only 22 red cars were resprayed at MCL's Sheerness facility in the UK. At the time, they were extremely unpopular. One car, currently owned by UK club committee member Clive Southern, had the green squares resprayed by the dealer, so his car is unique.

These cars were originally red before being resprayed in the UK. The engine was stripped out, but if you lift the carpets, the floor is still red.

↑ The Mazdaspeed 787B was the first Japanese car to win Le Mans. MCL celebrated by creating the MX-5 Le Mans. (LAT)

← The 1991 Le Mans limited edition MX-5 celebrated the famous win; this car is very original. (Dougie Firth)

↗ A Le Mans is masked up ready for addition of its Argyle-sock green diamond at Sheerness. (Mark Fryer)

→ Clive Southern's unique car had its green squares painted over by the dealer to make it more attractive! (Dougie Firth)

APRIL 1992–AUGUST 1993 SE
Built: 200
Price new: £18,686

Based on the 1.6i, and only available in Brilliant Black paint with SE badging, the SE ran on 10-spoke 7J x15 polished alloys with locking wheel nuts and low-profile 215/45/ZR15 tyres with ABS as standard. The cabin was trimmed with tan leather with a deep pile carpet, wooden steering wheel, gearknob and handbrake, along with stainless steel kick plates.

JUNE 1993–FEBRUARY 1994 1.8I SE
Built: 150
Price new: £18,449

As above, but with 6.5J x 15 wheels and now unpolished.

1994
Revised 130bhp 1.8 introduced.

APRIL 1995
1.6 reintroduced in addition to 1.8i and 1.8iS.

MAY–OCTOBER 1995 CALIFORNIA
Built: 300
Price new: £15,795

The California was a very desirable model marking the fifth anniversary of the MX-5 in the UK. Available as 130bhp 1.8i only, and 'in any colour as long as it's Sunburst Yellow,' it had power steering and an immobiliser but with manual windows, door mirrors and aerial plus five-spoke 7J x 15 alloys with wide 195/50VR 15 low-profile Dunlop tyres and a Clarion CRX601R radio-cassette. The California badge on the back panel had its own number plaque and the car came with a leather owner's wallet.

OCTOBER 1995–MAY 96 GLENEAGLES 1.8I
Built: 400
Price new: £16,995

Named after the famous Gleneagles Hotel and Golf Club near Stirling in Scotland, the Gleneagles special edition was based on the MX-5 1.8i, with Montego Blue paint, black carpet, champagne leather seats and steering wheel and Gleneagles logos everywhere. The tonneau cover was larger than usual, and tucks down just behind the seats. Other features include an impressive walnut-style dash with hinged centre compartment, Gleneagles tartan trim on gear lever gaiter and a Gleneagles crest showing the eagle landing on the centre of the steering wheel. Power steering,

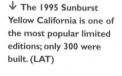

The 1995 Sunburst Yellow California is one of the most popular limited editions; only 300 were built. (LAT)

immobiliser, Clarion DRX8175R single CD player and five-spoke 15in alloys were also standard. The brochure read: 'The world-famous Gleneagles Hotel and Golf Club is steeped in tradition. These are values in common with the MX-5.'

The wood-effect console is actually just painted plastic, and the paint can fade or turn white if it has been in the sun or rain too much. Look for the matching Tartan wallet. It originally came with a pair of tartan caps for the driver and passenger, but these are very rare, although you can buy a tartan golf cap from Gleneagles.

One example was raffled and the proceeds helped send Scottish athletes to the 1996 Olympics in Atlanta.

MAY 1996–JANUARY 1997 MONACO 1.6l
Built: 450
Price new: £13,750
Based on the 90bhp 1.6i with five-speed gearbox, the Monaco featured special British Racing Green paint, body-coloured mirrors, Monaco graphics and a contrasting tan hood, along with Reflex five-spoke alloy wheels and locking wheel nuts. A Clarion ARB017E radio/cassette unit with removable front was also fitted.

JUNE–OCTOBER 1996 MERLOT 1.8l
Built: 600
Price new: £16,350
Launched alongside the Monaco, but based on the 131bhp 1.8i with power steering, the Merlot

Mazda MX-5

Gleneagles
Special Edition

↑ The 1995 Gleneagles celebrated the famous golfing hotel; one example was raffled to help send Olympic Games competitors to Atlanta. (Simon Farnhell)

← The 1996 Merlot limited editions were created around the batches of colours to be sent out by the factory. (Simon Farnhell)

was finished in Vin Rouge mica paint with Merlot
badging and matching mudflaps. Specification
included Phantom five-spoke alloy wheels with
locking wheel nuts, shod with Dunlop SP2000
tyres, grey leather seats (US version had tan
leather) and wood dash trim. The first 400 had a
leather-trimmed steering wheel, but the final 200
made do with polyurethane. Equipment included
a Clarion DRX8175R single-disc CD audio unit
RDS/EON and an immobiliser.

FEBRUARY–JUNE 1997 DAKAR
Built: 400
Price new: £17,210
The Dakar was based on a 1.8 with Twilight
Blue metallic paint, colour-keyed door mirrors
and rear mudflaps, grey leather upholstery with
dark blue piping and matching door panels.

Specification included a burr walnut effect dash
centre and console trims, chrome rear brace bar
and treadplates, Momo leather-trimmed steering
wheel, Dakar badging and floor mats, power
steering, Sony XR C500 RDS radio-cassette, and
immobiliser. It ran on 16-spoke 15in X 7JJ FOMB
Activa alloy wheels, with locking wheel nuts, and
Dunlop SP Sport 2000 195/50VR15 tyres. All
Dakar special editions sported a numbered plaque.

MAY–SEPTEMBER 1997 MONZA
Built: 800
Price new: £14,595
Named after the famous Italian racetrack, the
Monza wears British Racing Green with a Monza
logo showing a map of the circuit and a laurel
wreath on the nose and rear quarter panels.
These plastic transfers have a habit of peeling off

and no replacements are available.

It is based on the 1.6i, so in keeping with the racing cars that raced on the Monza banking, it has no power steering and the spec is basic. It even has wind-up windows. It has five-spoke 14 x 6JJ Aliseo alloy wheels with locking wheel nuts and a Clarion AR6270 audio/ cassette system.

MAY–SEPTEMBER 1997 HARVARD
Built: 500
Price new: £17,495
Named after the famous US college (Oxford and Cambridge would have reminded UK buyers of some rather different cars), the Harvard was based on the 1.8i and finished in Silver Stone metallic paint with Harvard badging and floor mats. It ran on five-spoke 15in x 7JJ Aliseo alloy wheels with

locking wheel nuts and 195/50 VR15 Pirelli P6000 tyres. Inside the driver sat on sumptuous, burgundy leather upholstery with grey piping and held a Momo leather steering wheel while facing a dark burr wood dash. Equipment included power steering, a high-power Clarion DRX8175R RDS audio/CD system, immobiliser, chromed brace bar and scuff plates, but ABS, airbags and power windows were all absent.

OCTOBER 1997 CLASSIC
Built: 400
The Classic was based on the 1.8i with black paint, 15in alloys, black leather interior with red stitching, wood trim, Momo leather-rim steering wheel, power steering, stainless steel brace bar and scuff plates. It had manual windows, an RDS radio cassette system and came with a Classic key fob.

↓ **This Classic Black MX-5 was the winner of the UK Owners' Club 'Hot 5' concours 2001. It has a supercharged engine and body kit fitted by Maztek. (Andrew Priest)**

JANUARY 1998 BERKELEY
Built: 400
Price new: £17,600
The Berkeley was the UK's final version of the Mk1, It came in Sparkle Green (turquoise) metallic paint with Berkeley decals on the front wings below the side repeaters. Inside were black leather seat facings with light grey centre door panels finished with black top stitching, a tactile Momo leather steering wheel and black leather gaiters on the gear lever and handbrake. An individually numbered plaque was mounted on the dark burr wood trim console and the key hung from a special Berkeley fob. Goodies included 15in five-spoke alloy wheels, power steering, a single CD player, immobiliser, stainless-steel brace bar and scuff plates, and a chrome boot rack, but no ABS, airbags or power windows.

↓ **Newly imported Sparkle Green MX-5s are transformed into Berkeley limited editions at MCL's Sheerness PDI centre in 1998. (Mark Fryer)**

Mk2 limited editions

DECEMBER 1998–1999 SPORT 1.8i (RED)
Built: 300
Price new: £22,535
In terms of performance and handling, the Sport is no sportier than the standard 140bhp 1.8iS on which it is based. Wearing a body kit with front fog lamps, it was available in Classic Red only and came with a colour co-ordinated hard-top. Kit includes air-conditioning, a wood interior trim kit and seats with black leather facings and Sport mats.

1999 SPORT 1.8i (BLUE)
Built: 300
The demand for the Classic Red Sport was such, that it was followed by a version in Racing Blue.

10TH ANNIVERSARY
Built: 7,000 (3,700 for Europe, 600 for UK)

This was the first limited edition to be offered worldwide. It celebrated the MX-5's 10th birthday and was based on the 1.8iS with, for the first time outside Japan, a six-speed close-ratio gearbox. Performance is enhanced with a sport-tuned suspension featuring Bilstein shock absorbers plus a Torsen limited-slip differential and a front strut-tower brace to decrease body roll. It came only in Innocent Blue mica paint with highly polished wheels. The seats had black leather side panels and headrests with suede-look blue material on the centre panels. A Nardi leather-covered steering wheel and gear lever were also finished in black and blue. The speedo and rev counter had chrome surrounds and red needles.

The 10th Anniversary edition is much sought-after, but try to get one with good wheels. The lacquer was notoriously thin, prompting a recall. Most were replaced, but the replacements often show

← The rare Mk2 10th Anniversary gift set included a pair of watches, a key ring and an exquisite model. (James Mann)

↓ The 10th Anniversary was the first limited edition available worldwide. It was also the first time a six-speed 'box had been offered outside Japan. (James Mann)

↑ The Jasper Conran platinum interior was plush Connolly leather, but the car was too expensive. (Mazda)

↗ Icon of 2000 had Art Vin paint. (Mahogany mica in the States)

→ Second generation California of 2000 is a great colour, but was available as a 1.6.

similar problems, and new ones are rare. Be sure to get your certificate and gifts, which were a pair of Seiko watches with logo, and a model car. German dealers didn't always give them out, so now they're worth a fortune.

2000 JASPER CONRAN
Built: 500

This special edition, based on the 1.8iS, featured interior enhancements care of fashion designer Jasper Conran. Of the 500 models produced, 100 were in metallic Platinum with a red interior and 400 were Classic Black with a black interior. Both had 15in BBS wheels and were trimmed inside with soft, aromatic Connolly hide as used by Rolls-Royce and Ferrari. Interior details included aluminium-effect fascia, gearknob and handbrake button. Entertainment came care of a Sony audio system with single CD and Minidisc changer. Each car was individually numbered and a donation for each car sold was given to the London Lighthouse. Price new was £21,000 for Classic Black, £24,000 for the Platinum, which also came with a set of smart Jasper Conran luggage. A lovely car, but this was far too much to pay for an MX-5 new. This edition sold like cold cakes.

2000 CALIFORNIA MK2
Built: 500
Price new: £16,000

Once again in Sunburst Yellow with body-coloured mirrors and optional body-colour hard-top, plus California interior mats, this time the special edition was based on the 1.6i with pretty much base-model standard equipment. Additions were air-con, a CD player and five-spoke 15in alloys. Fans of the Mk1 California regard this car as a misuse of the name.

JULY 2000 ISOLA
Built: 500
Price new: £16,000

The Isola is a 1.6i in Classic Red with matching hard top, Isola badges and 14in alloy wheels with 185/60/R14 82V Yokohama tyres and locking wheel nuts. The black canvas roof matches its black cloth upholstery. It was a very basic model and the audio specification was 'as per customer's choice', i.e. none as standard.

2000 DIVINE
Built: 500

The what? The Divine was exactly the same as the Isola, but you had a stereo as standard instead of the hard-top. In fact, the press office even sent out the same photograph with a different name on it. It was launched in July 2000.

2000 ICON
Built: 750
Price new: £19,200

The upmarket Icon was based on a 1.8iS, but with a six-speed gearbox driving the rear wheels through a Torsen differential (sharing the same gear ratios as the 10th Anniversary). On the outside it featured Art Vin (Mahogany mica) paint and 15in five-spoke wheels with low-profile tyres and optional body-colour hard-top. In the UK it had a black roof with a tan tonneau, overseas the roof was also tan. The cabin was beige with leather seats and unique Icon interior mats. A feeling of real class was delivered by the lacquer-finished wooden steering wheel, gearknob and handbrake handle, cream dials with chrome rings and orange needles plus chrome inner door handles and handbrake button.

The Icon was created in Japan, but its badges were sourced in the UK, and these tended to fall apart. Sadly, later Icon badges are quite different.

Mazda MX-5 Icon

Mk2.5 limited editions

2002 PHOENIX
Built: 1,200
Price new: 1.6i £15,995, 1.8i £16,595
(Titanium paint added £150)

The first pan-European limited edition was launched in March with a choice of Brilliant Black or Titanium Grey metallic paint and unique 15in alloys. Inside, heated Sienna Brown leather heated seats were matched by the door panels. The gearshift and handbrake lever were black leather, the steering

→ The 2002 Phoenix had Sienna Brown leather heated seats and a two-tone steering wheel.

↓ Phoenix, the first pan-European limited edition was the first Mk2.5 limited edition. (Mazda)

wheel a two-tone Nardi with Black or Sienna Brown hand grips, and the console was framed in aluminium. Extra kit included remote door locking with boot release, electric mirrors, an electric aerial and two additional tweeters for the stereo, plus a Torsen limited-slip differential for the 1.8 and an aero board for the 1.6.

2002 ARIZONA
Built: 1,000
Price new: 1.6 £16,095, 1.8 £16,605

This well equipped limited edition was launched for summer 2002, priced at a premium of £1,100 and £1,200 respectively above the price of the standard cars. It came in Sunlight Silver, sparkly Blaze Yellow mica (exclusive to the Arizona) or Eternal Red, although choosing one of the metallic colours would add another £250 to the price. Standard kit included unique 15in alloy wheels, style bars and windblocker, stainless steel scuff plates, aluminium centre console trim, remote central locking with boot release, electric windows, CD player and electric aerial. The heated sports seats, Nardi steering wheel gearknob and handbrake lever were trimmed in black leather with contrasting silver stitching. The 1.8 also had a Torsen limited-slip diff as standard.

2002 TRILOGY
Built: 333
Price new: £16,995

A girl's best friend? The Trilogy was launched in October 2002 in conjunction with Trilogy diamond

jewellery, and came with a solid silver key ring decorated with three .25 carat rocks. The press release announced that the trilogy diamond signified past, present and future, and the 'i' in the name was represented as three dots in a vertical line on the brochure. The high specification included Medici light grey Trilogy-branded high-backed leather seats, a Nardi two-tone steering wheel and gear knob, and leather handbrake lever. Interior glitz was provided by Trilogy badged scuff plates, chrome air-vent bezels and door handles and a chrome centre panel featuring the limited-edition number. For safety, twin airbags and ABS were standard. It was available only in black with a black soft-top, showing off its 15in chrome five-spoke wheels. When negotiating to buy one, knock 'em down if the keyring has vanished – as Marilyn sang: 'Get that ice, or else no dice.'

↑ ↑ Well equipped Arizona has style bars as standard. (Mazda)

← The 2003 Trilogy's silver keyring contained three (small) .25 carat diamonds; 333 were made.

↑ The 2002 Montana had Garnet Red mica paint and this one apparently drove itself.

2002 MONTANA
Built: 500
Price new: £18,995
Billed as an MX-5 for the winter (it was launched in October), the Montana came with a detachable hard-top, air-conditioning, heated seats and fog lamps as standard. It was available as a 1.8i only, in either Racing Green mica or Garnet Red mica (with no extra charge for metallic paint) and 15in five-spoke alloys. Inside, the heated leather seats and carpets were matching tan. The leather-wrapped wheel and gear knob by Nardi and 'wood-look' centre panel

– Cerion Silver or Strato Blue – with a dark blue or grey cloth soft top and cover, Nardi two-tone leather-wrapped steering wheel and gear knob, aluminium-look centre panel, a single CD with four speakers, remote central locking and stainless steel scuff plates. The seats are blue or grey cloth, but the 1.8i offered optional heated grey leather.

2003 ANGELS
Built: 500
Price new: 1.6i £16,500, 1.8i £17,000 (plus £250 for metallic paint)

The Angels edition was created to celebrate the film of the 1970s cult series *Charlie's Angels*. The colours were divided as follows: 1.6i 114 in Sunlight Silver, 61 Eternal Red; 1.8i 211 in Sunlight Silver and 114 Eternal Red. Kit included 15in alloy wheels, Medici black leather seats with subtle red stitching, tough-looking rear spoiler, style bars and wind blocker. The cabin glittered with a chrome effect centre panel, a radio and CD player, stainless-steel scuff plates with Angels badging, and there were also Angels exterior badges. The brochure suggests: 'If you want to be inconspicuous, try a nice little hatchback.'

2003 INDIANA
Built 250 £17,000

This extremely limited edition arrived in showrooms in mid-September, wearing a unique Garnet Red paintwork and 15in alloy wheels. All Indianas were powered by the 146PS 1.8 engine. Its comforts included a CD player, beige heated leather seats, tan carpets, a wooden steering wheel and luxurious wood trim. Fog lamps were standard, as were remote locking, a windblocker and MX-5 scuff plates.

↑↑ The 2003 Angels celebrated the film of cult TV series *Charlie's Angels*. It wore the famous silhouette of the Angels on its badges and scuff plates.

↑ The 2004 Euphonic had a premium Sony sound system, leather seats and carbon inserts for the console.

added a touch of ranch or maybe gentleman's club. Other goodies included a single CD player with two additional tweeters, scuff plates, chrome interior door handles and remote central locking. Twin airbags and ABS were standard.

2003 NEVADA
Built 2050
Price new: 1.6i cloth £15,995, 1.8i cloth £16,495, leather £16,995

Mazda billed the Nevada as 'great value for money'. It gained new 16in alloys, two metallic colours

2004 EUPHONIC
Built 2000
Price new: 1.6i £16,500, 1.8i £17,000

This is a special for the 'import tuner generation'. Its name means pleasantness or smoothness of sound, chosen because this little car boasts a big sound system. It has a premium Sony CD-MP80 CD/MP3 player set into an 'alpha GEL shock resistant system' and CDX-T69 six-CD changer, one Sony tweeter and one Xplod loudspeaker integrated into each door panel, capable of handling 150 watts each side. It takes cues from the RX-8 with its black and red heated leather seats, black leather steering wheel,

gearknob and handbrake lever with red stitching plus red door inserts. A carbon-effect centre panel and stainless steel scuff plates continue the 'tuner' theme.

A black cloth soft-top and windblocker were standard. It came in Velocity Red mica, Titanium Grey metallic, Brilliant Black and Sunlight Silver metallic (cheekily, metallic paint came at extra cost). ABS, EBD, limited-slip diff and central locking were standard.

2004 ARCTIC
Built 2000
Price new 1.6i £17,000, 1.8 £17,500

The Arctic's three metallic colours suggest a polar bear's habitat: exclusive Razor Blue, Sunlight Silver and Titanium Grey. All cars had unique multi-spoke 15in alloys, and the black cloth soft-top came with a blue cover to match the dark blue heated leather seats and blue door inserts. Black leather trimmed the steering wheel, gear knob and handbrake lever. Added goodies were: air-con, chrome side window mouldings and scuff plates, remote central locking and deadlocking, a single CD player with two additional tweeters and a wind blocker with two built-in additional speakers (normally an option on the 1.6i).

An accessory package consisting of a rear style bar, soundboard, chrome filler cap, chrome outer door handle finish and chrome door mirror finish at £499.95, a saving of £375.

2005 ICON
Built Unknown
Price new: 1.6 £16,674, 1.8 £17,100

Eye-catching Chilli Orange mica and Black mica paint were unique to the Icon, or you could choose Titanium Grey or Sunlight Silver from the standard palette. The wheels are 15in five-spoke alloys, and stylish front fog lights were standard. Heated black leather seats matched the black leather steering wheel, gear knob and handbrake lever, all with orange stitching. The single CD was boosted by two additional tweeters and a standard windblocker added two speakers (this was already standard for 1.8i). Other standard goodies were remote central locking and stainless steel scuffs. The price list included a host of tempting shiny chrome options and a body-colour hard-top for £999.95 rather than the usual £1,499.95. The Icon was launched in April 2005.

↑ The 2004 Arctic was named after its icy cool colour options. It came with 15in alloy wheels and a cloth soft-top.

Mk3

2005 3RD GENERATION LIMITED
Built: 3,500 worldwide
Price new: £19,999

The 3rd Generation Limited, also known as the
Launch Edition, marked the release of the all-new
MK3 (NC); it was only the second special edition
released worldwide (the first being the 10th
Anniversary). A limited run of 3,500 each had a
special plaque ahead of the gear stick. Global editions
show a number out of 3,500, but the UK kept things
cosy with a number out of 300 (the UK allocation).

Features over and above the 2.0i Sport include
a unique Velocity Red mica paint, chrome headlight
inserts and chrome rings around the fog lights and
front grille. The style bars are silver like those of
the Sport (the 1.8- and standard 2.0-litre's bars are
black). A chrome windscreen surround and chrome
door handles make it easy to identify from a distance.

The red and black leather interior has a satin silver
dash with chrome accents on the dials. The Bose
sound system features no fewer than seven speakers.
The unique 17in wheels have a new sword silver
finish, and were originally fitted with 205/45 R17

84W Michelin tyres, specially developed for the new
MX-5. Unfortunately many of these wheels had to be
replaced under warranty by Mazda due to the paint
surface bubbling around the centre cap.

UK enthusiast Paul Bateman has established a
register and website for this car featuring photos of
owners and their cars all over the world. See www.
mx5-3rdgenerationlimited.com. So far, though, no
one has registered with a number between 3,000
and 3,500, throwing doubt on how many were
actually sold.

3RD GENERATION LIMITED
0000 / 3500

2007 Z SPORT
Built: 400
Price new: £19,999

Loadsa bling and white lights. This 2.0-litre six-speeder came only in Radiant Ebony mica with a unique chrome grille surround and headlamp bezels, plus front fog lamps and a unique clear high-level brake light and side indicators with chrome side marker rings, chromed door handle covers and brushed aluminium style bar trim. Other kit included a black cloth soft-top, stainless-steel MX-5 scuff plates, Z-Sport branded luxury mats, BBS multi-spoke alloy wheels and stone coloured, stitched leather heated seats with matching co-ordinated door trim, steering wheel, gear knob and handbrake lever, plus brushed aluminium dash panel, chrome surround details and alloy pedals.

2007 ICON
Built: 1.8 – 875, 2.0 – 375
Price new: 1.8 5MT £16,825
2.0 6MT £17,825

Starting from the inside out, the 2007 Icon featured Icon-branded Medici leather sports seats with stitching co-ordinated with its exterior paint. Copper Red mica and Marble White cars featured red stitching, Stormy Blue mica cars had blue stitching. Extra kit included climate control, chrome style bars and Icon-branded mats.

2008 NISEKO
Built: 800, 1.8 Soft-top Roadster 240, 2.0 Hard-top coupé 560
Price new: 1.8 Soft-top £17,995, 2.0 Coupé £19,995

The Niseko was the first special edition available with a soft-top (1.8 only) or retractable hard-top (in 2.0 only). The link with the well-known Japanese ski resort of Niseko is its range of colours, which suggest snow and ice (as with the earlier Arctic). These were Icy Blue metallic (unique to the Niseko) and Sunlight Silver metallic. Both cars have special 17-inch alloys and a chrome pack including exterior door handle covers, side repeater surrounds, grille surround, front fog light surround and chrome headlamp bezels, plus body coloured style bar trim and Niseko exterior badging. The 1.8's soft-top is luxurious dark brown mohair. The cabin features dark brown heated leather seats, a dark brown leather steering wheel, with integrated audio controls, and matching handbrake and gear knob, plus door trim, all finished with blue stitching. Luxury mats have the Niseko logo in blue stitching. Both cars have climate control; the 2.0 coupé added a limited-slip diff and extra safety features such as DSC and side air bags.

↑ An unusual arrangement for a press shot: an MX-5 in the rain, but the driver of this 2007 Icon is probably still grinning under the black cloth hood.

↓ The Niseko was the first limited edition to be offered either as a soft-top or a hard-top. It was named after a Japanese ski resort, and this UK brochure shows off some cool detailing.

Desirability.

Only 800 individual Mazda MX-5 Niseko's will be sold in Britain. That makes them something really rather special.

A unique colour and trim combination means exclusivity comes as standard, while the choice of climate control air conditioning and heated leather seats assures your absolute comfort, whatever the weather. In response to rain, shine, or simply an open road, you can decide between the timeless roadster soft-top, or the world's fastest powered retractable hard top with the Mazda MX-5 Roadster Coupe, which rises or falls within just twelve seconds.

Given so much choice, the only real challenge is deciding which of the 800 is yours... quickly enough.

UK Limiteds gather

On 5 April 2009, an example of every UK limited edition made up to that date was gathered at the National Motor Museum, Beaulieu to be photographed for this book.

The event was organised by Paul Bateman, founder of the 3rd Generation Limited Register with the permission of Lord Montagu and a great deal of help from Beaulieu staff.

Just 35 cars were needed for the shoot, but Paul is a perfectionist and had lined up an entire set of understudies. In all 176 cars plus members drove through the gates and enjoyed a glorious sunny day out at the museum.

MK1

The UK Mk1 had a large number of limited editions over its long life, all created by the importer, MCL, as batches of a particular colour arrived. So the batch in rich red wine metallic became the Merlot, the sunshine yellow car became the California and so on. The rarest is the Le Mans, once described as looking like an Argyle sock – and it has to be said that the colour scheme looked better on the Le Mans-winning 787B quad-rotor racing car it commemorates.

The BBR Turbo was not actually a limited edition but a kit offered by Mazda dealers to anyone who wanted it. Around 200 were produced, although not all owners went for all the parts available. The BBR conversion is represented twice in this group – under the bonnets of the Le Mans and the SE.

MK2

The Mk2 brought in a second California, although this time it was a 1.6 rather than a 1.8, with fewer extra goodies than the original. The 10th Anniversary model was the first limited edition to be offered worldwide, and this was the first time the six-speed gearbox was offered outside Japan. The 2000 Jasper Conran was the most upmarket MK-5 ever.

MK2.5

The marketing department was working overtime during the lifetime of the Mk2 face-lift. The 2003 Angels edition was created in association with the film, starring Cameron Diaz, Lucy Liu and Drew Barrymore of the 1970s' cult TV series *Charlie's Angels*. The Trilogy of 2002 was created in association with jewelry maker, Trilogy, and it featured three diamonds in the keyring (which tends to disappear when a car is sold). For this generation, the yellow car became an Arizona.

MK3

The Mk3 began with a special edition, the 3rd Generation Limited, or Launch Edition. This was only the second special edition to be offered worldwide. Only three more specials, the Z Sport and Icon and Niseko appeared before the introduction of the Mk3 face-lift in 2008. The Niseko was the first special to be offered both as a soft-top roadster and a coupé with a retractable hard-top.

↑ Mk1 Back row: Merlot, Dakar, Monza, Harvard, Classic, Berkeley, Gleneagles. **Middle row: SE first release (this car also has a BBR Turbo kit), SE second release, California, Monaco. Front row: Limited Edition, Le Mans.**

→ (Top) Mk2 Back row: Icon, Isola, California, Jasper Conran. Front row: SE, 10th Anniversary, Sport.

→ (Middle) Mk2.5 Back row: Nevada, Angels, Indiana, Euphonic, Arctic, Icon. Front row: Phoenix, Arizona, Trilogy, Montana.

→ (Bottom) Mk3 Back row: Niseko, Icon, Z-Sport, 3rd Generation Limited. Front: Niseko Coupé.

plus it has Torsen limited-slip diff. The only options were air-con and a stripe designed by Mark Jordan.

POPULAR EQUIPMENT PACKAGE
Replaced A and B package from 1995, combining the features of both; adds Torsen diff from 1997.

1995 LEATHER PACKAGE
Replaced C package with tan leather interior and tan vinyl soft-top.

1996 POWER STEERING PACKAGE
Added power steering and wheel trim rings to standard cars. Montego Blue mica could now be specified on all cars in the range apart from R package.

1997 TOURING PACKAGE
Alloy wheels, power steering, leather steering wheel, electric windows, power door mirrors, door pockets.

US Equipment and Specials

1989 BASE MODEL
Steel wheels and manual steering; no audio system.

A PACKAGE
Power steering, leather-trimmed steering wheel, alloy wheels and stereo cassette.

B PACKAGE
As above, but adding cruise control, headrest speakers. From 1992 an electric aerial was added and the optional hard-top was given a heated rear screen. Colours were Classic Red, Crystal White or Mariner Blue; from Spring 1990 added Silver Stone metallic.

C PACKAGE
Loaded with desirable features such as BBS alloy wheels, cruise control, headrest speakers and a power aerial. Brilliant Black only in 1992; from 1993 became available in all colours except Mariner Blue.

R PACKAGE
Built: 1,218 (not limited)
The sporty R has a standard engine, but wears a body kit, alloy wheels and rides on stiffer suspension,

US Special editions

The rarest US specials are the 1991 'color cars', used to test customer reaction to colours. Each one is unique, and they are Orange, Teal Green metallic, Ice Green, Pale Yellow metallic, Electric Blue metallic and Raspberry metallic. The window sticker states, under 'Color of your Miata', 'Various Test Colors'. All had an X for the colour code.

1991 SPECIAL EDITION
Built: 4,000
Price new: $19,234
British Racing Green with B package, tan interior and part-leather seats, Nardi wood gearknob, stainless-steel scuff plates and CD player, brass plaque; Hard-top optional. Automatic offered at a slightly reduced premium. ABS brakes were optional.

1992 SUNBURST YELLOW
Built: 1,500
Price new: $16,770
Limited production, if not strictly a limited edition. Only available with A Package.

1992 BLACK MIATA
Built: 4,626 (not limited)
Price new: $18,800

Initially classed as a C package option. Brilliant Black exterior, tan leather interior with matching hood, BBS 14in alloy wheels. A hard-top, automatic, ABS, air-con, CD and limited-slip differential were optional.

1993
Miata suspension revised, new badge. 1.8 replaces 1.6

1993 LIMITED EDITION
Built: 1,500 limited edition
Price new: $22,270

This Brilliant Black model has front and rear spoilers and BBS alloy wheels on 185/60 R14 tyres. Red interior and red vinyl tonneau, leather steering wheel, Nardi leather gearknob, MSSS stereo system. Its sports suspension has Bilstein shocks and revised springs. All A and B package options included, plus limited-slip diff and anti-lock brakes.

1994 M EDITION
Built: 3,000
Price new $21,645

Luxury model in Montego Blue mica with tan leather interior and tan hood. Nardi wooden gearknob and handbrake handle, electric windows and mirrors, cruise control and central locking. Polished seven-spoke alloy wheels. Torsen diff was standard. Hard-top, ABS and automatic were optional, but ABS came as standard equipment with the auto.

1994 AND 1995 LAGUNA BLUE AND TAN
Built: 463
Price new: 1994 $20,155; 1995 $20,925

This was actually a standard C package Miata, but it is regarded as a special model by many enthusiasts. Air-con, hard-top, ABS, Premium Sound System, automatic transmission, all optional.

1995 M EDITION
Built: 3,500
Price new: $23,980

One of the most sought-after Miatas. Rich Merlot mica paint, 6J x 15in BBS alloys fitted with 195/55 tyres, ABS, limited-slip diff, leather interior trim, Nardi wooden gearknob and handbrake trim, air-conditioning and CD.

133bhp engine introduced

1996 M EDITION
Built: 2,968
Price new: $25,210

Featured Starlight mica paint, 15in Enkei five-spoke alloys. Tan leather seats with matching tan hood and hood cover, leather-trimmed wheel, Nardi wooden gearknob and handbrake handle. Lots of kit including power windows and mirrors. Automatic gearbox and hard-top optional.

1997 M EDITION
Built: 3,000
Price new: $24,935

The 1997 M came in Marina Green mica with tan leather trim and hood, polished six-spoke 15in alloy wheels, Nardi wooden gearknob and handbrake handle and air-conditioning. premium sound system with CD player and headrest speakers. Included Popular equipment package. Torsen limited-slip differential, rear subframe brace.

↓ The 10th Anniversary MX-5 had blue and black leather-trimmed interior, a six-speed gearbox and a Nardi steering wheel and gear knob. (Mazda)

↑ The SE and Shinsen were launched as a pair in 2003. The Shinsen was a step up from Base and had a five-speed transmission; the SE had a six-speed 'box.

1997 STO
Built: 1,500
Price new: $22,970

STO stands for Special Touring Option – or, according to its many fans: Still The One. Twilight Blue mica, wearing a rear spoiler, tan leather interior and tan vinyl top, 15in Enkei five-spoke alloy wheels and low-profile 50-series tyres, CD player and Nardi gear lever knob. Automatic and air-conditioning were optional.

1999 10TH ANNIVERSARY
Built: 3,150 to USA

Features included Sapphire Blue mica, polished alloy wheels, black and blue leather-trimmed Nardi steering wheel, blue suede seats, six-speed gearbox and Bose stereo system. See UK entry.

2000 MAHOGANY MICA

This popular limited edition, with a six-speed gearbox from the 10th Anniversary, has a cream interior, white dials with chrome trim rings, chrome door handles and stainless-steel scuff plates.

2001 SPECIAL EDITION
Built: 3,000
Price new: $26,195

Celebrating the 10th anniversary of the first special edition, the 2001 version once again has British Racing Green paintwork with tan leather upholstery and a tan convertible top. The cabin features a Nardi wood-rimmed wheel and polished wood gearknob. The list of standard features includes air-conditioning, power windows, mirrors and locks, fog lights, cruise control and chromed 16in alloy wheels. ABS and hard-top are optional.

2002 SPECIAL EDITION
Built: 2,500
Price new: $21,280

Available in two colour combinations: 1,500 in Titanium Gray metallic with Saddle Brown interior and 1,000 in Blazing Yellow mica with (for the first time) Classic Black leather seats with silver stitching, black dash and trim. Both cars have a six-speed transmission as standard. The body wears SE badges, a chrome-plated aluminium fuel filler cap, the wheels are new 16in alloys. Inside each cabin, the driver grips a Nardi steering wheel and is surrounded by aluminium-style details including vent rings and a leather handbrake handle with a silver release button. A Bose AM/FM six-disc CD changer provides entertainment.

2003

SE (SPECIAL EDITION)
Built 1,500 (Shinsen and SE combined)
SE price new $26,178
Lighter silver paint and five-spoke alloy wheels, six-speed manual transmission as standard, or four-speed manual was optional.

SHINSEN
Price new $21,458
The Shinsen was the SE's slightly less upmarket brother. It was a step up from Base, but still had a five-speed transmission (or optional auto). Power door locks and Cruise Control were standard.

2004–2006

MAZDASPEED MX-5
Price new $24,903
Introduced mid-year, the high-performance Mazdaspeed was powered by a turbocharged and intercooled 1.8-litre four-cylinder engine that pumped out 178 horsepower through an enhanced six-speed manual gearbox. It also came with beefed-up springs and dampers and 17-inch alloy wheels. The upscale cockpit featured black leather-trimmed upholstery and a Bose six-speaker audio system with CD.

2006 3RD GENERATION LTD
Price new $26,700
See UK version above.

2008 SPECIAL EDITION
Built 750
Price new $26,590 6-speed manual,
$27,340, 6-speed auto
The US cousin of the Niseko wore exclusive Icy Blue paint, complimented by a Saddle Brown soft-top. The cabin featured matching Saddle Brown leather with blue stitching for the heated front seats, steering wheel, parking-brake lever and silver-accented shift knob. A dark-silver finish instrument panel had

↑ **High-performance Mazdaspeed Editions were sold between 2004 and 2006. This 2005 Edition delivered 178bhp.**

← **The Mazdaspeed Edition's sporty cockpit had two-tone seats to match the body colour.**

chrome accents and housed an in-dash 6-disc CD changer for the Bose audio system with AudioPilot.

Shiny additions included chrome front headlight bezels, grille surround and fog lamp surrounds along with unique 17-inch alloy wheels.

↓ **The US Special Edition was the equivalent of the Niseko. The interior featured Saddle Brown leather seats with blue stitching.**

CHAPTER 8
THE ROADSTER

At its launch in 1990, the car we all love was called an MX-5 in the UK but a Miata in the US. From the third generation, Mazda tried to standardise the names, but the Americans have proved reluctant to lose the Miata name, so it has become unofficially the MX5 Miata. In Japan, it has always been the Roadster, but its branding changed instead.

In the late 1980s, Mazda launched three new brands: Autozam, Eunos and Anfini (also translated as Enfini). Anfini was the sporty brand while Eunos was the more luxury-orientated marque. Mazda decided to badge the new Roadster a Eunos, probably because it wanted to save the Anfini name for the more powerful RX-7.

The multi-brand experiment ended in the late 1990s, although Autozam and Anfini are still used for dealership chains. So, when the Mk2 arrived in 1998, it became the Mazda Roadster.

The original Eunos is now a common sight in the UK, and a number of Mk2 Roadsters are starting to arrive. Why? Well, the British and the Japanese have some important things in common: one is a love of Monty Python, another is the habit of driving on the left in cars with steering wheels on the right. There are some major differences, however, apart from opinions on the best way to eat fish (raw versus battered and deep fried). Where the Japanese like to impress their neighbours with shiny, brand-new cars, the Brits prefer to be seen as smart with money, and will happily boast that they bought all their Christmas cards in the previous January sale.

For the bargain-hungry British, a car that is almost exactly the same, but cheaper because it wears a different badge, is irresistible. So used Eunos Roadsters, discarded by the Japanese, became much sought-after in the UK. The prices of Japanese cars plummet after they are three years old because of the draconian 'shaken' inspection, the name of which describes how the owner feels once he's paid the enormous fee. So, from the

early 1990s, it became possible for the Roadster to be bought, shipped to the UK and still be sold for less than a second-hand Mazda MX-5. Some were brought in via Ireland using a loophole, now long-since closed.

Plenty of Roadsters also find their way to Australia and New Zealand, which share a preference for driving on the left, and which received fewer 'official' MX-5s than the UK. The MX-5 Club of New Zealand reports on its website that around 80 per cent of its members own a Eunos. However, in Australia these cars usually end up on the racetrack because of the continent's strict design rules governing road cars.

The Roadster tends to be better equipped than its European counterpart, offering standard luxuries such as air-conditioning and headrest speakers, electric windows and leather seats, plus many have a limited-slip diff as standard. It is also available with a separate series of limited editions and frequently sported different suspension set-ups. However, in most respects the MX-5 and Roadster are mechanically identical.

Naturally, the official Mazda line tended to stress the differences and difficulties of owning a Roadster, such as having a handbook in Japanese.

Company spokespeople insisted that the Eunos did not have the same rust protection as the UK cars, and buyers were advised to Waxoyl their cars. Specialists who are now stripping Eunos Roadsters and MX-5s for spares say this was total disinformation, the rust protection was the same. In fact, they find the Eunos frequently has less rust and corrosion than UK cars, so Eunos parts are frequently bought to help restore MX-5s. The reason why is uncertain, but some areas of Japan have a kinder climate than the UK.

The Eunos is labelled a 'grey' import, as opposed to a UK-spec MX-5 imported from Europe which is known as a parallel import. Mazda importer MCL actively campaigned against grey imports,

← The Japanese Mk1 Roadster wears the badge of Mazda's luxury Eunos brand on its nose. It offers a bargain to UK buyers. (Jonathan Elsey)

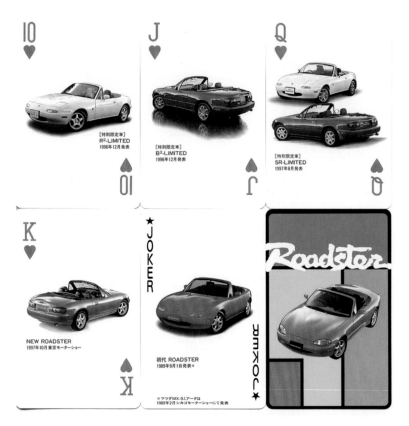

↑ It seems a little unkind to label the original Mk1 Roadster as the Joker; perhaps it means they're more fun? (Andrew Fearon)

and when they first started appearing in the UK, the Roadsters were unpopular with MX-5 owners because they brought down the residual values of the existing MX-5s. These days the Roadster is accepted on equal terms by the UK Owners' Club. This is vital for Roadster owners because insurance companies are often reluctant to cover grey imports, not knowing enough about them to be able to quote a realistic premium price. However, the club now offers insurance on an equal footing with UK cars. They remain cheaper than MX-5s and so are well worth a look. As with all older cars, however, the buyer needs to do plenty of reading and checking before buying.

There are now so many Roadsters in the UK, that a thriving specialist network has appeared to support potential buyers and owners.

Servicing should not be a problem, because most items used are identical. Roadsters have standard air-conditioning, however, and the 60,000-mile service will be more expensive to cover the changing of a slightly different drive belt. It will only cost the same as a service for a Mazda fitted with optional air-con though.

DID YOU KNOW?

Japanese cars are 'shaken' not stirred

Japanese cars must pass a regular rigorous inspection and repair procedure, carried out by a government inspection station on behalf of the Japanese Ministry of Transport.

After three years a car must undergo a 'shaken', which is a combination of inspection and minimal mandatory liability insurance, in addition a weight tax is charged. From then on the shaken is every two years. Altogether, the cost can be punishing.

Eunos Roadsters usually wear an inspection sticker in the top corner of their windscreen to show when they were last inspected. They should also have plenty of stickers under the bonnet. If one doesn't, it may have had its bonnet replaced following an accident.

Eunos Roadsters display Japanese Ministry of Transport stickers to show they have passed regular rigorous inspections. The 9 refers to the 9th year of the current Emperor (1999). (James Mann)

So, if anyone warns you that when they plug in the diagnostic machine it won't be able to read what's going on because the instructions come up in Japanese, say: 'Oh yes,' and 'you once picked up a hitch-hiker who disappeared'. It's nonsense.

It is true that the Eunos had a catalytic converter from launch, whereas the UK car only had one from 1992, and it has a different ECU (engine management system) which makes the engine run leaner to pass stricter Japanese smog regulations. Together, these emissions-reducing items will slightly reduce the performance of the car. The ECU rarely fails, but if it does, a specialist can order one from Japan, or you can buy a second-hand item.

Most spares are readily available new or second-hand. The only hitch is if you need a specific spare which is not in stock. Because the Mazda and Eunos have so many limited editions, all with different trim and suspension set-ups, your dealer or specialist will have to run a search to get the correct part

↑ **From the front, the only visible difference between the MkI MX-5 and Eunos Roadster is the badge. (LAT)**

← **The Eunos badge is quite distinct from the Mazda items (See Chapter 8). (James Mann)**

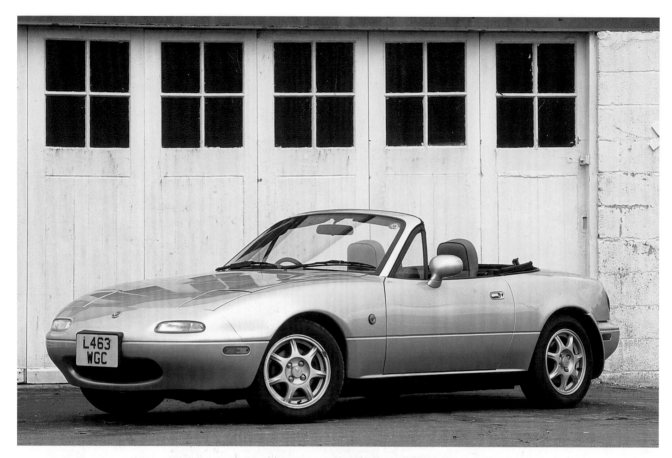

↑ A good support network has sprung up to cater for owners of imported Roadsters; they are also welcome in the UK Owners' Club. (James Mann)

→ The Eunos steering wheel is on the right and cabins tend to be better equipped than the UK MX-5. (James Mann)

number before it can be ordered.

Even if you decide you don't want a Eunos, it's a good idea to be aware of the main differences between the Roadster and the MX-5, because some unscrupulous sellers have been known

to switch badges and sell cars for higher prices. Some will also put a badge from a UK limited edition such as a California or a Merlot on a Eunos of the appropriate colour, even though the Roadster special editions were quite different. If you were caught out by either of these cons, you would still have a great car, but you'd have paid too much for it, and you'd lose out again when you came to sell it on.

Eunos in the UK

As with the MX-5, original, standard cars are sought-after but available only in small numbers. By far the most plentiful model is the V Special, manual or automatic, with its tan leather and wood package. The S Special is also around in quite large numbers and is a more desirable option.

Other limited editions, such as the RS have also reached these shores. However, specialists have spotted some oddities, such as a silver car with V Special options (it was never available in this colour, see details of special editions below).

The Japanese Mk2, called the Mazda Roadster is beginning to appear in the UK in numbers, but they tend to be more than 10 years old to avoid the cost of an SVO inspection.

The Japanese like to personalise their cars and spend plenty of cash modifying their Roadsters. So at least 80 per cent of the cars shipped over have some sort of mod, be it a simple strut brace, some added chrome or a truly appalling body kit.

The standard of workmanship demonstrated by Japanese modifying companies tends to be high, but obviously the mods themselves are a matter of taste.

Watch out if the wheels have been changed, though, because they could ruin your Roadster's deliciously balanced handling. Some of those fitted with suspension kits using Bilstein shock absorbers have an uncomfortably hard ride, too.

One serious concern is that a large number of Japanese sports cars, including Roadsters, are stolen in Japan and shipped abroad. BIMTA (British Independent Motor Trade Association www.bimta.co.org) can check your VIN (Vehicle Identification Number) against the stolen-vehicle register and run a mileage check for a small fee. If the car is stolen, the details will be passed on to the nearest police Stolen Vehicle Squad. However, if you already own the car, it may still be possible to negotiate legal title to it.

↑ Japanese owners tend to load their cars with visual and mechanical mods.

Spotting a Eunos

Apart from the badge on the nose, the most obvious difference is the back panel, which has a square indentation for the number plate, rather than the MX-5's rectangle. The side flashers will be red rather than amber. Looking inside the cabin, if an early car has air-conditioning, headrest speakers or an automatic transmission (only available on the MX-5 from the Mk2.5) then it's a Eunos. Some later models do not have airbags where the UK equivalent would.

The best way to make sure your 'Mazda' is not a dressed up Eunos, however, is to check the VIN number at the back of the engine bay. Genuine MX chassis numbers start with JMZ and have 13 characters; the Eunos chassis numbers begin NA. All

→ The major difference between the Roadster and MX-5 is the shape of the recess for the rear number plate (the later car also has a boot-mounted rear brakelight). (James Mann)

→ The VIN plate shows that this is a Mk1 Roadster imported privately from Japan. (Liz Turner)

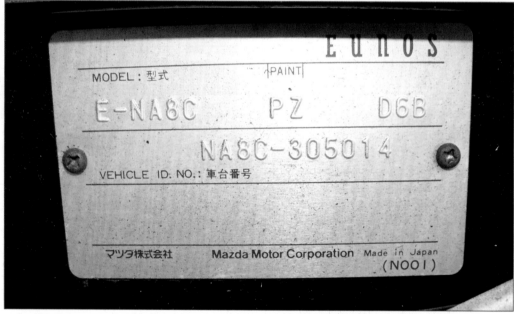

UK Mazdas are also listed at Mazda UK, so you can call to check on 0845 601 3147.

Naturally, any handbook that comes with the car will also be in Japanese, but English versions are available from specialists.

Around 15 per cent of all Japanese Roadsters were automatic, but this option was not offered in the UK until the Mk2.5 car. Automatics are extremely unpopular in the UK. All Roadsters have an airbag from 1996 onwards.

Conversion to UK spec

Any car up to 10 years old that is imported into the UK will need to pass a Single Vehicle Approval test.

This is a tough test which makes sure the car meets British safety standards, and to pass it cars must be fitted with items such as European-spec tyres and foglamps and a speedo in mph rather than kph. The Roadster can also fail if its vent and heater knobs protrude too far, so causing a risk of injury in an accident. (These can be changed.)

A small restrictor should also be slipped into the Japanese car's wider fuel opening, to make sure it can only take an unleaded fuel nozzle. The chrome rings around the dials often snap when the dial faces are changed, but reproductions are easily available.

Andrew Marriott of Autolink UK regularly imports Roadsters, but advised at time of publication that for some time the exchange rate has not been favourable enough to bring over cars young enough to need an SVO and all the changes it requires. Older cars tend to have had a speedo in miles fitted, however.

The standard radios have a different range of frequencies making it impossible to pick up some UK stations. Radio-band expanders can be fitted to the standard Panasonic unit to allow you to receive the majority of UK stations, or some people prefer to fit a new stereo. If the central console around the radio cracks while your fab new ICE is being fitted, don't kill the fitter, it happens a lot, and a replacement section is available.

Does the Eunos suffer any particular problems?

A large number of Eunos Roadsters have been in the UK for years, so you approach buying one in the same way you would a UK car. However, you need to be more careful about the paperwork if it has only just been imported. Many cars arrive in the UK without a service history or verification of the mileage, making it hard to know whether it has been well looked after. Even the age of your car may be a mystery, although you can probably find it on a sticker; check out the seat base, the white label on the door post or the label at the base of its seatbelt webbing. Some dealers will be able to offer a warranty, usually a mechanical breakdown insurance rather than the cover offered on a new car.

The Eunos is just as reliable and robust as its Mazda brother, but it's a good idea to give it an oil service immediately, if it has just arrived and the importer has not already done so. Oil pressure should be 1.8–6.0kg/cm. It should run at 2.0kg/cm at tickover when warm, or drop to 1.8 when the engine is hot.

Fit a new set of HT leads while you're at it. In common with the MX-5, these can fail after about 20,000 miles, and the catalytic converter can be damaged if the car runs too long with faulty leads. The car should accelerate and slow down smoothly,

← A large number of imported cars have been modified. This brochure shows just a few of the performance parts on offer to Japanese buyers. (Simon Farnhell)

so any hesitation may indicate faulty leads. Check that the cat light on the dash goes out when you start the car, to make sure you're not too late.

Some 1989–90 cars suffer from a crankshaft problem, which causes the car to cut out, or accelerate sluggishly, but this is rare.

Power-window motors seem to burn out or fail frequently, in common with the Mazda.

Most Roadsters have headrest speakers as standard as well as speakers in the doors. Many of these were incorrectly wired and sound very thin. See website www.Miata.net archives for a solution.

Check the tyres carefully, as you would on any older car. The Japanese tyres are made of a hard compound rubber and have a tendency to crack, particularly on the outer edges. If the car has been through an SVA, they may have been swapped already. Otherwise, budget for a new set of Yokohama A509s or A520s.

The plastic rear windows of cars in the hotter areas of Japan tend to go brown and crack, especially if careless owners have not bothered to unzip the window or fit the tonneau cover while the roof is down. Again, this is problem shared, although to a lesser extent, by older Mazdas.

The Eunos range

For more details of all the standard packages see the UK MX-5 Owners' Club site at http://ox.mx5oc. co.uk/guide_eunos.htm and http://en.wikipedia. org/wiki/List_of_Mazda_MX-5_colors_and_special_ editions

SEPTEMBER 1989

STANDARD 1.6i
Steel wheels, three-spoke Eunos steering wheel, manual steering, not very popular in Japan and quite rare in UK.

1.6 Special package adds power steering, seven-spoke alloy wheels, electric windows, leather trimmed Momo steering wheel. The Special package was always a popular option, accounting for almost half of all sales.

Optional extras: automatic transmission (n/a on base models from 1991), limited-slip differential, uprated suspension, Mazdaspeed five-spoke 6J ×

14in, SPA 17-spoke 6J × 14in wheels, polished cam cover, chromed door mirrors, front spoiler, air-conditioning, CD player, polished kickplates, alloy handbrake grip, wood trim package.

An extra brace bar was added to rear suspension after July 1991.

Colours available: Crystal White, Classic Red, Mariner Blue, Silver Stone metallic.

1990 V SPECIAL
Available as a manual or automatic. Neo Green, tan leather with matching hood cover, wood package with Nardi steering wheel, power steering, air-conditioning, power windows, CD player. Polished kickplates added by door speakers. From 1993 had the Sensory sound system as standard. Gains Nardi steering wheel from 1995. May have BBS wheels.

Optional extras: air-conditioning, hard-top, limited-slip diff, CD player, chrome door mirrors, polished tread plates, fog lamps.

1991 V SPECIAL
Also available in Brilliant Black, polished kickplates added. Side impact bars and option of an airbag added from July 1992.

AUGUST 1992 S SPECIAL
Price new: 220,000 yen

Sporty model in Classic Red or Brilliant Black with a rear spoiler. Manual only. Chassis stiffened with front strut brace, Bilstein dampers and BBS 6J × 14 alloy wheels with 185/60 tyres. Nardi three-spoke leather-trimmed wheel, gear knob. Mazda Sensory Sound Stereo (MSSS). Stainless steel kick plates and speaker grilles.

1993
1.8 replaces 1.6, chassis stiffened as for MX-5 and Miata. Model line-up as above continues; entry-level 1.8 has basic equipment as 1.6i above. Auto only available on Special Package and V Special.

V SPECIAL TYPE II
Price new: 2,486,000 yen

Adds a tan hood, chrome door mirrors and a set of highly polished seven-spoke alloy wheels to the existing V Special package. Nardi three-spoke steering wheel from 1995.

S SPECIAL
Price new: 2,111,000 yen

Now either Brilliant Black or Laguna Blue with Special equipment spec including uprated suspension with Bilstein shocks and thicker anti-roll bars, a front tower brace, a rear body brace, 14in BBS alloy wheels, Nardi steering wheel, polished kickplates and speaker surrounds, as above. Manual only.

1993/94
1.8 model introduced with extra chassis stiffening, Torsen differential added as Mazda MX-5 models.

1994
Brilliant Black added to basic colour line-up. S Special now also offered in Chaste White.

Spec changes 1995/96 include 133bhp engine, lightened flywheel, 4.3:1 final drive, standard airbag, rear-view mirror light. Roadster script on rear changes from red to green.

1995
M package takes Roadster line-up to seven. Steel wheels, three-spoke steering wheel, but power-assisted steering, electric windows and better stereo.

Special package can now be specified as manual or automatic, adding limited-slip differential with the manual version. Equipment as above: power steering, seven-spoke alloy wheels, electric windows, leather-trimmed Momo steering wheel; adds power mirrors, driver's airbag and improved stereo system.

S Special Type II adds 6J x 15 BBS alloys on low-profile Bridgestone Potenza RE010 tyres.

1996
All models adopted new Momo four-spoke steering wheel with airbag.

1998 Mk2 1.6 and 1.8 launched; Eunos becomes Mazda.

1.6
Standard package includes manual steering, manual windows, Mazda four-spoke steering wheel, five-speed gearbox, 185/60 tyres on 5.5J steel wheels. Colours: Chaste White, Classic Red, Highlight Silver metallic.

M package adds power steering, electric windows, Windblocker, automatic aerial, air-con, 5-speed manual or 4-speed automatic gearbox. Colours: as Standard package plus Evolution Orange, Twilight Blue mica, Brilliant Black.

Special package offers 5-speed manual or 4-speed automatic gearbox, power door mirrors, five-spoke alloys, 185/60 HR14 tyres on 6Jx14 rims. Torsen limited-slip differential on manual cars.

1.8

Standard package power steering, air-con, electric windows, windblocker, automatic aerial and power door mirrors. Manual versions of 1.8-litre cars had red needles for their gauges rather than white. ABS standard on auto and optional on manual. Torsen limited-slip differential standard on manual. Colours: Chaste White, Twilight Blue mica, Brilliant Black.

S 6-speed manual or 4-speed automatic, five-spoke alloys 185/60 HR14 tyres on 6J x14 rims, leather-wrapped three-spoke Nardi steering wheel, optional Bose radio/CD player, optional sat-nav. Colours: as Standard package plus Evolution Orange, Classic Red, Highlight Silver metallic.

RS 6-speed manual, five-spoke alloys, lightweight 195/50 VR15 Michelins on 6J × 15 rims, uprated suspension with Bilstein dampers and tower brace, leather-wrapped three-spoke Nardi steering wheel, polished treadplates optional Bose radio/CD player, optional sat-nav.

VS 6-speed manual or 4-speed auto, five-spoke alloys 185/60 HR14 tyres on 6J x14 rims, three-spoke wood Nardi steering wheel with matching gearlever and handbrake, tan interior trim and hood, polished treadplates, standard Bose radio/CD player, standard remote central locking, optional sat-nav.

Special colour: Grey Green mica.

2000 FACE-LIFTED ROADSTER ANNOUNCED IN JAPAN (MK2.5)

1.6

Basic level dropped, so M became the entry-level. It came with power steering, power door mirrors and windows, an electric aerial and 14in alloys.

SP added ABS, Torsen diff, Nardi wheel, windblocker and remote central locking.

1.8

S came with power steering, power door mirrors and windows, electric aerial 14in alloys.

SP Adds a Torsen diff, Nardi steering wheel and leather gearknob, windblocker and AM/FM stereo radio with two speakers. Remote central locking optional. ABS standard on auto only.

RS 16in wheels, limited-slip diff, uprated suspension with front strut bar and Bilstein dampers and rear mudguards, Nardi leather wheel and gearknob, stainless treadplates, AM/FM stereo radio.

RS-II adds red cloth seats and two-tone Nardi wheel, remote locking, Bose sound system and windblocker.

VS had 14in 5-spoke alloys, a Torsen diff, tan leather trim with a matching hood and hood cover, a Nardi wood-trimmed wheel, wooden gearknob and handbrake grip, windblocker, stainless scuff plates, power door locks with remote control, plus chrome internal release handles. Bose radio/CD.

Colours were: Crystal blue met, Classic red, Supreme Blue mica, Pure White, Brilliant Black. The RS-II didn't have blue options, VS had no red or silver, but a unique Grace Green mica.

JULY 2002

Minor revisions: all cars gained ISOFIX child seats for the passenger seat and a revised A-pillar to protect against head injuries. The Bose sound system became optional for the 1.6.

VS was split into two variants. Combination A came with black leather upholstery, a black cloth hood (instead of vinyl), all black interior with aluminium highlights. Combination B had a beige interior, a beige fabric hood and darker wood trim.

Colours: Crystal Blue was replaced by Splash Green mica and Garnet Red mica.

LATER ROADSTERS

Sooner or later, examples of more recent Roadsters will almost certainly arrive in the UK although full specifications are beyond the scope of this book.

Roadster limited editions

Here follows a summary of Roadster limited editions spanning all three marks of the Eunos and Mazda Roadster.

AUGUST 1991 J LIMITED
Built: 800
Price new: 1,900,000 yen

Based on Special package. Sunburst Yellow paint; wood trim package for interior plus stainless steel kickplate. Optional hard-top. Auto available for an extra 40,000 yen. Entire 800 allocation was sold within the first day.

DECEMBER 1992 S LIMITED
Built: 1,000
Price new: 2,350,000 yen

Based on S Special. Brilliant Black with gold-coloured BBS alloy wheels; red leather interior and Sensory Sound System.

NOVEMBER 1993 TOKYO LIMITED
Built: 40
Price new: manual 2,458,000; automatic 2,508,000 (the M2-1002 was 3,000,000 yen)

Brilliant Black with gold BBS alloy wheels and tan hood. Used high-quality interior parts left over from the unsuccessful M2-1002 including cream leather interior and trim details and (see Chapter Three) Sensory Sound System.

DECEMBER 1993 J LIMITED II
Built: 800
Price new: manual 2,030,000 yen; auto 2,080,000 yen

Based on the Special package, in Sunburst Yellow with a black windscreen surround. Bucket seats with separate headrests, high-power audio system with CD player. Available as manual or automatic. 6J x 14in seven-spoke alloy wheels with Pirelli P700-Z tyres.

JULY 1994 RS LIMITED
Built: 500
Price new: 2,215,000 yen

Sporty Roadster based on S Special. Standard 1.8 engine, with lightened flywheel and lower 4.3:1 final drive. Montego Blue mica paint with RS decals on front wings. BBS wheels with Bridgestone Potenza RE010 P195/55 HR15 tyres. Recaro bucket seats, Nardi leather-rimmed three-spoke steering wheel.

JANUARY 1995 G LIMITED
Built: 1,500
Price new: manual, 1,900,000 yen

Based on M package, available with manual or automatic transmission. Satellite Blue mica paint

↑ **This 2002 VS Combination B wears the luscious Garnet Red mica paint introduced to the range that year. (Mazda)**

and dark blue hood with seven-spoke alloy wheels. Low-back bucket seats as used for the J Limited II. Momo leather steering wheel, uprated audio system.

FEBRUARY 1995 R LIMITED
Built: 1,000
Price new: 2,175,000 yen
Like RS Limited, this sporty model had a lightened flywheel and 4.3:1 final drive ratio. Satellite Blue mica (894) or Chaste White (106) with a blue hood and 15in BBS alloys on Bridgestone Potenza tyres. The interior was trimmed in red leather with a three-piece wood trim package.

DECEMBER 1995 VR LIMITED
Built: 1,500
Price new: 2,080,000 yen
Available in two guises, both based on the S Special Type I:
Combination A (700) Vin Rouge mica paint with tan hood and matching leather trim, alloy gearknob, shift plate and handbrake lever. Five-spoke 6J x 15in alloys.
Combination B (800) Excellent Green mica with dark green hood, black leather upholstery, alloy gearknob and handbrake handle as Combination A, plus five-spoke 6J x 15in alloy wheels.

DECEMBER 1996 B2 LIMITED
Built: 1,000
B2 stood for Blue and Bright; as the Twilight Blue mica bodywork and dark blue hood were complemented by polished seven-spoke, 14in alloy wheels, chrome mirrors and dial surrounds shone from the dash. The buckets seats were trimmed in black moquette, a CD player was standard and air-conditioning optional.

R2 LIMITED
Built: 500
Launched at the same time as the B2, the R2 stood for Racy and Red, although only the interior was red with black trimmings, the bodywork being painted Chaste White. Five-spoke, 6J x 15 alloy wheels wore Bridgestone Potenza tyres. Equipment based on the S Special Type I; alloy gearknob, shift plate and handbrake grip, chromed dial surrounds.

AUGUST 1997 SR LIMITED
Built: 700
Price new: 1,978,000 yen
The SR celebrated the eighth birthday of the Roadster. Based on the M package, either manual with Torsen differential or automatic transmission. Sparkle Green (316) or Chaste White (384) with highly polished seven-spoke alloy wheels and chromed mirrors. Black leather upholstery with light grey nubuck-type inserts, chromed dial rims, Momo steering wheel, Nardi gearknob, CD player.

Mk2 Mazda Roadster

1998
M-SKY (Anfini Southern Tokyo Limited)
The name was an acronym made up from the names of the team that created it: Mazda Anfini South Tokyo, Sinsuke Saito (the famous Japanese motor journalist who tuned the car), KG Works and Youare's Sport (tuning shops). Just 30 were custom-made for dealer Anfini Southern Tokyo Limited.

10TH ANNIVERSARY
Offered worldwide, see details of UK model.
Optional extras – automatic transmission, anti-lock brakes, air-conditioning, hard-top, limited-slip differential, CD player.

JANUARY 2000
NR Limited
Built: 500
Based on the 1.8-litre S-model with a 6-speed manual gearbox, the NR Limited wore the same Mahogany mica as the US Special Edition and UK Icon with buffed aluminium wheels. The beige soft-top matched the interior, which had classy leather seats, a Nardi wooden steering wheel and shift knob, and white dials surrounded by chrome-plated rings. Other goodies included a Bose sound system and power door locks.

DECEMBER 2000
YS Limited
Built 700
YS stands for Youthful and Sports. Based on the 1600M model, this edition was available in Brilliant Black, Pure White or Sunlight Silver metallic with blackout headlamps. Inside it had a sporty black and titanium two-tone interior colour scheme with

a titanium-accented centre panel and door trim and leather-wrapped Nardi steering wheel and shift knob. Standard equipment included front airbags, a keyless entry system and power locks. Four-wheel ABS with the EBD function was standard for the automatic.

2001
Sunburst Yellow
Built: 450

Not exactly a special edition, but when Mazda launched its online store, the Web Tune Factory www.w-tune.com, this special colour was offered only if you ordered your new car using the website. (You had to go to a dealer to complete the paperwork). The offer was limited to 450 cars.

Facelift (Mk2.5)

MAY 2001
Mazdaspeed Special Edition
Built: 200

Based on the RS, but its 1.8-litre engine had a custom exhaust to improve breathing and give a nice growly sound. The suspension was tightened up with stiffer rubber bushes and a mechanical four-level adjustable damper. Reinforced mounts were provided for the engine and six-speed manual transmission.

The Mazdaspeed certainly stood out: it was painted Starry Blue with gold wheels and its aerodynamic accessories included front air dam and side skirts, a rear under skirt and rear spoiler. The front suspension tower was blue to match the body.

The cabin had a carbon tone centre panel, blue metal-plated gauge rings and a blue steering wheel and gearknob. Its MP3-compatible CD system was manufactured by Kenwood and had four speakers.

DECEMBER 2001
MV Limited
Built: 300

Based on the 1600 SP, the MV was billed as the Roadster 'for customers who seek an ever higher level of style, interior and exterior feel'. It came in Titanium Grey metallic with dark red leather seats, aluminium highlights for the centre panel, and aluminium pedals (5MT model only).

DECEMBER 2002
SG Limited
Built 400

Based on the performance-enhanced 1600 NR-A and 1800RS, the SG Limited featured special equipment designed to create a more luxurious feel. The new package combined the custom exterior colour of Celion Silver metallic with cool, blue tones throughout the interior and a matching blue soft-top. The exclusive aluminium wheels used larger disc brakes, and the SG had Bilstein dampers and larger brake discs. The cockpit featured aluminium toned parts, a Nardi leather-wrapped steering wheel and a Bose sound system.

OCTOBER 2003
Roadster Coupé
Built 350, Type A 200, Type E 150, Base Roadster Coupé and Type S not limited

Three years before the world saw the retractable hard-top, Japanese buyers were offered a fixed-head coupé.

Mazda's team didn't simply weld on an accessory hard-top, design chief Shigenori Fukuda went back to the drawing board with CAD and clay models, and revised the body structure to enhance rigidity and give even sharper handling. The sheet metal was new from the doors back, and created a slightly deeper boot and a long, flat shelf behind the seats for extra storage. Headroom was about on a par with a normal MX-5.

↓ Tweaks to the suspension of the facelifted MK2 sharpened its handling.

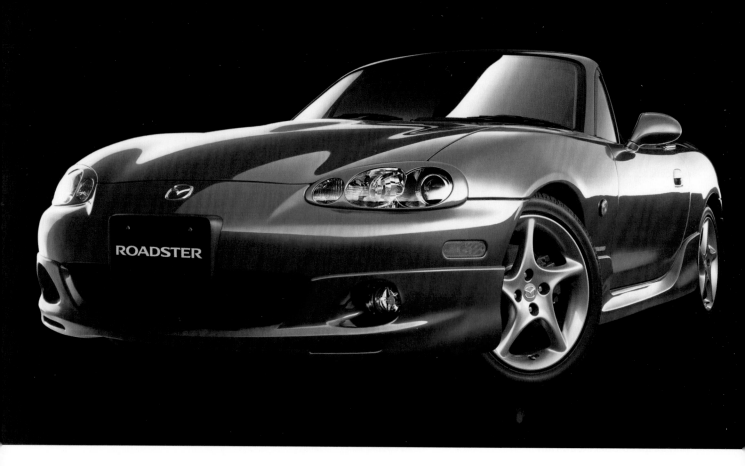

didn't just look loud, it had
a special sporty exhaust. Its
suspension was stiffened by
Mazdaspeed and its cabin
had carbon-tone panels
and an MP3-compatible
CD system.

The result was the only domestically produced
rear-drive coupé with an engine size less than two
litres. Its new hard top featured a rear quarter
window and rear window with a defroster.

The Roadster came with a mind-boggling choice
of four grades with three package types:

The base Roadster Coupé and Type S both
retained the same front design as the Roadster,
but the Roadster Coupé was based on the 1600
SP (125PS 1.6-litre, 5MT), while the Type S was
based on the 1800 RS (160PS 1.8 6MT). Both were
available in Pure White, Sunlight Silver metallic, and
Classic Red.

The Type A was described by Mazda as having
an 'authentic design reminiscent of traditional
racing cars' and by British journalist Peter Nunn
as a 'mini-Maranello', the new look being achieved
using fibreglass-reinforced plastic body sections. Its
long nose had fancy headlamps in three circles of
decreasing size; a large grille and prominent fog lamps
housed in the deep front bumper/air dam. It wore
flares over the wheelarches and a rear spoiler above
rear combination lamp bezels.

It was based on the 1800RS (160 PS 1.8-litre
6MT) and came in Lightning Yellow and Velocity Red.

The Type E was based on the 1800VS
Combination B (154PS 1.8-litre 4AT). It was

described as having a 'refined and elegant design' and
has a distinct Jaguar flavour. It shares the long nose
and front grille and fog lamp arrangement of the Type
A, but its headlamp design was a simpler one-piece
affair, and it didn't have the wheelarch flares. Like the
Type A, it came in Lightning Yellow or Velocity Red.

Peter Nunn was lucky enough the drive the
Coupé in 2003 and wrote: 'Although it rides on
205/45 R16 Bridgestones, the Coupé's still not hugely
endowed with grip so it's a car that's more than
up for the sideways challenge. The benign way the
tail drifts out is one of the great things in life. The
intuitive steering, superb gearshift, strong brakes and
decent ride also come together to make the Coupé
feel impressively all of a piece.'

DECEMBER 2003
Roadster Turbo
Built: 350

The Turbo's 1.8-litre engine achieved 172PS at
6,000rpm and 154lb ft of torque at 4,500rpm
courtesy of a single-scroll turbocharger limited to
7.25psi and an air-to-air intercooler. The power
reached the wheel via a 6-speed manual gearbox.

An aggressive bodykit added a front air dam with
an extra-large air intake and recessed fog lamps, a
boot spoiler and lower rear spoiler.

The car rode on 17in alloy wheels (with 205/40 R17 tyres) and the visible standard MX-5 brake callipers were painted red.

The tweaked suspension gained modified Bilstein shocks, 20% stiffer springs (giving a 7mm-lower ride height), larger-diameter anti-roll bars (up 1mm front and 2mm rear). A torque-sensing limited-slip differential helped keep the beast on the road.

Other mechanical upgrades included a larger radiator, upgraded clutch, prop shaft and differential, plus beefier rubber engine and diff mounts, and a larger exhaust outlet. A quicker steering rack (2.3 turns lock-to-lock instead of 2.7) made it feel even more fun to drive.

The Turbo was available in Velocity Red mica (exclusive to this model), Pure White, Sunlight Silver metallic and Grace Green mica. Inside, it had new seat trim with a red insert, drilled aluminium pedals, stainless steel scuff plates and a centre dash featuring a swirl alloy finish. The air-vents, door handles and the gearbox surround also had an alloy-look finish.

The Turbo was also sold in Australia as the SE.

Cover of 2003 Roadster Coupé brochure shows the base model, which shared the same nose as the soft-top. (c/o Andrew Fearon)

← The Type A was the most radical look of the hard-top coupés sold in Japan in 2003, its long nose has a touch of Ferrari about it. Just 200 were made.

← Type E – E-type? This 2003 hard-top coupé has a touch of Jaguar about the nose, and an elegant rear design. Only 150 lucky owners were able to buy one.

歓びを分かち合う
「日本カー・オブ・ザ・イヤー受賞記念車」、登場。

クルマと心を通いあわせて駆ける「人馬一体」の走り。
ロードスターがずっと追い続けてきた
その価値に与えられた、「日本カー オブ ザイヤー」。
この歓びを、ロードスターを愛する人々と分かち合うために。
いま、日本カー・オブ・ザ・イヤー受賞を記念した特別仕様車、登場。
洗練を極めた上質がオーナーとなる歓びを深くする。

↑ **The upmarket 2007 Blaze had lightweight 17in BBS forged alloy wheels with a chrome finish and style bars.**

↓ **The Japan Car of the Year Commemorative Edition was launched to mark the Roadster winning the 2005–06 Japan Car of the Year Award. Colour choices were either Brilliant Black with a red interior or Copper Red mica with a black interior. (c/o Andrew Fearon)**

Mk3

2005
3rd generation limited
Built 3,500 worldwide, 500 for Japan
See details for UK car.

JANUARY 2006
Japan Car of the Year Commemorative Edition
Numbers not limited

Launched to mark the Roadster winning the 2005–2006 Japan Car of the Year (JCOTY) Award. This special edition came with either Brilliant Black paint and a red interior or Copper Red mica with a black interior. The bucket seats were leather, the cloth hood black. The engine was a 2.0-litre mated to a six-speed manual 'box or six-speed automatic.

Standard extra goodies are a Bose sound system with a six-CD changer and seven speakers, keyless entry and engine starter system, front fog lights and scuff plates.

DECEMBER 2006
Blaze Edition

Launched as a soft-top, a Power Retractable Hard-top followed in April 2007. Mazda's press release said it came from the idea of sparkle and 'fiery color'. It was painted an exclusive deep wine-red called Radiant Ebony mica, or the deep Highland Green mica recently added to the standard model's colour range, and it shone with plenty of chrome. The front indicators, side indicator lenses and high-mounted brake light had smart clear lenses.

The BBS 17in wheels were forged alloy with a chrome finish. They were lighter than the wheels of the base Roadster, so reducing unsprung weight and improving driveabilty. (The 6-speed auto featured both increased diameter 'inch-up' wheel rims and a front strut tower bar.)

The classy cabin used sand beige and black leather and alloy highlights. The steering wheel, parking brake cover and manual gearlever cover were black leather with beige stitching.

OCTOBER 2007
Prestige Edition
Numbers not limited

This suave soft-top was based on the top-spec Roadster RS RHT and Roadster VS RHT hard-top coupés, but added heated leather bucket seats, 17in aluminium alloy wheels by BBS Japan, fog lights and Dynamic Stability Control. A front strut tower bar (cowl connecting type) was added to the six-speed automatic transmission model.

BLACK×RED

RED×BLACK

Japanese Hard-top Coupé Concepts

It's clear the idea of a Roadster with a hard-top was rumbling around for quite a while before the Retractable arrived. After all the MGB GT had one, and the BMW Z4 Coupé has a solid fan base. A fixed head coupé is always going to be stiffer than an open-topper for racing, too.

Mazda had shown the M Coupé at the New York Auto Show in 1996, and the Limited Editions had been offered in 2003.

At first glance more evidence of a plan to produce a hard-top is presented in the form of two motorsports-related Coupé concepts shown at the Tokyo Auto Salon 2004 and '05. The Roadster Coupé TS Concept was shown at the Tokyo Auto Salon 2004 in orange with two small stripes across the wing of white and green. It was followed at the 2005 Salon (December 2004) by the extremely cute Roadster Coupé Circuit Trail in blue with smart Oz wheels. This was described rather unfortunately by the translated press release as giving 'an image of a feisty, slightly retro-looking weekend racing enthusiast in his or her 50s' (is it the car or the enthusiast who's feisty and retro-looking?).

However, this pair of coupés was produced not by Mazda, but by an affiliate tuning company Mazda E&T. A spokesman for Mazda Japan states: The fixed-hard-top Roadster was not part of Mazda's plan, and Mazda was not considering its launch'.

The Roadster Coupé TS Concept was shown at the Tokyo Auto Salon 2004. It was based on the Roadster Coupé Type S 1800 sold from December 2003. (Mazda)

The metal was new from the doors back, but headroom was about the same as the soft-top. The coupé body made the body more rigid to sharpen its handling. (Mazda)

Retro racer taunted Japanese viewers at the Tokyo Auto Salon 2005. It was intended to appeal to slightly older weekend racers. (Mazda)

CHAPTER 9
CHOOSING AND BUYING AN MX-5

If you have decided to buy an MX-5, you've already made the right decision. The Mazda is tough, reliable and likely to have been loved and cared for by its previous owners. Plus, it holds its value better than most, so you won't be throwing your money away.

It may have brought the spirit of freedom and enjoyment of the classic roadsters from the 1960s, but it left behind the rust, the bad-tempered electrics and reluctance to go out in the wet. If well looked after, it must be one of the most reliable cars on the market.

The engines are happy to rack up hundreds of thousands of miles and – unusually for a sports car – there are plenty of dealers to keep up that collection of regular dealer service stamps.

Running costs are surprisingly modest. The Mazda's simplicity also means that servicing and regular parts are comparable with a basic hatchback, and thanks to forward planning by its creators, insurance premiums are low. The owners' club will also be able to offer you a very good insurance deal.

Your local owners' club can also help you find your car, so it's a good idea to sign up even before you get your hands on a set of keys. You'll be able to find general advice on club websites and in the magazine, which will also have ads for cars for sale. And you'll find a friendly ear if you need help.

Make sure you look through plenty of classified ads to get a good idea of what to pay (again the owners' club websites should be able to give you up-to-date estimates). Prices tend to dip in winter as buyers aren't in the roadster frame of mind, and as Christmas approaches buying a car gets pushed to the back by the need to tracking down whatever toy is essential but impossible to find that year. As the bulbs start to come up in spring, so do MX-5 prices.

However, one of the greatest advantages the MX-5 hunter has is that there are so many very good cars around to choose from. Close to 900,000 had been made by 2009. So, if something vital appears to have been mislaid, or the condition is not perfect,

you have no reason to waste the owner's time. Just walk away and find a better one.

The number produced also means that there are plenty of good, reasonably priced used parts. The only parts you might not be able to find are those specific to low-volume limited editions, such as the badge for the original Icon or the ECU for a BBR Turbo.

Where to buy

For later cars, a dealer will be able to offer you more protection in case that peach turns out to be a lemon. It will be more expensive, but Mazda has a pretty good approved used scheme with a decent warranty.

You still need to do your homework, however. It would be dangerous to assume that the salesperson will have an encyclopaedic knowledge of Mazda's back catalogue. So, for example, if you want power steering or other 'invisible' features, check out the details of the models with the owners' club or a book before you buy. Every dealer should have a reference book giving all the specifications and chassis numbers of every model and limited edition, so if you have any doubts about a car once you are at the showroom, you can suggest firmly that they dig it out.

Specialised dealers are another relatively safe option. Or there are auctions, but the best advice here is DON'T, unless you really know what you are doing.

You'll get more for your money if you buy privately, but be careful as there are some tatty cars out there. Again you'll need to read up about the model you are buying, and be on your guard in case that nice lady owner who left her son-in-law in charge of selling the car (shortly after losing all its documents) is off riding one of the pigs just flying past.

eBay can be a good option if you're careful. Look for an owner who has put up photographs of every

← The Mk2 appears to be a Mk1 that has toned its muscles in the gym, but both models have their ardent fans, and both hold their value very well. (Courtesy *Miata Magazine*)

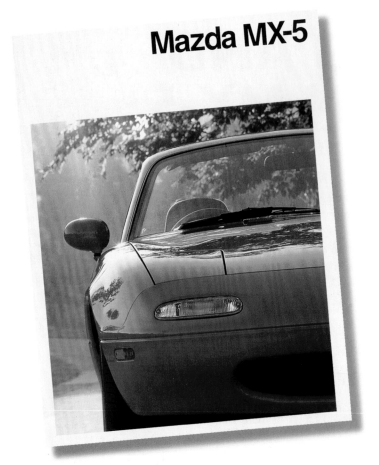

Mazda MX-5

Read up before you buy; early cars like this MkI are now officially classed as classics. (Simon Farnhell)

more than two exclamation marks in one sentence. If possible, go and see the car before you bid and check all the usual details.

If you're buying an older model, it's definitely worth considering a Eunos (see Chapter 8).

Be sure of your car's history

Sadly, desirable sports cars like the MX-5 are irresistible to thieves, and you don't want to be one of the mugs buying a stolen car – you could end up losing both the car and your cash.

Paperwork is vital, and the more of it the better – preferably strewn over a table in the seller's house with a mug of tea in your hand if you're buying privately, so you know the seller really lives there.

You need to know that the car really is what it is claimed to be, with all the right trim and options. In Europe, you also need to be sure you're not paying Mazda money for a Eunos (see Chapter 8).

If you're answering a classified ad, always say you're calling about 'the car'. If the seller has to ask 'which one?' then they could be a dealer.

When you're inspecting the car, make sure the vehicle identification number (VIN) at the back of the engine bay corresponds to the numbers on the registration documents and look to make sure there are no signs that it has been tampered with or replaced with a different plate.

fault and plenty of detail about where they bought the car and any work that has been done. You can usually spot a dealer posing as a private owner from common phrases such as 'drives superb' (dealers never use ly), 'nice, tidy example', 'presented in Brilliant Black', 'absolute bargain!', or anything with

→ The vehicle identification number (VIN) at the back of the engine bay will record exactly which model it is. (James Mann)

It's always advisable to get a vehicle condition check when buying used, and if you are a member of a breakdown service, this will include a history check. If you don't go for the full check, you can also get a history check separately from HPI Equifax, Experian, or *What Car?* History Check in the UK.

This will run your VIN against a number of registers held by the police, finance companies and the insurance industry to make sure it has not been reported as stolen, or as an insurance write-off and that there is no outstanding finance on it. In the latter case you could lose the car because it still belongs to a finance company.

If it comes up as a write-off, your MX-5 could either be hiding accident damage, or worse it could be a 'ringer', that is, it's a stolen car wearing the ID taken from a damaged vehicle.

A history check may turn up disturbing details, which may also point towards an accident or a 'hot' car. For example, it may give the wrong colour or trim level, or perhaps it may have a record of the mileage that is strangely higher than the odometer says now. In this case it could also have been 'clocked'.

What to look out for

BODYWORK

Older cars may have some rust problems, but it's not a linear progression, i.e. the older the car, the more they are likely to suffer. The years have proved the Mk1 (known as the NA) to be more resistant than the Mk2 (NB).

The usual place to rot is the rear sill ahead of the wheelarch, usually because the hood drains are blocked and water has been sloshing around inside the wing. So even if you can't see any rust, damp carpets in the cabin and the boot may be a giveaway. Have a look at the soft-top drains, too (see Chapter 10).

If you catch it in time, the damage can be repaired with some minor welding. If the rust has been allowed to spread, however, it can rot out a complicated box section, and, because it's near the seatbelt mounting point, this could lead to an MoT failure in the UK. (Experts argue that it won't affect the mounting point, but convincing your garage might be difficult.)

↑ **This rare BBR Turbo** spent most of its life near the sea. (Simon McInerney)

← **This typical damage to the rear wheelarch** was caused by blocked drain holes and retained rainwater. A repair section is available for this area. (Simon McInerney)

Repair sections of the back of the sill and front of the wheelarch are available at a reasonable cost, but if you can't do it yourself, you'll have to factor in the cost of labour and a respray in that area.

Mk2 bootlids began to rust when the cars were relatively new. One cheaper fix in the UK is to buy a Japanese replacement.

Hidden accident damage is more of an enemy than rust in a car that encourages such enthusiastic driving. You should scour ever inch of the bodywork, as you would any used car or classic. Only go to see a car in good light – never in the rain – and take a

→ Pop-up headlamps can
suffer stone chips; if they
are winking, it's probably a
dodgy relay. (James Mann)

magnet to hunt for filler. Look down the line of the car, check for uneven shutlines, bulging filler or poorly matched paintwork.

Another clue that the car has had a respray is overspray on rubbers or on the inner wings under the bonnet. The rubber around the windows is particularly difficult to mask up.

On a Mk1 the paint should have a rougher texture below the distinct midriff crease, because of the antichip coating beneath, and the sill is black on most models. On a Mk2, the paint is rougher up to about a foot from the bottom of the door.

If the car has had a respray, it's reassuring if the owner has photographs of the restoration project showing what's beneath the new paint. Or, if the work was completed a couple of years ago, any filler will probably have started to swell.

The MX-5's original paint was thin on early models, so beware a car that has been polished too hard – patches of primer may start to show.

On some early cars, the silver and some white paint wasn't keyed properly to primer, and flakes off – sometimes in sheets. If this is happening you do, at least, know the car is original!

Small dents on the nose, probably from careless

parking, are difficult to tap out and can cause paint to flake off, so even though the damage is minor, it's best to walk away. Also, if the owner has been sloppy about parking, what else have they been careless about?

The chassis rails are likely to have a few dings, and that's okay, but give them a poke with a screwdriver to make sure they're not rusty. Obviously they shouldn't be completely mangled – that could indicate accident damage.

The Mk1's pop-up headlamps are very reliable, so if they're winking, your car may have suffered frontal damage, although it could simply be a dodgy relay. When you go to see a Mk1, raise and lower them a few times. If they are slow, it may be because they have not been used for a while, but it could also be an indication of damage.

You may decide you can live with minor scrapes if the price is right, but check hard for evidence of major damage which may ruin the way the car drives, or could even be dangerous. If you are unfortunate enough to find yourself in a hedge, be aware that replacement panels can be quite pricey.

Colour can affect the price significantly. Red cars are always popular, the bronze, white and blue will be cheaper to buy, but harder to sell in the UK. A lot of early white cars were actually resprayed blue by their original dealer because they proved so difficult to shift.

Demand for different colours can change according to country or state. Generally, in sunnier climates brighter colours are more popular, but in colder, wetter places, bright yellow can stand out like a sore thumb. The Sunburst Yellow is always popular, but the owners' clubs reckon they are usually bought by the more outgoing (and/or crazy) personalities among their members. White is popular in Japan because it is the national F1 racing colour, equivalent to British Racing Green. In the UK this is Crystal White, the Eunos Roadster is painted a prosaic Chaste White.

HOOD

Although the hood is simple to erect and put down again, it can suffer from rough handling and will be expensive to replace. A large number of Mk1s have scratched, creased or even torn plastic rear windows. So put the hood up, check the plastic and the zip for fraying, loose threads or loose teeth. You can get the zip replaced by a hood specialist, but it can be quite

a good bargaining tool. Hoods can also shrink and leak, so look for water damage on the doors and the sides of the windscreen.

Make sure the owner still has the tonneau cover, too. People frequently put this away in a cupboard to create more boot space, and then forget to replace it when they sell.

If it is at the back of a cupboard, this is also a good indication that they haven't been using it. So check the underside of the hood for fading or rain damage.

Hard-tops are interchangeable between the Mk1 and Mk2 and even between Mazda and Eunos, but the rubber seals will be different and can leak if they are not swapped for the correct items. The early versions, produced by TWR don't fit very well and do leak around the side windows.

Soft-tops are also interchangeable from Mk1 to Mk2, but some owners find the glass panel heavy and difficult to manoeuvre while it is being zipped in and out, so this is not a popular swap.

If you put a Mk1 hard- or soft-top on to a Mk2 car, you will have to have a new section of wiring loom put in to link up with the heated glass window.

INTERIOR

Cabins last very well, but check for cracked plastic, or wear on the outside of the seat, which can be costly to fix. The early fabric was prone to bobbling (technical term 'pilling') so owners often consider retrimming them in leather. If the interior and pedal rubbers look worn and the clock has only recorded a low mileage, suspect 'clocking'.

Check all the electrical items such as power windows, lights and stereo to make sure they work as they should. The windows do close quite slowly, but they should raise and lower smoothly.

The central locking units of 1994-onwards 1.8iS models have been known to be 'lazy' and not lock the doors properly, but this can be sorted.

Air-conditioning is a very desirable option. It won't add to the price, but it will help you hook a buyer when it's time to make a change. Check that it works and give it a good blast regularly once you own the car to keep it in good nick. All air-con systems need recharging after five years, and corroded condensers in front of the radiator can prove costly.

As you open the door, have a look at the stainless steel kickplate to make sure that it has a protective strip underneath and that there is no rust bubbling

↑ Some MX-5s will have been driven hard; look out for signs of rough treatment. (LAT)

→ **Rust can bubble up at the end of the kickplate if there is no rubber strip underneath it. (James Mann)**

When this happens, the key quickly gouges a wider keyway in the crank and the engine loses power. It's a gradual process, but in extreme cases the nose of the crank can fall off.

The usual fix is to replace the crank (or the engine), although some experts suggest welding in some new metal or filling in the damage with Loctite Quick Metal (see the Garage section of Miata.net).

If you simply want to avoid buying a car with a short-nose crank, look for cars with a VIN ending 127442 or higher in Europe, or 209447 in the US. You can also count the slots on the front of the crank pulley. The early cars have four slots, the later 'long-nosed crank' has eight.

If you're looking at an early car, a wobbling crank may give away a munching Woodruff key – but the only sure way to check is to get your hands grubby and inspect the crank pulley, but if you're only shopping, the owner may not be too pleased.

Always test drive the car from cold. Look out for blue smoke in the exhaust, which means it's burning oil. A happy engine will be quiet and clicking tappets indicate sloppy maintenance. Standard plug leads can fail, too, causing misfires.

The cambelt needs to be changed every 60,000 miles or five years. So make sure it has been done, and if it's coming up, haggle the price down to compensate.

The catalytic converter has been known to fail on older cars and is expensive to replace, so get an MoT or emissions certificate to make sure yours is working. The exhaust heat shield can also work loose and rattle, but this is not hard to fix. Californian models had a second cat, which can be a problem.

Batteries last for years, but they are a special gel-filled unit and are expensive to replace. Mazda can fit a conventional battery by modifying the fixing brackets. If these are not modified and the battery is loose, it can short and cause a fire. Finally, be aware that 1999 and 2000 models have some electrical issues.

up at either end. These kickplates were fitted to protect the sills from damage, but early examples had no protective strip and the metal-to-metal contact causes the paint to bubble up.

This is very localised and is surface not structural, but it looks tatty. The best solution is to have the plates removed, and the affected area treated and repainted. The new replacement plates have a strip of rubber underneath to prevent the same thing occurring again. If the car still has warranty this should be carried out free of charge, or if you are buying from a dealer you could insist that this is done before you buy.

ENGINE

All MX-5 engines are strong and reliable and should pass six figures easily if they are well maintained. When you go to see a car, the colour of its various fluids should indicate whether the current owner has been giving it appropriate TLC. The only Achilles heel affects early 1.6-litre cars fitted with the 'short-nosed crankshaft'. In some cases, possibly due to parts being assembled incorrectly, the pulley comes loose and the load of the belts is transferred to a Woodruff key only intended to provide alignment during assembly.

GEARBOX

The gear lever should slide silently through the gate. Clunking or whining is a sign of severe misuse. Early cars up to K registration have a very notchy first-to-second gearchange. This is due to the use of a single-cone synchromesh on the second gear, which has since been changed to dual cone to ease the problem. This notchiness should go away once the

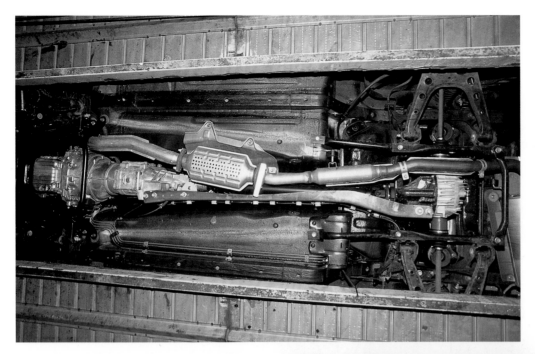

car has warmed up, so test drive the car long enough to make sure it does. Running synthetic gear oil is a good, but pricey solution if you can't live with it.

A stiff, notchy gearchange may also be due to a torn gasket underneath the lever. The ball at the bottom of the gear lever is supposed to sit in its own bath of oil, but if the gasket has torn, it may have leaked out. This is a cheap and easy fix (see Chapter 10).

Many cars have a noisy clutch release bearing, but this should disappear when the clutch is depressed. If not, get it checked or negotiate a price reduction. Clutches also get squeaky if the car doesn't leave its garage very often.

High-mileage cars are likely to need a new clutch soon if they haven't already had one.

WHEELS

The MX-5 has been fitted with an extraordinary number of different wheels, and not all are easy to replace, so make sure the car you are looking at has a perfect, unkerbed set. As well as looking awful, scuffed wheels don't say anything good about the driving or the attitude of previous owners.

All base models had steel wheels, the S models and limited editions had alloys, and some of these, such as the BBS wheels, do suffer from corrosion and pitting. Both the 10-spoke alloy of the 1992 Mk1 Black SE and the Mk2 10th Anniversary wheels were lacquered to protect them, but the lacquer was

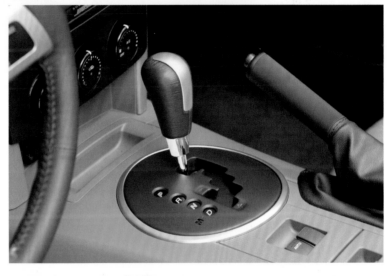

too thin and so corrosion gets started underneath. Most of the 10th Anniversary cars had their wheels replaced under warranty, but the replacements will probably also suffer problems.

The standard Minilite-lookalike wheels are only lacquered on the outside, so they can corrode on the inside. The best solution is to take them off, get rid of the powdery white corrosion with some wire wool and elbow grease and have some lacquer put on by a wheel specialist.

Badly pitted and corroded wheels can also be sandblasted and refurbished by a specialist. Wicked Wheels in the UK has a mobile service to do this (www.wickedwheels.co.uk). You should knock the cost of this procedure off the purchase price.

While you're checking out the wheels, have a look at the brake discs too, because these can corrode and are quite pricey to replace.

TYRES

Check tyres for tread depth, and use this as a bargaining point if you are going to have to replace them soon.

MX-5's are generally gentle on tyres, so uneven wear may indicate steering or suspension damage.

Make sure the jack and tools are present and correct, and that the spare tyre has not been damaged.

SUSPENSION

The major suspension parts should not need any major work, but if you buy a high-miler you may want to change the shocks and check the suspension bushes to keep the handling up to scratch.

POWER STEERING

Manual steering is fine above around 20mph, but it does get heavy for low-speed manoeuvring and parking. Therefore power steering is a desirable option and although it won't necessarily add to the price of a car, it can make it easier to sell. Don't assume all limited editions will have power assistance; those based on entry-level models will not.

Which model?

MKI (NA)

There are two quite different buyers for the Mk1 (known in the company as an NA), and what you have to look for depends to some extent on which one you are. If you want a cheap roadster, perhaps your first sports car, then a high-mileage MX-5 or Eunos Roadster is an excellent choice. To keep the price down, you might have to put up with a few minor scrapes on the paintwork and fabric seats might be a little fluffy, but it is still guaranteed to be a reliable, everyday fun car.

On the other hand, the Mk1 is now officially a classic. If you are buying with this in mind, then your ideal car should be a low-mileage, early 1.6 in original condition. Mk1 fans love the simpler, more retro shape, with those Elan-style pop-up headlamps and delightful details such as the chrome oval door handles inside and out.

Its fans will also tell you that the Mk1 is the best of the bunch to drive. The Mk1 also handles more like the roadsters of the Sixties, and for those who enjoy a bit of controlled oversteer, that's great. But it can catch out the unwary on damp or icy roads. In particular, drivers who have grown up at the wheel of an understeering hatchback, may find it disconcerting when the tail starts to twitch. The worst-case scenario on wet or icy roads is a pranged MX. Best

↑ **The Mazda badge changed to the more modern 'owl' for the Mk2. (James Mann)**

advice is, buy the car, but take a skid course.

The early 1.6 delivers 114bhp and 100lb ft of torque, and its performance is very similar to the first 1.8 which replaced it. The rather coarse 1.8 unit, taken from the Mazda 323 GT delivered 115bhp and it took a second longer to sprint to 60mph than the 1.6, although it overtakes the smaller-engined car at higher speeds. The 1.6 introduced in 1995 had been downgraded to 88bhp to differentiate it from the 1.8.

Mazda produced limited-edition models almost every year, and these vary in desirability (see Chapter Seven), but generally they fetch more than standard cars.

Just because the Mk1 is older than the Mk2 and 3, doesn't make it any less reliable. This little

← **The Mk1's chrome oval door handle is a beautiful piece of design, but the body-coloured Mk2 item snaps fewer fingernails. (James Mann)**

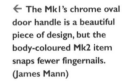

← **The Mk1's outer chrome handle was echoed in black plastic inside the door; the modern theme continues inside the Mk2. (James Mann)**

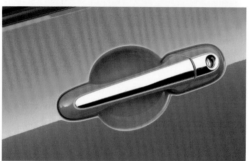

↑ The third generation has simple lines, in the mould of the Mk1, but it has followed later-model 911s by sprouting larger wheel-arches.

→ Mk3 external door handle has a circular recess and a splash of chrome.

↓ ↘ The spare wheel and battery took up a large chunk of luggage space in the Mk1; these are stowed beneath the floor in the Mk2. (James Mann)

hood catches. On the Mk1 they last forever, but he describes the equivalent part on the Mk2.5 as seeming to be 'made out of some kind of cheese'.

MK2 (NB)

There was a storm of protest when the Mk2 arrived in 1998, sans pop-up headlamps and with a far more modern look. However, fans have now grown to admire its slimmer lines and its slicker handling. Because it is newer, a Mk2 will probably have fewer miles on the clock and will hold its value better than an average-condition Mk1.

MK2.5 (NB FACELIFT)

The 'sharknose' slipped in surprisingly quietly, and its face-lift was so subtle that it was quickly nicknamed the Mk2.5. (Officially it's called the M2 Facelift.) Inside it added white dials and touches of chrome in the cabin.

Its variable-valve-timing engine is more efficient from the point of view of emissions, but offers no significant performance advantage over the Mk2. It has a six-speed gearbox as standard, and, for the first time in the UK, it was offered as a four-speed automatic. At the time, road testers claimed its handling was sharper than ever, but most people agree that the Mk2 and 2.5 driving experience is about the same. Unfortunately, this model seems to have had some less robust parts than its predecessors.

car was seriously over engineered, and the sheer number of them still roaring around tells you they can run and run. In fact, as engineers had to add more power and safety equipment without adding seriously to the overall weight, some components became less robust. One specialist who regularly breaks Mk1 and 2 cars gives the example of the

MK3 (NC)

The Mk3's fans prefer its simple lines to the more fussy styling of the Mk2. Many enthusiasts felt the Mk3's wider arches ruined it (echoing the complaints of 911 fans who hated its ever-growing arches). Mazda's aim was to make it more masculine, but actually it is less overtly sporty to drive and more civilised than the Mk2.

MK3.5 (NC UPGRADE)

The facelift gave the car the family look, following a number of radical concept cars. Better than that, Mazda engineers reacted to complaints about the too-civilised nature of the Mk3 (the more harsh critics would even say boring) and livened up the handling. Even if you prefer autos, the auto isn't the best choice.

COUPÉ

As above, but a hard-top pops out of the boot at the touch of a button. We never thought the MX-5 would need it, but it looks great with the roof down, and who can complain about too much convenience?

Road Tester's choice

Alisdair Suttie, ex-Road Test Editor for *What Car?* (seen kicking up sand in a Mk2 page 56):

'Original is best when it comes to MX-5s. The first Mk1s with the 115bhp 1.6-litre engine always felt the most lithe and willing, especially compared to the later detuned 1.6-litre. All Mk1s handle with a deft nimbleness that is almost impossible to find in other roadsters.

'This character was carried through to the Mk2 models, which managed to retain the original's ability to change direction at the mere thought of it, even if the power steering didn't have quite as much sensitivity as the earlier car's. The Mk2 offers a bit more cabin space and refinement, but it's essentially still the same lovable package of pert styling, superb handling and just enough performance to entertain.

'The Mk3 is an altogether more sophisticated car thanks to its revised rear suspension design and the option of a folding metal roof. However, Mazda has pulled off the trick of making the latest MX-5 handle and reward just as the first cars did. No other car maker has managed to keep the bloodline of a sports car so pure throughout its evolution and that's why the MX-5 remains such a huge hit with magazine road testers and the buying public alike. If you want a driving treat that won't cost a fortune to run, the Mazda MX-5 is unbeatable.'

Gavin Conway, ex-editor of *4Car* and *Automobile*: 'My favourite generation of the MX-5 is the very first one. I'll admit, this has more to do with a nostalgic memory of the impact that little car had – I doubt

All three generations have their fans for different reasons.

even the most hidebound enthusiast would argue that the current car isn't a much better proposition in terms of refinement, safety, equipment and performance.

'But that first-generation MX-5 was a revolution, a car that had as much impact for me as the E-type's launch would have had for enthusiasts in the early '60s. You see, Canada in the late 1980s was a bit of a wasteland when it came to proper sports cars. Domestic 'sports cars' such as the Mustang, or Camaro, or Firebird were, frankly, an embarrassment. Porsches were unaffordable and the usual European suspects were either not sold there or, again, too expensive.

'And then the MX-5 arrived – the local Mazda dealers put a couple of dozen demonstrators on the road, just tooling around town to announce their arrival in dealerships. I remember the thrill of seeing my first one (on St Laurent Boulevard in Ottawa). Here, at long last, was the modern equivalent of my friend's Triumph Spitfire. Lightweight, affordable, pointy, and something that the Triumph never was: reliable and very well built.

'I left for the UK not long after the little Mazda's launch, and finally got to drive one in 1991. And I was so happy that the MX-5, unlike so many motoring icons that I'd subsequently drive, met and then exceeded my expectations.'

John Simister, ex-Road Test Editor of *Car*, contributor to *EVO, Octane* and *The Independent* and Car of the Year juror:

'The first versions of cars are usually the ones that most closely reflect the designers' and engineers' intentions, and that's certainly true of the MX-5. So the Mk1 is the most raw, pure and viscerally entertaining, as well as looking the tidiest and tautest and having the neatest detailing. The Mk2 was a more 'polite' version of the Mk1 (so said the engineering chief at the time), still good fun and requiring fewer corrective inputs in fast, bumpy corners. The styling lost its tension, though; it looked like it was beginning to melt.

'The Mk3 went off the rails despite a press launch adamant that all the MX-5 virtues were not only intact but enhanced. The steering was oddly viscous, and its weighting was inconsistent as you finally discovered an explosion of oversteer. The engines felt lacklustre, too. The MX-5 crispness and intimacy had gone. But the Mk3 has just had a facelift and, joy of joys, it's back on form. The third generation has always looked good, and now it drives properly thanks to revised front suspension geometry and smoother, keener engines. It feels just as a modern MX-5 should, as long as you avoid the horrid automatic.'

CHAPTER 10
OWNING & MODIFYING YOUR MX-5

The purpose of this chapter is to help owners avoid common problems or to recognise their symptoms if it's already too late. It also indicates whether the problem is likely to be something you could tackle yourself, or whether it's a deal breaker if you've spotted it on a potential purchase. However, restricted space means we can't go into too much detail. For step-by-step instructions, see Paul Hardiman's *Do it Up! Mazda MX-5* (Haynes) or Keith Tanner's excellent *Mazda Miata MX-5 Performance Projects* (US).

Protecting the body

Early MX-5s (and Eunos Roadsters) have proved to be well protected against rust, but a Waxoyl kit is still a good investment to protect your car for the future.

The only serious problem occurs if the soft-top drains get blocked. Rain water will eventually creep into the cabin, soaking the carpet underlay. Worse, it can get trapped in the wings and sills so the car rusts from the inside out (in another unexpected homage to the MGB). The areas affected tend to be the front of the rear wheelarch and the rear of the sill. In the most serious cases, the trapped water can rot out the complicated box section close to the seatbelt mounting point, and in the UK this will probably mean an MoT failure.

If the damage has already been done, repair sections are available at reasonable prices, but if you can't do the welding yourself, it can get expensive.

You can avoid the problem by clearing the drain holes regularly, or asking your garage to do it at every service. You'll find the top of the drain holes, about the diameter of a pencil, under a small carpet flap one either side of the cabin behind the driver and passenger's shoulders. Find a long rod (or a straightened coat hanger if it doesn't have a sharp point at the end) and push down through the hole until it comes out on the ground.

If you are getting rain water in the boot, your drain gutter rail is probably blocked. This runs along under your rear window as the roof material joins onto the car body.

Mk1 rear wings may also suffer from strange outward dents, as though something has been trying to escape from the boot. In fact, that's exactly what has been happening. The thin metal of the rear wing has nothing to protect it from golf clubs or other heavy items sliding into it as the car takes a corner. If you're likely to carry such loads, you can buy a little black pad from accessories companies to protect it (or you could use a rolled up picnic rug).

Another weak point of earlier cars is the door mirror. The swivel bolt tends to corrode until the mirror simply snaps off. Spraying it with oil may extend its life. Or, if you already have a mirror unit sitting on the table as you read this, you have several options. You can buy an entire new mirror, you can replace it with a used item, or repair your existing unit with used parts which are available separately.

An accessory front grille not only looks smart, but it also protects the vulnerable radiator. Stones thrown up from the road have been known to go right through the aluminium rad, landing owners with a large bill. Note, too, that the 'eyes' inside the front 'mouth' are tie-down hooks to secure the car on a trailer; they must not be used to tow the car.

If you own a Mk1, it's a good idea to clear any snow or ice off before raising your headlamps to avoid overloading the headlight motor.

UK club members have been impressed with Wonder Wax by CarPlan, for polishing and protecting paintwork. Be aware that paint on early cars is quite thin, and if you polish it too much you can go right through to the primer.

Alloy wheels were frequently only lacquered on one side, and so consider taking them off, and cleaning them up to inspect their condition. It may be worth having them sandblasted and lacquered

← You can enjoy your Mazda out of the box or modify it to suit your personality – there are plenty of companies offering parts and accessories. (Magic Car Pics)

to protect them in the future. It's a very good idea to have a set of plain steel wheels to use during the winter to protect your alloys from damp and salt.

Mechanical

Make sure the oil is changed every 3,000–5,000 miles (5–8,000km), and opt for a synthetic. On a normal MX-5 10W-30 is fine, but some owners believe 5W-30 synthetic reduces noise on older engines. The debate about the best oil raging on internet forums could fill this book, but everyone seems to agree that you can never change the oil too frequently.

If your car suddenly starts puffing blue smoke, don't panic. Before you start looking for a replacement engine, check out the PCV (positive crankcase ventilation) valve on the side of the cam cover, take it out and blow through it. You should only be able to blow one way. If you can't, good news, it's stuck and the fix is an inexpensive replacement.

Coolant should be changed every two years or 30,000 miles. HT leads usually only last 30,000 miles (48,000km). If you have any kind of misfire, the leads should be the prime suspect.

Mk1s have a small battery in the right-hand side of the boot, which goes flat very easily, so make sure you don't leave the lights on, even for a couple of hours.

The MX-5 loves to be driven, and hates to stand for long periods. If you don't drive your Mk1 regularly the clutch will get squeaky, the battery

can go flat and the spark plugs can flood when you fire it up again.

The throttle body can get gummed up with black oil deposits. These should be removed gently with mineral spirits or carburettor cleaner. However, be careful not to clean off the coating Mazda put inside the bore to assist the blade seating, otherwise you'll suffer leaks, rough idling and poor driveability.

Treat your transmission to a synthetic transmission oil made by a well-known name such as Redline, Mobil or Amsoil. Make sure it meets the API service GL-4 or GL-5 rating.

If your older five-speed gearshift seems stiff and notchy, it may be more than age. The ball at the bottom of the gear lever is supposed to sit in its own bath of oil, but if the gasket has torn, it may have leaked out. Luckily removing the gearlever, and replacing the rubber is a simple job.

If you can't select a gear at all with the clutch fully depressed, it's likely the clutch slave cylinder seals have gone and it's lost all its fluid. Check the fluid level in the master cylinder reservoir (on the bulkhead inboard of the brake master cylinder). As a get-you-home fix, top up the reservoir and it may work again for a little while. Replacing the slave cylinder is a fairly easy job and nine times out of 10 it will bleed itself so you can do it without an assistant to pump the clutch pedal.

If your car has a noisy release bearing you'll hear it when the car is idling and the noise will stop when you depress the clutch. Note that the spiggot bearing can give exactly the same symptoms, so when replacing the clutch it's a false economy not to change the flywheel spiggot or pilot bearing, too.

↘ **Wing mirror can snap off, but new parts are cheap. (Simon McInerney)**

↓ **If your car starts smoking, check the PCV valve first. If it's stuck, this inexpensive part can fool you into thinking there's a costly problem. (Liz Turner)**

If your car starts vibrating at around 65mph (100kph), check the tyre pressures. The MX-5 is very sensitive to tyre pressures, and the car will be happiest with 28psi at each corner.

Vibration can also be caused by a stiff spot on the tyre where the belts inside the tyre carcass overlap. Try a tyre with a jointless nylon band, and have wheels balanced to 1/10 of a gram. These problems are most likely to affect cars made before the chassis was stiffened in 1994.

To keep your car handling crisply, the shock absorbers should be changed every 30,000 miles. However, some aftermarket items last longer or even offer a lifetime guarantee.

Think about your bushes, too. These little pieces of rubber dry out with age, become solid or crack so they lose their bounce. It's a gradual process, but the ride will deteriorate and the car will simply feel old and rattly. Some people recommend changing them as early as 60,000 miles.

If you are making a change, you could consider long-lasting polyurethane or harder rubber bushes which reduce suspension deflection without affecting the firmness of the ride.

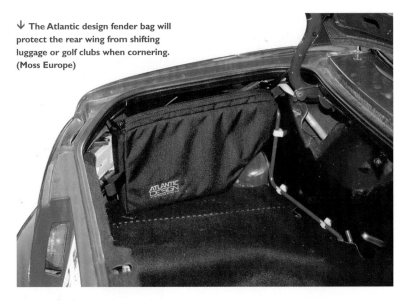

↓ The Atlantic design fender bag will protect the rear wing from shifting luggage or golf clubs when cornering. (Moss Europe)

Inside the cabin

If electric windows have slowed to a snail's pace, the problem is probably lubrication. The cheapest – and extremely simple solution is to remove the door trim to spray the mechanism and winder cables with grease.

↓ An accessory grille will protect the aluminium radiator from stones. Tie-down hooks inside the 'mouth' must not be used as tow hooks. (James Mann)

If your leather seats are looking tired and dried up, UK club members recommend the leather restoration kit offered by Woolies of Market Deeping, near Peterborough (Tel. 01778 347347).

Air-conditioning needs to be used regularly if it is to stay healthy. If you are inspecting a car you want to buy and it has air-conditioning, check that it produces a fridge-like blast for a couple of minutes with the vents set to recirculating.

The engine revs should change as the air-con is switched on, indicating that the pump is working.

Cars usually need recharging every seven to 10 years because of leaks in the system. Regular use will extend the time between recharges.

Hoods

If your Mk1 has a zip-out window, NEVER fold the roof without zipping it out and laying it flat, otherwise your window will soon become creased and dented. The correct method is to unlatch the top, unzip the window and lower it. The reverse procedure is to put up the top, zip in the rear window and then latch the top. This takes the strain off the zip, otherwise you may find the teeth coming loose.

It is a good idea, too, to check the zip for fraying or any loose threads where the teeth are stitched on to the backing, as this can sometimes foul the zip and jam it.

If you regularly drive roof-down without fitting the tonneau, the exposed underside of the roof can become dried out, damaged by hot sun, or it may go mouldy after a sudden shower of rain.

In the winter, scraping ice off the plastic window will scratch it, using warm water is a much kinder option.

Mild fogginess and minor scratches on the rear window can be cured with Meguiars Plastic Polish (available through the UK club).

If your hood has come to the end of its life, you have plenty of choices about how to replace it. You can avoid all the problems associated with plastic windows or zips by fitting a glass window or a later hood (see page 145 for more details).

The hard-top is very easy to put on, but you need somewhere safe to store it. Accessory companies, including Moss offer a trolley to move it, or you can have a hoist inside your garage.

↑ The Mk1 battery can go flat very easily so make sure you don't leave your lights on. (James Mann)

→ Accessory trolleys or an in-garage hoist will keep your hard-top in top-notch condition. (James Mann)

Mods and Accessories

The MX-5 might be a volume seller, but you never see two the same. The urge to add just a little personal touch is irresistible and the scope for making your car individual is enormous.

You can smarten it up by retrimming the seats and adding bright touches to the interior, you can add a body kit, choose from a vast mass of accessories, or stoke up the engine.

The engineers had their way when they were building it, so this is a tough little car and its chassis and structure can handle a phenomenal amount of power. Now the older models are getting cheaper and younger buyers can afford them, the number of seriously hot cars is rising. Keith Tanner from US performance specialist Flyin' Miata says: 'The great thing is that it's so reliable, you can afford to spend the money on mods, rather than just keeping it healthy.'

What owners do to their cars can depend on where they live. In America, boosting power is popular, but in Switzerland, regulations forbid any serious engine work, so enthusiasts go for wild body kits. In Germany, too, TUV regulations forbid a change of brakes or ECU, so again, the conversions tend to be for show rather than go.

The Japanese love to dress up their cars, too, so most of the wildest body kits and brightest chrome goodies come from Germany or Japan.

The best place to look for inspiration, new or used parts is on the net. A number of club and enthusiasts' sites offer reviews of parts people have bought with praise or complaints about their user-friendliness. Miata.net has reviews of products, and a chart showing which parts from the MX-5 Mk1 and Mk2/3 are interchangeable. Or www.mx5.mods.co.uk has a running top 10 (usually headed by the good old K&N filter). This site also provides a forum for modifiers to show off their engineering triumphs, or warn of their disasters. If you register here, the team will also answer your queries on line.

Just for fun, Keith Tanner's site www.eunos. com/keith/wheels lets you try different stripes or wheels on your car to see how they look, but he doesn't sell either, and the products shown may not be up to date.

↓ **Modified cars spotted by Andrew Fearon in the USA; one has an M Speedster-style aerodeck. (Andrew Fearon)**

ROADSTER
Shop Options

↑ **Japanese suppliers offer an incredible range of mods and accessories for the Roadster.**

There are also plenty of companies offering wood steering wheels, gear levers and handbrake handles. Think hard before interfering with a steering wheel fitted with an airbag, however. It may not look stylish, but your safety is more important, and you might find your car is harder to sell on.

Alloy gear levers are more fashionable in new cars at the moment, following the example of racing cars. Perhaps the most extreme option, though, comes from KG Works, which produces a Ferrari-style metal open gate.

Touring

It's great to let the MX-5 really stretch its legs over twisting mountains roads; the difficulty comes if you don't have a butler to drive ahead with the luggage.

However, a number of companie have come to the aid of the determined tourer. One option is a bag to fit behind the seats, although sticking up slightly from the rear deck. You can opt for a complete set of bags which fit together like a three-dimensional jigsaw to use up every inch of boot space. Or, if you have a Mk1, which carries its spare wheel in the boot, there are circular bags tailored to fit into the centre of the spare.

Of course, another option is the good old rear boot rack, and there are a number to choose from which do not require any drilling into the lid.

Owners of early cars may love wind in the hair, but it's good to stop the cold wind down your neck by fitting a windstop. Again, there are a number on the market, but most people's favourite is the Oris Windstop available from Moss. Although quite expensive, it virtually eliminates wind buffeting, and is reckoned to be better than the standard item provided on the Mk2 or Mk2.5. It fits easily with two screws, and can be left in place when you put the hood up. Serious Automotive also offers an Oris Windstop incorporated into a Hard Dog roll-over bar.

Dressing up

One of the most popular body decorations in the States is a set of front-to-rear white stripes, echoing Carroll Shelby's colours for the famous Cobra. You can buy stripes from most graphics suppliers, or try specialists, The Mroad.

Cabin

The MX-5's cockpit is neat and orderly, but it doesn't live up to the promise of the gorgeous curvy exterior.

It says a lot that one of the most popular MX-5/Miata mods is a pair of chrome air vent rings. Another favourite is a set of white dials, as fitted to the production Mk2.5. You can actually have them in most colours, or go for a fluorescent look. The walnut dashboards of the 1960s may have been outlawed by safety legislation (and the realisation that you don't want to headbutt a plank in the case of an accident), but there are plenty of other options now. Companies such as Autotech Designs and Moss can sell you dash and console veneer inserts in burr walnut, carbon fibre, brushed aluminium or pearl-effect.

↑ Charlotte Nadin
transformed the interior
of her Mk2 California into
what she believed it should
have been. (Dougie Firth)

← Some go even further.
This Japanese owner didn't
understand the phrase
'over the top'. (Andrew
Fearon)

→ This impressive European Dodge Viper lookalike was spotted in Bruges by Clive Southern. (Clive Southern)

→ The European MkI has M Speedster-style twin headlamps and Shelby stripes. (Clive Southern)

Body kits may add aerodynamic effects, or simply give a more individual look. Some of these pick up on ideas showcased by MX-5 concept cars, for example, twin-headlamps peering from beneath half-closed pop-ups echo the muscular M Speedster of 1995. This conversion is offered by BrainStorm, Donutz and Moss.

Some owners pay homage to other more expensive sports cars. For example, MX-5s have been spotted in Europe giving good impressions of a Dodge Viper, a miniature Ferrari, or even a Lotus Elan.

Sporty whale-tail boot spoilers are another popular option. For outrageous body kits, have a look on the web at Eribuni Corporation, and KG Works.

Roll-over bars are also popular either for safety or style. In fact, because of litigation concerns in the States, these are usually referred to as style bars. A true roll-over bar needs to be bolted to the chassis with bars reaching back.

A number of companies offer single or double

hoops bolted behind the seats. If you're racing, however, you may need a heavier-duty roll cage, such as those produced by Hard Dog Fabrication.

Soft-tops

Hoods will generally last eight to 10 years although sadly the binding around the edges tends to dry out and crack long before the hood fabric wears out. When the time comes to replace it, you could buy a new standard replacement or splash out on an attractive high-quality hood in duck or canvas.

The Mk1 and Mk2/2.5 hoods are similar apart from their rear windows. On the Mk1, the plastic window has to be zipped out and laid flat before the hood is folded to prevent creasing and damage. The hood fabric is fixed to the hoops, and is pulled back with it.

As you push the Mk2 hood back, the fabric slides over the hoops and the glass window is lowered to lie flat behind the rear seats. So the Mk2 hood and window can be made to fit the Mk1 frame with a relatively simple alteration to allow it to slide over the hoops. (However, it will need a new section for the wiring loom to operate the heated rear window.)

Matt Developments used to offer a glass window conversion for a Mk1 hood using 2CV rear glass which could be sewn-in Mk2 style, or with a zip. Another interesting option was an easy-lift system kit for the hood, featuring small gas struts. A number of UK cars still have these hoods, although the company no longer exists.

Hard-tops

Hard-tops for the Mazda MX-5 and Eunos Roadster and the Mk1 and Mk2 are interchangeable, but their rubber seals are different. So they will fit without any modification, but will probably leak unless you change the seal.

Hard-tops are only available from dealers in the colours current at the time, so you will probably have to fork out for a respray whether you buy new or second-hand.

Moss can also offer a budget glassfibre hood if you really want to keep the weather out, but don't want to stump up for a full factory version. This is, of course, lighter than the factory original, which is a plus for economy and performance, but it won't keep the body as rigid as a metal top.

↓ A whale-tail boot spoiler is fitted to Allan Legg's Mk2 Anniversary. (James Mann)

↙ Oris Windstop is reckoned to be better than the standard item in the Mk2 and Mk2.5. (Moss Europe)

↓ ↓ A luggage rack that can be fitted without drilling is the best option. (Moss Europe)

↑ Richard Ducommun found an old-stock Finish Line body kit intended for the Le Mans; his MkI is lowered and uses Tokico adjustable springs and dampers. (Dougie Firth)

→ A Jackson Racing supercharger with a pacecharge cooler boosts Richard's 1.6-litre engine to 200bhp. (Dougie Firth)

Performance Modifications and Tuning

Owners have been hotting up their MX-5s since it first roared out of the factory and, as prices fall and younger people are getting behind the wheel, the conversions are becoming wilder, both in looks and extra power.

The MX-5 can handle plenty of power; it won't fall apart, and it will still handle tidily even with a V8 under the bonnet. That said, every mod will affect the way the car drives. So it's best to sit down and come up with an overall plan before starting to add performance parts on an ad hoc basis.

Obviously, if you hot up the engine, you'll have

to look at your suspension and your brakes, or you won't be able to exploit the power.

However, one way to gain more power instantly is to rev the car far higher than most owners ever do. The redline is way up at 7,000rpm, and letting the needle hit it won't damage a well maintained engine, even if it will be letting out quite a roar. Try it before reading on.

Engine tuning

Mazda's engineering team will probably have beaten you to most of the traditional methods of squeezing a few more horsepower out of an engine. Both the 1.6 and 1.8 are extremely efficient 16-valve units each benefiting from excellent ignition and fuel injection systems and a highly tuned intake manifold. The team also had some pointers from the proven 323 GTX turbo, so just like its boosted cousin, the MX-5's engine was given lighter rotating components, a windage tray for the sump and a high compression ratio. Nevertheless, there are areas in which you can cut into the margins left by the original engineers

to make sure the car is smooth and economical for everyday use.

The MX-5's weakest point is its low-rev pull, so the cheapest way to tweak a little more out of your car is to change the basic ignition timing from the stock 10 BTDC (before top dead centre) to 18 BTDC. This should give about 20 per cent more torque at 1,000rpm, but you will have to stick to petrol of 92 octane or greater to avoid detonation or 'knock'. If you regularly rev above 6,500rpm, then 14 will suit you better. It will give you around two more horsepower and move the power band up by around 400rpm.

More juice?

A traditional way to boost power is to pump in more fuel, but if anything the Mazda runs a little too rich, and you won't have enough air in the chamber to burn the extra fuel unless you opt for forced induction (either supercharging or turbocharging). Then you can either fit a high-performance fuel pump, increase fuel rail pressure or go for the more expensive option of fitting larger injectors.

↓ Jonathan McCormack's 130bhp hillclimbing Roadster rides Mazdaspeed racing shocks and springs and 15in OZ Racing F1 alloys. (Jonathan McCormack)

Let it breathe

The most effective way to hot up your engine is to help it breathe more easily, although how far you go depends on how much power you want, and how much you are willing to spend. The aim is to allow your Mazda to suck in more clean, cool air to help the fuel burn efficiently, creating a nice big bang in the combustion chamber and then to expel the burnt gases as quickly as possible.

In fact, the best way to start is back to front, because there's no point in your engine gulping in air, if it is then trying to push the burnt gases out through a restrictive stock system. You'll just end up with an asthmatic Five.

The same principles apply as you replace sections of the exhaust system. If you don't want to splash out on an entire system all at once, then start by replacing the rear box (or muffler in Yankee-speak) first, then slot in a performance cat, and if you still want more power, invest in a performance exhaust manifold (header). With the exception of 1999–2000 cars, the factory header is well regarded by enthusiasts, but an aftermarket version can still make a difference. US readers should be aware that the California-spec 1999–2000 cars have an extra catalytic converter which makes the job more challenging and may raise emissions issues.

Replacement rear sections often include a 'cat-back' system, which has a larger-diameter pipe leading from the catalytic converter. It's well worth considering a high-flow cat if your car has done 50,000 miles or more, because the original will be giving up the ghost soon anyway.

Plenty of power figures are bandied around by the various parts manufacturers, but replacing your entire exhaust system can boost your output by close to 20 per cent. A simple item such as a cat-back muffler alone can add 7bhp and 5lb ft of torque.

There are a large number of stainless-steel systems promising maximum airflow on the market, but it is best to invest in a well-known name such as Jackson Racing, Moss or Borla. Cheaper systems can set up an annoying resonance or boom, which can ruin the driving experience. You should also look for a system with a minimum of twists and bends or welds because these will simply add resistance.

→ **A Mazdaspeed tailpipe is a good place to start. (Mazdaspeed)**

Breathing in

Aftermarket parts to help your MX-5 inhale range from a simple, less-restrictive air filter to turbochargers and superchargers. The popular K&N filter gives the engine a slightly more growly note as well as boosting power and improving throttle response. The Jackson Racing dual-stage air filter is made of pre-oiled foam. It promises an extra 3bhp and you can buy a cleaning kit to keep it effective.

A number of suppliers also offer a tuned induction unit to replace the stock air-filter box, which gives the air a smoother journey.

These changes may simply shift the available power up the rev range, but mid-range power is what you need if you want to overtake that caravan and get a free stretch of road.

The next step up is to fit a cold-air induction kit. This replaces the stock intake tract up to the

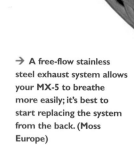

→ **A free-flow stainless steel exhaust system allows your MX-5 to breathe more easily; it's best to start replacing the system from the back. (Moss Europe)**

throttle body. It incorporates a high-performance air filter, and works by directing cold air from ahead of the radiator into a tuned air box. It passes through an airflow meter to let the engine's ECU know what's going on and then into the throttle body with increased velocity. These kits are offered by a number of suppliers. They can gain a significant boost of 12–14bhp for a very reasonable price.

If this doesn't quench your thirst for power, then the next step is forced induction – bolting on a turbo or a supercharger.

Supercharging versus Turbocharging

The debate about which method of getting that surge is best has been raging since 1989. Rod Millen and BBR went for the turbo option, but when layout engineer Norman Garrett left Mazda in 1989, he approached Eaton Superchargers to create a small unit specially for the Miata. This is still around, now known as the Jackson Racing Sebring supercharger and is sold by Moss among many others.

Both methods work by forcing more fresh air into the cylinders to burn more fuel and so create more power. Turbos are driven by exhaust gases from the engine and are usually used in conjunction with an intercooler, which chills the air before it goes into the engine to boost power even further. Superchargers are powered directly from the engine via a belt. Jackson Racing has produced upgrades for its supercharger to set it spinning even faster, so increasing boost by up to 20 per cent.

Superchargers, or blowers, deliver more low-down grunt, so their enthusiasts claim they are better for everyday use. With a turbo, the extra oomph kicks in higher up the rev range, and there can be a delay between your right foot pressing the pedal and a fierce kick in the back – the dreaded turbo lag – but the turbo keeps on pushing long after the supercharger has run out of breath. In fact, even the BBR and Le Mans turbos deliver their power very smoothly, with no obvious lag, and modern turbos are improving all the time.

A water injection system can be used with either the turbo or the blower. This sprays water through a fine nozzle into the intake charge where it atomises and soaks up the heat created by either system.

If it is not controlled, this heat can cause damaging detonation. Another method of controlling this is simply to retard the timing, but the result can be a sluggish, low rpm response. Using water injection to cool the air down allows more ignition advance, and so better throttle response.

The sophisticated 21st century turbo seems to be winning over the 'blower'. Both Keith Tanner of Flyin' Miata in the States and Richard Ducommun of Maztek in the UK (sadly, no longer in business) reported independently that a large number of owners were coming in to have their superchargers stripped out and replaced by turbos.

One reason, Keith suggests, is that the Sebring supercharger is not ideal for later models, and far more development work has been done on the various turbo systems. He told me: 'The main advances being made now are in the electronics rather than the turbos themselves, which are well-

↖ This BBR Turbo engine is tidy but very original. (Dougie Firth)

↑ The same engine in this Le Mans is a work of art. (Dougie Firth)

↑ **This Eunos Roadster in Australia has been boosted by the turbo from the Mazda's Familia 1.8 engine. (Roger Trethewey)**

understood technology; we don't just rechip, we put in a full replacement ECU.'

A second factor is that, as the prices of used MX-5s go down, younger owners are demanding the increased top-end power delivered by a turbo.

Keith says: 'Turbos are very hard to beat for "bang for the buck" and they're typically more trouble-free and powerful than supercharged cars. The boost can be increased (to a certain point) with the adjustable wastegate actuator, beyond that you'll need external boost control, be it electronic or manual. Properly set up (on an FMII), you can go from 6psi to 14psi with the flick of a switch. And, contrary to popular belief, a turbocharged Miata makes a great autocross car!'

Turbocharging is also a popular option in New Zealand, because the Mazda 323 GTX 4WD Turbo models are frequently imported, and it is reasonably straightforward to strip out the turbo and fit it to the MX-5, although a new manifold and a few other mods are required.

A trip to the machine shop

One way to optimise your engine's breathing is to make sure the intake and exhaust manifold ports mate precisely with those of the cylinder head. Slight variations in the casting process may mean that the head ports will not quite match, but you can have

them both removed and machined. To check for a mismatch, remove the manifold, make a 'gasket' in cardboard and then hold it up to the cylinder head.

While you're at it, the cylinder head can be 'ported' to make the transition between the combustion chamber and the ports as smooth as possible.

If you want to increase the compression ratio, you can have the cylinder head milled. The minimum cylinder-head height quoted by Mazda is 133.8mm, which is as low as you can go for some racing classes. It is possible to take it lower, though, because the cambelt has a tensioner that can take up the slack of a lower cam-pulley-to-crankshaft dimension.

Every 0.065in you mill off the head removes about 0.15cu in (2.5cc) from the chamber and increases compression approximately half a compression-ratio point.

If you're going for a forced-induction engine it's best just to have the head smoothed over with a very light milling, because you'll need the greater volume in the combustion chamber.

CAMSHAFT

You can buy aftermarket high-lift cams from companies such as the Japanese performance specialists. The improvements will not be dramatic, but if you are going for ultimate power, they will shift the power peak a little higher up the range. Racers should also consider having the cam-bearing bores align-honed or align-bored.

CRANKSHAFT

The life of your hard-working crankshaft can be extended by nitriding. Micropolishing with ultra-fine emery paper will reduce surface friction with bearings.

For smoother running, you should also get the con rods balanced and cleaned up. They should all weigh the same, and all rough casting marks should be removed. Shot peening will create a stronger, harder surface.

If you are fitting a turbo or supercharger, you should consider a set of heavy-duty rods, for example, those from the 323 GTX are stronger than those of the stock MX-5, but they are heavier.

FLYWHEEL

A lighter flywheel allows the engine to spin more quickly because of its reduced rotational inertia. The engine revs will drop faster between gearshifts, too.

The stock item weighs 18lb (8kg), but you can buy much lighter replacements, including aluminium versions weighing just 4lb (1.8kg). Try performance suppliers such as BrainStorm and Racing Beat.

More cubic inches

Both the MkI 1.6 and 1.8 engines have enough metal in them to allow you to overbore the cylinder and gain more capacity. You can bore out the 1.6 by 0.040in to give 24.992cu in (409.6cc) per cylinder, 2.549cu in (41.8cc) more than the stock engine, which is worth about 3 horsepower. The new compression ratio will be up to 9.6:1.

On the 1.8, the 0.040in overbore will give you an added 2.770cu in (45.4cc) and about 3.3 more horsepower and a compression ratio of 9.2:1.

Swap shop

Mazda redesigned the head of the 1.8 engine in 1999. The new head was fundamentally the same (and even used the same head gasket), but it used solid tappets, had an improved intake port angle and was more efficient than its predecessor. So this later head can be used to boost the performance of an earlier car, although you need to know what you are doing. Turbocharged and supercharged cars in particular will benefit from this swap. Ideally you should use a Mk2 (NB) intake manifold, it will match up to the port and simply bolt into place. An NA manifold will also work, but will need some modification.

The best donors are 1999 or 2000, because VVT was introduced in 2001 and the head, intake manifold and intake all changed.

Another option is to swap the entire engine. Retrofitting a 1.8 engine into a 1.6 is relatively simple because the 1.8 is just a stretched version of the 1.6. NB engines will also fit. The increase in power from an early 1.6 to a 1.8 isn't massive, but the 1.8 has more torque and the potential for further power increases.

The ECUs for the two engines are different, but it's easier to adapt a 1.6 ECU than to rewire the car to run on a 1.8 ECU. You'll also need a 1.8 exhaust manifold (needing some modification of the flange at the end) and catalytic converter where fitted.

↑ A 5.0-litre Mustang V8 fits nicely in the Miata engine bay and the chassis can handle it. (Andrew Fearon)

Creating a Monster

Carroll Shelby did it with the Cobra and Sunbeam Tiger and, remarkably a V8 engine slips happily into the Mazda's engine bay.

David Hopps of Monster MotorSports in California eased a 5.0-litre Mustang V8 and a Borg-Warner T5 transmission into a Miata shortly after the car first arrived in the USA, creating the first Monster Miata. It sounds like a recipe for terminal understeer, but the 302cu in Ford V8 fitted relatively easily beneath the Mazda's bonnet and weighed only 250lb (113kg) more than the four-cylinder unit it replaced. With sufficient reinforcements to the body, the Monster proved a balanced and nimble sports car capable of sprinting to 60mph in 4.8sec. Next came the Mega Monster with a Kenne Bell supercharger boosting power to 400bhp and torque to 375lb ft. A Ford Thunderbird limited-slip differential and a number of frame reinforcements helped the car deal with the extra power. The five-bolt hubs, rotors and callipers from the third generation RX-7 R1 made sure it stopped again.

In February 1994, *Motor Trend* magazine ran a test of the best 'tuner cars' on the Market, pitting the Mega Monster against a fearsome field. The figures for the 0–60mph test ran: Bittle Mustang 4.2 sec, Monster Miata 4.2, Farrell RX-7 4.4, Dodge Viper 4.5, Vortech Mustang 4.6, Stillen

300 ZX 4.7, Morrison Camaro 4.8, RSA Supra 4, Corvette ZR-1 5.2.

The Mega-Monster achieved the quarter-mile in 12.6 seconds at 111.6mph, compared with the Viper's 13.2/112.1 and Corvette ZRI's 13.6/106.

As this book goes to press, Monster Miata Inc in San Marcos, California offers V8 conversion kits from $3,995 (plus car and engine). The company is run by Martin Wilson, who previously worked for the now defunct Monster Motorsports and set up Panache. For more details and photos, see www. monstermiata.com.

Other V8 fans have followed the Monster lead. In Britain, the more compact ex-Buick Rover V8 is plentiful and cheap. An English contributor to www.MX5mods.co.uk, calling himself simply 'Bob', has fitted one in his Eunos Roadster, and reckons his 220bhp 3.5-litre car is 'a pussycat' to drive, compared with a TVR.

The New Zealand owners' club recently held an entire meeting of V8 Mazdas using either Holden V8s, or the 4.0-litre Lexus LC400 (Toyota Soarer) engine.

In Australia, regulations forbid a straight transplant. However, Bullet Cars, now owned by AEC, offers an extreme alternative. To create its Bullet Roadster, the company imports MX-5 bodyshells from Japan, stretches the wheelbase by 70mm and constructs its own box-section chassis. It then fits the all-alloy quad-cam 4.0-litre Lexus V8. For the muscular SS, it then bolts on a supercharger. The prototypes for both have undergone rigorous homologation tests and the Bullet V8s are sold as new cars.

With a 429bhp and 405lb ft, the pounding SS could give a Porsche 911 Turbo a fright. However, thanks to a 53/47 per cent weight distribution and the slightly longer wheelbase, it retains much of the MX-5's supreme balance (it has some serious Brembo brakes, too). You can snap up a normally aspirated Bullet Roadster for $98,000 or the SS for $118,000.

Nitrous injection

If you really want your MX-5 to fly, then you can join the growing number of drivers who have turned to the drag racer's favourite tipple: nitrous oxide.

As mentioned above, the key to getting more power from your engine is to burn more fuel, and this is usually accomplished by adding air.

Nitrous oxide contains more oxygen than normal air, so you effectively feed your car 'super air'.

At the high temperatures inside the cylinders of your engine, the nitrous oxide molecule breaks open, releasing its oxygen atom. This oxygen allows more fuel to be burned, creating higher cylinder pressures, and more power.

The leftover nitrogen acts as a buffer to keep the reaction under control, and is then ejected with the rest of the exhaust gases.

A separate, very useful feature of nitrous is its cooling effect. When liquid nitrous oxide at the nozzle is released into the intake stream, it instantly turns into a gas. The boiling temperature of nitrous oxide is 127°F (88°C). This has a serious cooling effect on the entire intake charge. Since an 11°F drop in charge temperature correlates with roughly one per cent gain in power, this cooling effect alone can produce a 58 per cent gain in power.

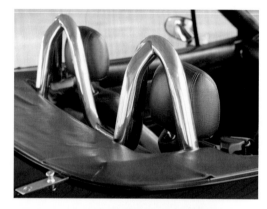

→ Most chrome bars are added mainly for style, they may prevent the standard tonneau cover from being fixed at the front. (Magic Car Pics)

↓ More serious roll-over bars are needed for racing, and have to be secured to the chassis. (Magic Car Pics)

← Panasport Minilite-lookalike wheels are comparatively light, and so should not upset your handling like other aftermarket alloys. (Moss Europe)

Chassis rigidity

A stiff chassis allows the suspension to do its job. Mazda stiffened up the chassis in 1992 and more seriously in 1994, mainly to reduce vibration. Earlier cars can easily be fitted with braces for the front and rear subframes, plus cockpit braces, which run between the shoulder harness mounting points.

Another popular option to stiffen up the rear bulkhead is to fit a roll-over bar (in the litigious USA these must be known as 'style bars') which can usually be fitted to the seatbelt turrets.

For ultimate stiffness, you can opt for a full roll cage, and there are several on the market, including the well-known Hard Dog item. However in the UK, the height of the cage required for sport makes the soft-top difficult to fit with one in place.

Wheels

If you're worried about preserving your car's supremely balanced handling, then think hard before changing your car's wheels. Enough space was provided inside the wheelarch to use snowchains, so it is possible to fit up to an 18in wheel with low-profile rubber. This will look handsome, but you'll ruin the finely tuned handling of your Mazda.

The Mk1's original alloys are some of the lightest ever fitted to a mass-production car and they were fitted with special lightweight Dunlops. Both were commissioned to reduce unsprung weight, so even the alloy wheels fitted to special editions by local distributors such as MCL in the UK, can spoil the optimum balance created in Hiroshima.

So, if you are going to change the wheels, go for the lightest possible option.

The 1994 seven-spoke wheels weigh just 10.3lb (4.7kg), or even less if polished, and are highly prized, but unfortunately rare.

The BBS 15in wheel, created using a high-pressure forging process weighs just 9.6lb (4.4kg), or the polished M-Edition wheel is also a good choice if you can find one. (Polishing reduces weight even further.)

The Mk2 MX-5 has 15in tyre and wheel combinations available from the factory, which can be retrofitted to Mk1s.

Wire wheels tend to be heavy and so are best avoided. (They're a menace to clean, too.)

The rolling diameter of the stock Miata wheel and tyre combination is 22.7in. The bigger the wheel, the lower the profile of the tyre must be. If you go higher than 23.2in, it will affect your speed readings and your gear ratios.

The taller the rolling height, the taller the overall gear ratio will be and the less brisk your acceleration will be.

The collar that keeps the wheel centred is 54mm in diameter. So it is essential that the hubcentric collar diameter of an aftermarket wheel matches this.

The original wheels have a 45mm offset to make room for the brake callipers and to fit into Mazda's family wheel system; however, this is not a standard size. Most aftermarket wheels have an offset of 35–37mm. This will fit the car and look pretty smart, but will create some unacceptable handling quirks and lead to premature wear of your suspension bushes. Just listen for the rattles and crashes over potholes.

A good compromise is the Panasport 14 or 15-inch eight-spoke Minilite-lookalike, which is light, has a 45mm offset and an attractive polished aluminium finish (available from Moss).

If, having read all this, you just want some knock 'em dead alloys, you'll be spoiled for choice.

Tyres

You can sharpen up the MX-5's handling even more with a set of performance tyres. The US Miata Owners' Club favourites in the inexpensive bracket are the Dunlop D60 and Yokohama A509.

Or you can upgrade to a premium tyre such as the Dunlop SP-8000 or Michelin Pilot 4. These will provide even greater grip and performance.

Remember that fitting a wider tyre doesn't necessarily mean more grip if it is not staying flat on the tarmac; it may just change the shape of the contact patch rather than putting more rubber on the ground. So if you're going this route, you also need to alter the suspension.

Remember, too, that a larger tyre weighs more and takes longer to get warm. The widest tyre a MX-5 can wear is 195mm of tread width.

Suspension

↑ **Remember that stiffer suspension means sharper handling but a less comfortable ride.**

Ride comfort and superb handling are natural enemies, one requiring a softer set-up, the other needing a firm platform, and well-controlled body roll.

It is a compromise engineers have to struggle with, keeping a close eye on their customers. National tastes are quite different, too. Americans drive on long straight roads for hours at a time, and so Europeans find the typical yank's ride too wallowy. US drivers find European suspension set-ups, designed for wriggly roads strewn with hairpins, very hard on the backside.

Mazda's engineers achieved something quite extraordinary with the MX-5. The ride is firm, but far from uncomfortable, and its body control is supreme as it rails around the tightest bends.

You may get more out your MX-5 simply by having the suspension alignment fettled by a specialist once a year. Mazda specifications are vague, and some experienced technicians have their own favourite settings for caster, camber and toe.

If the engine's power has been boosted, however, some extra tweaks may be required to keep the new set-up under control, or owners may choose to sacrifice a little comfort for even sharper handling.

Keith Tanner of Flyin' Miata reckons a set of upgraded anti-roll bars 'give the best bang for the buck of any Miata modification'. They will make the car more responsive on turn-in and corner flatter without a significant effect on the ride.

Anti-roll bars connect the left- and right-hand sides of your suspension front and rear. They reduce body roll by transferring some of the load from the compressed side of the suspension to the expanding side as you take a corner. The stiffer they are, the flatter the ride. Eventually, though, the ride will become harsher.

You can also play with the handling balance of the car by firming up the front and rear bars. If you make the rear bars softer, the car will grip better at the back than the front, increasing understeer. Softer bars at the front lead to more oversteer.

When you replace the bars, you may as well replace the rubber bushes with a firmer set to decrease deflection. Most aftermarket anti-roll bars with come with a polyurethane set.

Beware, the anti-roll bar mounts for the Mk2 are not as strong as those for the Mk1, and can break if you overstress them by fitting too firm a set of bars and going for it on the track.

Fitting shorter, stiffer springs and performance shocks will also firm up the suspension to give flatter cornering. If you are racing regularly, a number of companies offer short springs for the MX-5, which will lower the car by up to 2in. However, if you drop it by more than an inch, you'll have to raise the steering rack to avoid 'bump steer'. Go down another 0.25in and you will have to trim the rubber bump stops, too.

If your springs are too stiff, you will actually lose traction as the wheels need enough travel to clamber over bumps – wheels in the air don't grip or steer. The best way to lower your MX-5 is by fitting adjustable shock absorbers, such as the popular Koni. In fact, after a set of performance tyres, the next best way to improve ride and handling quality is to fit performance shock absorbers.

The Konis are adjustable for damping and allow you to lower the ride height of your car in seconds while still using the stock springs. An added benefit is that when it starts to wear, a turn of the knob will dial back in any lost damping force.

A number of shocks, including those by Carrera also have an adjustable lower cap or spring perch which can be moved up and down to easily change the ride height.

You can also buy threaded sleeves to create a finely adjustable lower spring perch.

When the Mk3 arrived, plenty of owners felt it sat too high. The solution adopted by a number of British enthusiasts was the Mazda Eibach lowering kit, which lowered the car by about 30–35mm and greatly improved the handling (Mazda Part Number (Eibach Lowering Kit) 4100-77-774A). The springs could also be purchased from specialist suppliers.

Legal LSD

A limited-slip differential prevents one wheel from spinning uselessly under power, while the matching wheel is stationary. It helps the car grip in extreme conditions such as an icy road or a sharp corner on a race track.

The first to be offered for the MX-5 was a simple viscous limited-slip diff made up of a set of plates connected to each axle, running in a bath of silicone fluid. The plates don't touch, but as one spins faster than the other, the silicone firms up under the shearing force and resists the differing speeds. This was an option, but can be retrofitted without too much of a problem.

From 1994, the Torsen gear differential was introduced, and this long-lasting and tough unit provides excellent traction. Again, it is relatively simple to retrofit to an earlier car. However, if you are fitting a Torsen differential from a 1996 or later car into a 1994 or 1995 car, you'll need to use the later-style halfshafts introduced that year. That will mean swapping the diff, halfshafts and driveshaft.

From 1997, Mazda introduced the Torsen Type 2, which was cheaper to manufacture (and sell) than the Type 1 and has a higher-bias ratio, so this is a better option. The part number is MM02-27-200A.

In 2001 the Toshiki-Fuji unit was introduced, based on the same principles as the iconic Torsen, but with a stronger carrier.

Transmission

The MX-5's gearbox is quite simply one of the best on the market. Its quick-shifting action is a delight, and it is strong, so it is best left just as it is, so long as it has been well cared for. However, you might consider a stronger clutch if you are going for a radical power hike.

A number of gear sets are offered by the aftermarket manufacturers to allow you to change up a little later, but changing the final drive is probably best left to serious racers.

Brakes

If you're seriously increasing your go, you need to make sure you can stop. Mazda brakes grew from 9.25in at the front and 9.1in at the rear on 14in wheels to 10in front, 9.9in rear 1994–2002 and then up to 11in for the 2001–2002 Sport and all cars from 2003. The Mk3 front discs swelled to 11.4in (290mm) front and 11in (280mm) rear. Retrofitting larger brakes is relatively simple, or there are also numerous aftermarket brake kits.

Bigger brakes will be more resistant to fade and will scrub off speed more quickly. You may also like to see a pair of brightly coloured callipers through an open-wheel design.

It's essential to consider your new set-up carefully, however, as bigger brakes add unsprung weight – as will the larger wheels you may have to fit in order to use them. Make sure your chosen brakes and wheels are compatible, too. Just because they seem to be the right size, the design may mean they don't fit together.

As usual, the best way to choose is to look at the internet forums, or chat to other owners at shows about their experiences.

↑ 4-pot vented big brake kit (Moss part no. MXV2110) suitable for Mk1–2.5 MX-5 models. Visit www.mossmx5.co.uk for more information. (Moss Europe Ltd)

CHAPTER 11
OWNERS' CLUBS

Like birds of a feather, MX-5, Miata and Roadster owners have a tendency to flock together. There are owners' clubs all over the world, swapping tips and ideas for mods, or addresses for aftermarket suppliers over the internet.

Plenty of owners arrange their holidays to join in with events thousands of miles away on different continents. Some even arrange to borrow one another's cars when they arrive.

Events vary from relaxed tours to competitive autocross meetings and concours shows, but they all offer the opportunity to see some wonderful cars. Plus, on occasion you may bump into one of the car's original designers or current Mazda executives.

Tom Matano is an enthusiastic attendee and is always willing to spend time with owners telling inside stories, whether he's in the USA, Europe or Japan. He's also signed a lot of engines with his 'Always Inspired' tag (sometimes countered by Bob Hall's 'Perpetually Perspiring').

The ex-publisher of *Miata Magazine* in the States, Barbara Beach described four categories of owner: 'Wine and Cheese', people who like to drive somewhere nice, essentially to socialise; 'Rally and touring types', who enjoy a bit more action from a gymkhana when they arrive; the 'Racers' are autocross fanatics who get very serious about their times; and finally there are the 'Modifiers', who may be looking for performance, or who may just get satisfaction from the engineering that goes into their hot power plant.

Owners in the USA and Canada are probably the most serious when it comes to holding autocross events on shopping mall car parks or airfields, any old piece of tarmac all over the country, and most American club events will include a driving event. In the UK, Europe and down-under in Australia and New Zealand, an exhilarating drive usually forms part of the route, and although there may be a driving event when members arrive at their destination the event tends to be smaller and often on grass.

Owners' clubs the world over offer vital services, such as technical advice and preferential insurance schemes. Club events also attract stallholders, offering accessories and showing off their expertise with superbly modified cars.

The exchange of information between clubs has blossomed as more members get online. There is now a flourishing worldwide community of owners and fans on the internet, through Miata.net, the Miata Ring and hundreds of individual club sites and blogs. To join in, just get online.

USA and Canada

It's sad to report that as we go to press there is no Pan-American club for the Miata. The original Miata Club of America (MCA) was established before the car was launched, and US executives frequently took the opportunity to canvas the club for opinions about future product development.

The Californian team working on the original car knew that as soon as their creation escaped into the world, it would have a club. The idea was chewed over by Tom Matano, layout engineer Norman Garrett and his friend since college, Vince Tidwell, who had gone into aviation while Norm headed towards automotive design.

As the Miata's launch approached, Garrett was moving back East to work for Volvo, and he and Vince thought they'd have a go at running the club as an entertaining hobby. As a keen BMW owner, Vince had already been a member of an enthusiasts' club, and to make sure this one was successful, he critiqued a number of existing sports car clubs.

One benefit was that, instead of a newsletter, club members should receive a glossy magazine, sharing the production values of a newstand title and the result was the excellent *Miata Magazine*.

Mazda provided the club with a list of proud new owners every month and the response was

← All three generations line up on Madeira Drive at the end of a UK Owners' Club run from London to Brighton. (Paul Bateman)

↑ Tom Matano signs Clive Southern's boot lid at a meeting of European clubs in Bruges. (Clive Southern)

astonishing. Norman and Vince soon knew that they would not be able to do this alone.

Meanwhile, Barbara Beach and her friend Lyn 'Sky' Vogel had also come up with the idea of starting a club. Barb claims she had originally lost her heart to the RX-7, which she describes as a 'monster with a rotary engine', but a friend had seen some spy shots of a cute little curvy roadster, so very different to American muscle cars or 1970s wedges of cheese and she wanted to be involved. She says: 'When I first saw the Miata, it was smiling at me. I got to take one to an SCCA event in 1989 and everyone was staring and stopping me, because it was so special.'

In fact, it was so special that around 60 people approached Mazda, all suggesting a club, but when Wayne Killen and Rod Bymaster met Barbara, they could see she was clearly someone who could get things done, so they put her in touch with Norman and Vince.

She and her husband bought *Miata Magazine* in 1997, but Mazda North America took over the club in 2000 renaming it the Miata Owners' Club. Both the club and Miata magazine disappeared shortly afterwards. However, there are hundreds of enthusiastic local clubs in the US linked by Miata.net.

Some local clubs drive regularly through deserts, others get to try out the handling on mountain roads. One of the most spectacular events is the biannual Miatas in Moab meet in Utah. Another is Miatas at the Gap, an unofficial gathering of keen drivers at Deal's Gap, a serpentine section of road between North Carolina and Tennessee. Or, because Mazda owns the Laguna Seca race track in California, Miata drivers are regularly given the opportunity to try out its curves.

Autocross, also known as gymkhana or Solo II is the US favourite driving event, but a number of keen drivers go in for track events. Members of the Wild Rose Chapter in Edmonton, Alberta, however, have also been known to have a go at ice racing.

Uk MX-5 Owners' Club

The UK Owners' Club members define the word 'enthusiast'. Its members love nothing more than to simply get in their cars and drive, top-down whatever the weather.

This island may be small, but The UK club is one of the largest MX-5 Owners' clubs in the world.

Membership is open not only to all owners of MX-5s, Roadsters and Miatas, but also to enthusiasts of the car who have yet to acquire one.

The club is organised by Area across the country. One of its greatest strengths is the network of Area Co-ordinators who arrange local meetings, runs, track days, social gatherings and other events.

Surprisingly, it was a late-starter – a UK Club hadn't even been thought about until 1994. The Miata Club of America allowed overseas membership, however, and UK members Paul and Jayne Grogan saw a picture of another British MX-5 owned by Tim Robinson in *Miata Magazine*. The club put them in touch and they met in June 1994 to plan their own club.

Following a mail shot and advert in *Exchange & Mart*, 28 owners, all eager for a UK club, met on September 18 1994 at Billing Aquadrome in Northamptonshire. The first newsletter – a single A4 sheet – was sent out a couple of months later. Mazda's UK importer MCL also came to Billing, to assist and support the Club. This allowed support for rallies and, eventually, colour photos in the Club magazine, *Soft-top Hard-top*. Vitally, MCL agreed that

← **US owners enjoy motorsport and those in California also get to keep their hoods down more than most.** (*Miata Magazine*)

↓ **Shelby stripes look great in the native land of the Cobra.** (*Miata Magazine*)

its dealer network would let owners know about the Club when they booked their cars in for service or repair. Crucially this lead to Membership packs being put into all new MX-5s sold in the UK.

Membership numbers rose rapidly and help was enlisted from fellow members Clive and Maureen Southern and Andy and Gill Whitlow. The first birthday event at Solihull in September 1995 drew 112 cars, and numerous other events were organised throughout the year, including European Club meets, treasure hunts and track days.

By 1998, membership had climbed to more than 4,500 and MCL sadly decided to remove their support following a change in marketing strategy. The original committee had also decided it was time for a change, so the reins were handed to a new team.

As this book goes to press, membership benefits include discounts on servicing, parts and accessories across the country, plus a recommended car insurance scheme.

Most Areas publish a bi-monthly newsletter for local members, and Area websites and forums provide up-to-date information on forthcoming events with reports and feature on past get-

together. *Soft-top Hard-top* is a glossy bi-monthly, and maintains a consistently high standard of content and design. It was named Club Magazine of the Year 2008 by *Classic and Sports Car* magazine.

The Club's online forum is the heart of the UK community and the first place to check for MX-5 technical advice, Club news and events.

Members frequently take their cars across the Channel to MX-5 meetings in Europe, and a number have travelled to events in Japan and the US at Laguna Seca and Monterey. Visit the website at www.mx5oc.co.uk for more information.

New Zealand

New Zealand owners generally like to use the car the way Mazda intended, and enjoy the country's wonderful twisty roads. Even though there are relatively few MX-5s and Eunos Roadsters in New Zealand, there are plenty of club events, usually involving a great drive, but occasionally with a hillclimb or track day, so members can really let rip. Local groups also arrange occasional autocross events, but they are usually fairly light-hearted gymkhanas. Website: www.mx5club.org.nz

↑ Members of the new South Wales Owners' Club pose before a driver training day by Ian Luff Motivation Australia. The instructors are John Boston (left) and Ian Kimber in yellow shirts. (Ian Luff)

 ↑ **Fifty MX-5s and their owners from the South Australia Owners' Club attend a wedding at Martindale Hall. (Roger Trethewey)**

→ **Roger Trethewey, president of South Australia Owners' Club, puts his right foot down. (Roger Trethewey)**

Australia

→ **A thousand Roadsters, many of which have been modified, are seen parked up around the Hiroshima test track. (Andrew Fearon)**

The vast Australian continent has a single overall owners' club divided into chapters based in the different states. As you can imagine, Australian club activities involve a lot of socialising and barbecues, but also lots of enjoyable driving.

The most popular club driving event is known as a motorkhana. This test of precision driving uses four different circuits, each circuit takes just under a minute and involves reversing and handbrake turns as competitors try to beat the clock. Website: www. MX5.com.au

Japan

Japan has a large number of local roadster clubs, but no overall umbrella organisation. One of the largest is the Roadster Club of Japan (www.open-inc.co.jp/rcoj). Another is ROCK's (Roadster Owners' Club Kids) (rock-s.hp.infoseek.co.jp). The founder Tak Yamamoto explained that he gave the club this name because it's for people who retain the curiosity and enthusiasm they had when they were boys. (He also likes rock music).

Japanese owners like to dress up their cars with plenty of accessories and performance parts, and

they frequently turn up to events in fancy dress themselves.

Plenty of Roadster drivers go in for circuit racing, sprints, autocross and hillclimbs, and are serviced by a thriving aftermarket parts industry.

← You could ask why he didn't just buy an Elan, but then again he probably prefers a car that always starts… (Andrew Fearon)

↑ Japanese owners go in for wild body mods. (Andrew Fearon)

CHAPTER 12
THE MX-5 ON THE TRACK

Club racing was always in the back of the engineers' minds when designing the MX-5, and the car has proved to be just as nimble on the track as they'd hoped. Since its launch, its owners have put the car through adrenaline-pumping events just about every weekend and it has collected an embarrassment of trophies.

Owners can choose between a number of fiercely contested autocross events, time trials, sprints and endurance races. You have to spend money if you want to lift the silverware, though, and most competitors are very serious indeed.

More recently, drifting has joined the list of choices. If there was a car suited for a sport where the aim is to go sideways, this is it. Google MX-5 and 'drifting' and you'll find plenty of amusing clips on YouTube. See the smokin' pictures on www.doristars.com, too. The MX-5 doesn't have the power to be a top-ranking drifter, but it's still a lot of fun.

USA

Motorsport in the US was varied and widespread from day one. It always included Autocross, endurance and road racing.

For details see the Sports Car Club of America (SCCA) website www.scca.com (Tel: 1-800 770 2055). Or there's the National Auto Sports Association (not to be confused with the space programme) see www.proracing.com. Drifting comes under the NASA.

Mazda owns the legendary Laguna Seca Raceway in California and gives plenty of support to MX-5 Miata racing. It also has links with the excellent Skip Barber Racing School.

Communications officer for Mazdaspeed Motorsports in the US, Dean Case, told us: 'The heart of Mazdaspeed is in supporting club racers. There are over 9,000 Mazda customers who compete in club racing with the SCCA and NASA.

More than a few of them have aspirations of racing professionally and Mazda has directly assisted a number of club racers with the leap to the professional ranks.'

He suggests that a young driver can begin in karts and progress through the Skip Barber series, Club Racing Formula Mazda, professional Star Mazda and finally to Formula Atlantic, all with Mazda.

Autocross

Also known as Solo II, Autocross is the US favourite, and most events are sanctioned by the SCCA. This amateur event is cheap to enter, and it is part of the deal that all drivers must help marshal another group.

Competitors drive against the clock around a small road course marked out with cones, usually in a large parking lot or on an airfield. The style and length of the course varies considerably by region, but usually contains many linked tight turns, often of increasing or decreasing radii, a few small straight sections and often a slalom section or two. Courses are generally designed to be very tight in order to keep speeds to a safe level.

All sorts of cars compete in appropriate classes, which can include big and powerful machines such as Cadillacs and Lamborghinis, but the compact, agile Miata is perfect. Amateur racers must first participate in two SCCA driving schools before they can compete in regional races. After six regional events, they can move up to enter national competitions.

Road racing

Confusingly for Europeans, this doesn't mean street racing or rallying. In the States, road racing means on a track, and the Miata has also seen plenty of action in endurance races, time trials and production saloon races on race circuits all over the USA.

← They take drifting seriously in the States. (Mazdaspeed)

↙ Dave Larkman keeps it crabwise at the British Drift Championship. (Ross l'Anson, doristars.com)

exploding in your face halfway round a corner
could be disastrous.

The serious Pro Road racing is for Touring Cars
in which the engines are built to an exacting spec,
with intakes and exhausts tuned for maximum
horsepower. The biggest event for these cars is the
SCCA Pro Racing Speed World Challenge. See the
following websites: www.world-challenge.com, www.
sccapro.com, or www.speedvisionwc.com.

Koni Challenge

Miatas also frequently appear in the Grand-Am Koni
Sports Car Challenge see www.grand-am.com/koni
or www.konisportscarchallenge.com. This is Grand-
Am's showcase for the latest high-performance
sports cars, coupés and sedans straight from the
dealer showroom floor. Major modifications are
permitted only in the area of safety, so the KONI
Sports Car Challenge is home to the same cars seen
on roads around the world. It was known as the
Grand-Am Cup Series from 2001 to 2006 and the
KONI Challenge Series from 2007 to 2008.

The starting fields typically feature more than
60 cars competing for both class honours and
overall victory. The two classes are: the big-bore
Grand Sport (GS) class, which allows exotic

In all, the SCCA has 24 categories for road
racing, not all of which would suit a Miata (the
sedan class, for example).

The least modified category is the Showroom
stock class, which is designed for mass-produced
cars under seven years old. Small tweaks are
allowed, for example, you can change the brake
pads, exhaust systems, steering wheel and driver's
seat. Roll cages and a harness are compulsory,
and steering wheels with airbags should be
removed because cars do touch, and an airbag

Miata Mono-Posto Concept 2000

The Miata Mono-Posto Concept was inspired by endurance racers of the 1950s such as the Jaguar D-type and Lotus 11.

It was launched by Mazda's North American Operations at the extreme SEMA (Specialty Equipment Manufacturers Association) show at Las Vegas in 2000. However, its job was to show Mazda's commitment to endurance racing. The press release reminded readers that Mazda was sponsor of the annual four-hour endurance race at the Tsukuba Circuit (Party Race). Entrants that year included Japanese automotive media teams, US and European automotive media teams, the Roadster (Miata) Owners' Club of Japan (RCOJ) and Team Mazda.

The Mono-Posto was also an important milestone because it was the first concept based on the second-generation Miata, following in the footsteps of the 1989 Club Racer, the 1995 M-Speedster and the 1996 M-Coupé.

Sports custom bodywork included half doors, air intake in the bonnet, a one-piece valence, front and rear fascias, cowl-mounted rear-view mirror, a minimalist windscreen and aluminium rollbar. Only the headlights and taillights were stock. The paint finish was a custom Red Pearl mica.

Mods under the bonnet included an HKS turbocharger and intercooler, HKS intake and exhaust manifolds and an HKS stainless steel exhaust, which result in a 36 per cent increase in horsepower (to 190hp @ 6,100 rpm) and a 104 per cent boost in torque (to 243lb ft @ 4,100 rpm).

Other performance modifications included Racing Hart three-piece, five-spoke, 18in wheels (18 x 8in front and 18 x 9.5in rear), Baer Racing four-wheel disc brakes and HKS Hiper Damper Coil Over Suspension.

The cockpit featured a Formula One-style Momo® steering wheel, Sparco® lightweight, one-piece racing seat and custom gauges.

'The Miata Mono-Posto is for one who wants to be alone with the road, focused purely on driving,' said Tom Matano, in his role as Executive Designer in charge of global advanced design, based in Hiroshima. 'The idea of this concept was to take the fun of driving a Miata to the extreme.'

The stunning 1999 Mono-Posto was inspired by endurance racers such as the Jaguar C-type.

↑ Most serious American road racers even do without the luxury of a windscreen. (*Racer*)

→ Miatas battle it out wheel-to-wheel in the States. Hard-tops add rigidity for racing. (*Racer*)

international machines like the Porsche 996 and 997, Nissan 350Z and BMW M3 to go head-to-head with American iron such as the Camaro and Dodge Challenger. The smaller Street Tuner (ST) class is Grand-Am's offering to the import and compact car crowd, including the Mazda RX-8 and Mazda MX-5, Chevrolet Cobalt SS, Dodge SRT4, Mini Cooper S, Acura TSX and a variety of BMWs. From 2009, the GS and ST classes ran separately in six of 11 event weekends.

Spec racing

Spec Miata is the largest road-racing class in the world. In 2009 more than 1,500 first- and second-generation Miatas were tearing up America's racetracks, making it the most-raced production car in the world.

This class is designed to provide an affordable nationwide class in which all regions are using basically the same rules and regulations. This allows for crossover Division to Division racing with a year-end championship event of all Divisions. Spec Miatas currently race both sprints and endurance races where available.

The 1990–1993 1600cc and 1994–1997 1,800cc Miatas have been approved by the SCCA for regional racing in all Divisions. The cars use a Bilstein shock with an adjustable coil-over suspension with Eibach springs and sway bars (front and rear, adjustable), steel braided brake lines. Toyo, Kumho and now Hankook tyres are in use in the various regions. For more details see website www.Specmiata.com. Specific rules for the various regions are posted in the Specifications section.

MX-5 Cup

The SCCA Pro Racing Mazda MX-5 Cup replaced the former MAZDASPEED Miata Cup in 2006. Featuring identical Mazda MX-5s on spec Kumho tyres, the MX-5 Cup gives drivers the opportunity

← Low-cost Spec Miata class encourages close racing. (Mazdaspeed)

↓ Playboy MX-5 Cup is a great proving ground for young racing drivers with professional ambitions. (Mazdaspeed)

to run on high-profile weekends in an economical, entry-level racing series.

Originally the series was open only to SCCA National Runoffs champions. NASA National Championship winners were added to the mix for 2007, and NASA Spec Miata Teen Driving Champions became eligible to compete in 2008.

Typically there are eight races at prestigious events across North America with grids composed of roughly 30 cars at each race. The season champion is awarded a factory-supported Mazda ride in the series. Visit www.mx-5cup.com to learn more.

As this book goes to press, the event is sponsored by *Playboy*, and all the cars wear bunny ears on their screens. This was never a shy and retiring series, however. When the Mk3 appeared, an example turned up in full race trim and Le Mans colours. Sadly, we understand that it has since been crushed because it was a prototype and could not be sold.

For 2007 Mazdaspeed supported the Humane Society of the US, and cartoon characters Earl the Dog and Mooch the cat attended races and the MX-5 appeared in the famed newspaper cartoon strip.

↓ **The famous Le Mans colours are seen again on a Mk3 prototype at Laguna Seca. (Mazdaspeed)**

UK

Motorsport didn't take off for MX-5s in the UK in the same way as it did in the US from launch probably because it had more inexpensive rivals. A few were always seen having a go at hillclimbs or track events, but the MX-5 went head to head against souped-up, nimble Minis, Vauxhall Novas or Caterhams and Westfields – and couldn't compete. An official one-make series was hard-fought in 1991, but not repeated.

Track racing began to gain popularity at the end of the noughties. One reason was that Mk1s and early Mk2s were now cheap to buy. Another was that racing an MX-5 was extremely inexpensive compared with other series, and as the credit crunch hit, some racers 'downsized'.

MaX5 Racing was formed in 2003 and set up a one-make championship based on US Spec Miata racing, then Ma5da Racing split off in 2008 and set up the Ma5da MX-5 Championship. Both championships welcome drivers with a wide range of experience from novice up to skilled and extremely competitive.

Drivers rep for MaX5, Jonathan Halliwell said:

'We will help drivers get a race licence, we can offer track days and instruction with Mazda On Track. We'll hold the driver's hand to help them get started.' In 2009 he reckoned that a driver could buy a car, kit it out and race for a season for £78,000. In 2009, MaX5 also introduced a new invitation class for modified MX-5s of all generations. For more information see MaX5 www.max5racing.com, tel 07831 331777 email jon@maxracing.com

Mazda On Track offers tuition in car control and drifting plus private events at UK tracks and the Nürburgring (tel: 01295 771 831, Website: www. mazdaontrack.co.uk).

Ma5da Racing wanted to stick to the basics: cars entering the Ma5da MX-5 Championship are all 1.6-litre Eunos Roadsters with limited-slip diffs. Control engine parts and tyres make sure it's all down to the driver to get ahead of the pack. Championship Director Jonathan Blake reckons a newly prepared car would cost £6,500, or a second-hand race-prepared car £5,000. Racing for the year would add another £56,000 plus, of course, repairs following contacts or expeditions off the track. He compares this extremely favourably

with the Renault Clio Cup costing around £85,000 for a year (all figures 2009). For details see: www. ma5daracing.com, email jblake@ma5daracing.com

A small number of owners use their MX-5s for hillclimbs or drifting, but the cheapest way to find out what your car can do in the UK is to take it on a track day. Circuits are booked by clubs or groups who are given a certain amount of time or number of laps. The only kit needed is a crash helmet.

Rather than risk their own cars, some enthusiasts club together to buy and sort an old

↑ Control parts and tyres guarantee nose to boot excitement in the Ma5da MX-5 Championship. (Lewis Craik)

car to share on the track, and many of them were inspired by Project Merlot. The Merlot in question was heading for the scrapyard when three members of the MX-5 Owners' Club's Eastern region set it up as a track car and kept an enthusiastic blog (See www.merlotmotorsport.blogspot.com). As this book goes to press, the Merlot is still going strong, having been thrashed by dozens of members of the Eastern region. Team Merlot has even attracted commercial sponsorship.

Japan

Mazda Japan showed it truly understood the Roadster buyer when it supported the 'Roadster Party Race Series' known as the friendliest race in Japan. This is a low-cost, one-make circuit race run by the Japanese NR-A. (see http://partyrace.nr-a.com) The NR-A category races are designed to give drivers a chance to test their driving skills under equal conditions in vehicles registered for daily use. As only a limited number of modifications are required to

→ Japanese racers show they mean business.

equip vehicles for racing, drivers can participate in 'real' races at a reasonable cost.

Surprisingly, given the title, the Party Race is an endurance event. However, it's only four hours long and good manners are apparently as prized as speed. Families are encouraged to come, mingle with friends and have lunch together. Teams have sometimes joined in from Australia and New Zealand.

Mazda makes entry extremely easy by selling a fully prepared Party Race Roadster with height-adjustable Bilstein dampers.

Contact details: JAF Japan Automobile Federation (like the FIA) is responsible for safe motoring in Japan (website: www.jaf.or.jp/e/index.htm). JNR-A (Japan NR-A Race Association), Ikejiri Setagaya-ku, Tokyo 154-0001 Zip 2-37-2-3F, telephone 03-3424 7871, email info@nr-a.com.

← The Japanese certainly know how to do cute. (And it's good to see a woman driver on the top step of the podium).

← Friends and family are all welcome at the Party Race.

↓ Manners are highly valued at the Party Race.

Australia and New Zealand

Australian MX-5 enthusiasts can enter a number of different racing formulas overseen by the Confederation of Australian Motor Sport (CAMS) www.cams.com.au including Production Sports Car racing and Supersprints. The latter is a form of circuit time trials, in which cars from stock to fully developed racing cars compete in different classes in races of between five and 12 laps.

Clubs also organise Regularities, where a driver nominates their expected lap time and endeavours to complete eight laps of the circuit keeping as close to that lap time as possible.

One cheap option has been to buy an early-

NR-A Roadster

The first Roadster NR-A went on sale in Japan in late 2001. This new model was designed to be a registered for the road, but designed for owners who might want to try it out on the track at the weekend.

It was unveiled to Roadster fans in a test run during the 'Roadster Festa' on Saturday, 8 September at the Tsukuba Circuit of Ibaraki Prefecture.

This 1600 five-speed manual model featured a larger radiator, tougher engine and diff mounts, a limited-slip diff, Bilstein dampers, stiffer suspension and an anti-roll bar and larger brakes with 15in rotors.

If buyers wanted to enter the one-make series, they had to buy the Mazdaspeed NR-A pack. This consisted of a six-point roll cage (detachable at the door), four-point seat belts/seat belt anchors and front/rear large pulling hooks (authorised by JAF).

The NR-A was available in Crystal Blue metallic, Pure White, Sunlight Silver metallic, Brilliant Black, Supreme Blue mica or Classic Red. The standard interior had red seats and a Nardi steering wheel. Mazdaspeed bucket seats were also optional.

A new NR-A Roadster went on sale in April 2006 with the introduction of the Mk3. It came with a 2.0-litre engine and five-speed 'box with height-adjustable Bilstein dampers, a torque-sensing Super LSD and front strut tower bars. The wheels became 16in steels (or aluminium if you didn't want to race). The pedals were lightweight aluminium and the steering wheel was leather-wrapped.

Japanese buyers can pick up the Roadster NR-A at a Mazda or Anfini dealership, register it for the road and race it at weekends.

model Roadster imported from Japan, which could not be registed for the road because they do not conform to Australia's Design Rules. Trim, carpets, etc. are stripped out to reduce weight and a solid roll bar fitted. Most competitors will invest in competition springs, shocks, brakes, anti-roll bars, and a limited-slip differential and wider wheels, and the standard engines will be tweaked and tuned for more power.

Aussie clubs also organise practice days for members. Naturally, there's drifting, too

Although New Zealand members are keen drivers, not many MX-5s were imported to New Zealand, so although individual members may enter production saloon races, motorsport tends to be limited to local motorkhanas and hillclimbs.

APPENDIX A
Inspired Sensation by Tom Matano

In 1984, I created this story to express our philosophy…

A car starts to draw more attention than another, either it passes you on a freeway, or you see it for a split second on a TV screen. It makes you want to find out what it is.

You start to develop some expectations about how it feels to drive, how you look in it, or the lifestyle you may lead with it. After a while, you discover that it was a Miata.

Then you may want to go to the dealership for a closer look. Upon closer inspection, you are satisfied that your expectations and excitement were justified.

You open the door, and the sight of the interior is so inviting, that you can't help but sit in it. From the first turn of the key, the engine starts, and it sounds and feels exactly how you imagined it would.

The first turn of the wheel … how it corners, and the way it stops. The car goes beyond initial expectations.

By the end of the test drive, we would like you to become a Mazda owner…

In the past, our product development efforts ended at that very moment. However, our new philosophy really begins here. We went on describing the type of life our customer would lead after the purchase.

The customer takes the car home, and, of course, takes the family for a ride, shows it to their neighbours and friends. Just before retiring to bed, you stop for one last look, and even say 'goodnight' to the car, or maybe even sit in the car one last time.

On your daily route, you start to think about more challenging roads … Or new routes in order to spend more time with the car.

On your first out-of-town trip, you discover other aspects of the car's personality that you didn't realise from your daily routine. You discover the depth of the car more and more, as days, months, and years go by.

Of course, even with the most prolonged driver-car relationship, there comes a time when the owner has to part with the car. You part with fond memories, which you will treasure for a long, long time.

And further down the road, the customer seeks out and finds the same model, buys it again and restores it.

Miata was the first product developed under this philosophy, and all the other Mazda cars that followed were products of this philosophy.

Tom's signature
on a bootlid.
(Andrew Fearon)

SPECIFICATIONS AND PERFORMANCE FIGURES

NA/NB/NC These refer to the three generations, the codes coming from Mazda's own designations for the cars.

The NA is the original, produced from 1989 to 1997 with the pop-up headlights. It was sometimes referred to as the M1 or Mk1.

The NB arrived in 1998 (1999 in North America), also known as the M2 or Mk2. The facelifted 2001–05 models are sometimes referred to as the NB-FL; this model also quickly became known as the Mk2.5 (strictly unofficial).

The all-new NC was introduced as a 2006 model. For obvious reasons, 'M3' has not been widely used. It is known as the Mk3, and Mk3 Facelift or Upgrade. Unofficially, of course, it's the Mk3.5.

1990
MAZDA MX-5 1.6

Engine	Inline 4-cylinder, water-cooled, DOHC, 16 valves, longitudinal
Displacement	1,598cc
Bore x stroke	78 x 83.6mm
Max power	114bhp @ 6,500rpm
Max torque	100lb ft @ 5,500rpm
Compression ratio	9.4:1
Induction system	Electronic fuel injection
Cylinder block	Cast iron
Cylinder head	Die-cast aluminium
Fuel tank	45 litres (9.9gal)
Fuel	Unleaded (min 91 ON)
Transmission	Five-speed manual
Gear ratios	1st 3.136
	2nd 1.888
	3rd 1.330
	4th 1.000
	5th 0.814
	Rev 3.758
Final drive ratio	4.300
Clutch	Hydraulically operated single dry plate, diaphragm spring
Diameter	200mm (7.87in)
Steering	Rack and pinion, power-assisted
Turns lock-to-lock	2.8
Turning circle	9.14m (29.99ft)
Brakes (front)	236mm (9.29in) ventilated disc
Brakes (rear)	231mm (9.09in) solid disc
Disc thickness	Front – 18mm (0.71in)
	Rear – 9mm (0.35in)
Vacuum servo	8in
Parking brake	Mechanical on rear wheels
Chassis and suspension	
Body	Monocoque
Suspension (front and rear)	Independent by double wishbone and coil spring

Shock absorbers (front and rear)	Cylindrical double-acting, gas-filled
Stabiliser	Torsion bar
Tyres	Dunlop P185/60 R14 82H steel radial
Wheel size	5.5JJ x 14
Wheel material	Aluminium alloy
Spare wheel	Space-saver
Dimensions (external)	
Length	3,975mm (156.5in)
Width	1,675mm (65.9in)
Height	1,230mm (48.4in)
Wheelbase	2,265mm (89.1in)
Track (front)	1,410mm (55.5in)
Track (rear)	1,430mm (56.3in)
Ground clearance (laden)	115mm (4.5in)
Dimensions (internal)	
Front legroom	1,085mm (42.7in)
Headroom (top closed)	942mm (37.0in)
Shoulder room	1,280mm (50.3in)
Kerb weight	995kg (2,193lb)
Weight distribution	52:48 f/r unladen
Towing capacity	
Braked trailer	700kg
Unbraked trailer	350kg
Performance (per Mazda Motor Corporation)	
Max speed	121mph (195kph)
0–62mph (96.5kph)	8.75sec
Fuel consumption	Urban – 29.4mpg (9.6l/100km)
	56mph (90kph) – 46.3mpg (6.1l/100km)
	75mph (121kph) – 36.2mpg (7.8l/100km)
Standard equipment	Momo leather steering wheel
	Power-assisted steering
	Electric windows
	Tachometer
	Sun visors with passenger vanity mirror
	Clarion CRH60 stereo radio/cassette (detachable front)
	Manual aerial
	Front door speakers
	Lockable central storage box
Colours (UK)	Classic Red
	Mariner Blue
	Crystal White
	Silver Stone metallic
Interior	Black cloth

JULY 1993
MAZDA MX-5 1.8i (Replaces 1.6i)

Engine	(1.8 from Mazda 323F GT) Inline 4-cylinder, water-cooled, DOHC, 16 valves, longitudinal
Displacement	1,839cc
Bore x stroke	78 x 83.6mm
Max power	130bhp @ 6,500rpm
Max torque	110lb ft @ 5,000rpm
Compression ratio	9.0:1
Camshafts	Hollow, for lighter weight
Induction system	Electronic fuel injection
Cylinder block	Cast iron
Cylinder head	Die-cast aluminium
Fuel tank	45 litres (9.9gal)
Fuel	Unleaded (min 91 ON)
Transmission	Final drive ratio 4.10:1
Brakes (front)	254mm ventilated discs
Brakes (rear)	251mm solid discs (larger diameter from 1994)
Chassis	Body shell stiffened. Steel rod between front suspension assemblies, stiffer rear anti-roll bars, brace between seatbelt anchor points behind the driver
Suspension	Stiffer springs and brushes, Bilstein sports damper, thicker anti-roll bar from 1994
Tyres	Pirelli P700-Z tyres available from December 1993
Wheels	Seven-spoke alloy
Wheel size	6 x 14in standard on 1.8 models from 1994
Kerb weight	1,020kg (2,249lb)
Weight distribution	51/49 f/r unladen
Interior	Seats with separate headrest replace those with integral items Passenger airbag available

Performance (Mazda Motor Corporation)

Max speed	120mph (193kph)
	0–60mph – (96.5kph) 8.5sec
Fuel consumption	Urban – 22mpg (13l/100km) Motorway – 27mpg (10.5l/100km)
Standard Equipment	Momo leather steering wheel Power-assisted steering Electric windows Tachometer Sun visors with passenger vanity mirror Clarion CRH60 stereo radio/cassette (detachable front) Manual aerial Front door speakers Lockable central storage box Electrically adjustable mirrors Electric aerial ABS optional Alarm optional

1995
MX-5 1.6i (New lower-powered 1.6 introduced April)

Price new	£12,995
Engine	1,598cc, inline 4-cylinder, water-cooled, DOHC, 16 valves, longitudinal
Max power	90bhp @ 6,000rpm
Max torque	97lb ft @ 4,000rpm
Max speed	109mph
0–62mph	10.6sec
Fuel consumption	Urban: 30.1mpg Constant 56mph: 42.2mpg Constant 75mph: 31.4mpg
Wheels	14 x 5 5JJ
Tyres	185/60 R14
Standard Equipment	Immobiliser Laminated windscreen Halogen headlamps Body colour bumpers and exterior mirrors Side protection beams Manual convertible top Door and luggage area trim Foot lights Vanity mirror Driver's footrest Manual aerial Door speakers Tachometer Lockable glove box Rear console

MX-5 1.8i

Price new	£14,495
Engine	1,839cc, inline 4-cylinder, water-cooled, DOHC, 16 valves, longitudinal
Max power	131bhp @ 6,500rpm
Max torque	114lb ft @ 5,000rpm
Max speed	123mph
0–62mph	8.6sec
Fuel consumption	Urban: 28.2 Constant 56mph: 40.9mpg Constant 75mph: 31.0mpg
Standard equipment	As for 1.6i, plus suspension brace bar, door pockets, locking centre console

MX-5 1.8iS

Price new	£17, 395
Engine	As 1.8i
Standard equipment	As 1.8i plus power steering, electric mirrors, electric aerial, anti-lock brakes, 14x 6JJ alloy wheels, 185/60R14 tyres, locking wheel nut set, driver's side airbag, leather steering wheel, electric windows, digital clock with standard RDS audio unit, stainless steel scuff plates

Dimensions

Length	3,950mm
Width	1,675mm
Height	1,230mm
Wheelbase	2,265mm

Kerbweight	990–1,018kg
Turning circle	9.14mm (30ft)
Fuel tank	48 litres

In 1995 the 1.8i engine's flywheel was lightened to make the engine more free-revving. From August, 133bhp standardised worldwide. Final drive 4.3:1 optional for those wanting acceleration rather than a higher top speed, became standard from 1995. BBS 6J x 15in alloy wheels with P195/55 HR15 tyres offered as an option. Recaro seats become optional

1996
Rear badges become green Dials lose chrome surrounds

1997
Spring, high-level brake light added to bootlid Final drive – 4.10

1998 (1999 in US)
MK2
Prices from new 1.6i £15,520, 1.8i £16,650, 1.8iS £18,775

1.6i, 1.8i	
Engine	Inline, 4-cylinder, water-cooled, DOHC, 16 valves, longitudinal
Displacement	1,597cc, 1,839cc
Bore and stroke	78 x 83.6mm, 83 x 85mm
Compression ratio	9.4:1, 9.5:1
Max power	110bhp, 140bhp @ 6,500rpm
Max torque	99lb ft @ 5,000rpm/119lb ft @ 4,500rpm
Power to weight	108bhp/136bhp per tonne
Gearbox (five-speed)	
Gear ratios	1st – 3.14
	2nd – 1.89
	3rd – 1.33
	4th – 1.00
	5th – 0.81
Final drive	4.10

Gearbox (six-speed) – 10th Anniversary and Icon models	
Gear ratios	1st – 3.760
	2nd – 2.269
	3rd – 1.645
	4th – 1.257
	5th – 1.000
	6th – 0.843
	Rev – 3.564
Final drive	3.636
Wheels	Steel or cast alloy (Space-saver spare)
Tyre size	with steel wheels 14 x 5.5JJ, with alloy 15 x 6JJ
Tyres	1.6i – Yokohama A-460 185/60 HR14 1.8i – Michelin Pilot 195/50VR15 SX GT

Dimensions (external)	
Length	3,975mm (156.5in)
Width	1,680mm (66.1in)
Height	1,225mm (48.2in)
Wheelbase	2,265mm (89.2in)

Dimensions (internal)	
Headroom	942mm (37.0in)
Legroom	1,086mm (42.8in)
Shoulder room	1,263mm (49.7in)

Luggage volume	144 litres (5.08cu ft)
Kerb weight	2,255lb (1,025kg)
Weight distribution	50/50 f/r unladen

Performance		
Max speed	1.6i – 118mph (191kph)	
	1.8i – 127mph (203kph)	
0–60mph (96.5kph)	1.6i – 9.7sec	
	1.8i – 7.8sec (*Autocar*)	

Fuel consumption	
1.6 five-speed	Urban – 26.7mpg (10.6l/100km)
	Extra urban – 42.8mpg (6.6l/100km)
	Combined – 34.9mpg (8.1l/100km)
1.8 five-speed	Urban – 25.2mpg (11.2 l/100km)
	Extra urban 40.4mpg (6.9 l/100km)
	Combined 33.2mpg (8.5 l/100km)
1.8 six-speed	Urban – 24.1mpg (11.7l/100km)
	Extra urban – 39.8mpg (7.1l/100km)
	Combined – 32.1mpg (8.8l/100km)

UK Standard equipment (1.6i and 1.8i)	
	14in steel wheels
	Driver and passenger airbags
	Power steering
	Seatbelt tensioners
	Heated glass rear window
	Remote boot opener

Optional equipment	Metallic paint, 14in alloy wheels, Leather seat facings, Air-conditioning Windblocker, Detachable body colour hard-top, Rear spoiler, Stainless-steel scuff plates, Front and rear mud flaps (ABS not available)
1.8i	Adds: Power windows, Aero board (windblocker)
1.8iS	Adds: Torsen differential, Anti-lock brakes, Nardi leather steering wheel, Power door locks, Central locking, Stereo radio cassette and electric aerial, Stainless steel scuff plates, Mud flaps
Colours at launch	Bronze, Blue, Silver (metallic), Green (metallic), Red, Black

US Model
The US had the 1.8 only, prices from $19,770
Power: 140hp @ 6,500rpm or 138hp @ 5,000rpm in California

Base model	5-speed manual gearbox 5.5J x 14in steel wheels, 185/60 HR14 tyres Dual air-bag with passenger side deactivation AM/FM/CD stereo Glass rear window with defogger Black cloth upholstery Removable cup holder Remote fuel door/trunk release Sport tuned exhaust
Options:	Air-conditioning Power steering Automatic transmission

Detachable hard-top with rear defogger
Fog lamps
Bose audio system
Carpet Floor Mats
Cassette Player

Touring Package
added to above: Power steering, 6J x 14 in alloy wheels, Power windows and mirrors, Nardi three-spoke leather-wrapped steering wheel

Popular Equipment Package
added to above: Torsen® Limited slip differential (manual only), Cruise control, Windblocker, Power Door Locks, Upgraded sound system, Electric aerial

Options: Bose stereo
ABS (only if stereo was also ordered)

Leather Package
added to above: 6J x 15 inch alloy wheels, 195/50-VR15 Michelin Pilot SX GT tyres, Tan leather-trimmed upholstery, Tan coloured hood, Bose audio system

Option: ABS

Sports Package
(manual trans only) As Popular Equipment package, but added: 15 inch alloy wheels with195/50-R15 tyres, Sport suspension with Bilstein shocks, Rear spoiler, Front air dam, Front strut brace

Appearance Package
(not available on Sports Package) added: Front air dam, Rear spoiler, Rear Mud flaps, Foglights

Standard colours: White, Brilliant Black, Classic Red, Twilight Blue mica, Highlight Silver metallic, Emerald mica

MK2.5
Launched September

	1.6i	1.8i	1.8 auto	1.8i Sport 6-speed
Prices at launch	£14,995,	£15,495	£16,495	£17,495
Engine	Inline, 4-cylinder, aluminium alloy, DOHC with sequential valve timing			
Displacement	1,597cc	1,839cc	1,839cc	1,839cc
Max power	110bhp @ 6,500rpm	146bhp @ 7,000rpm	139bhp @ 6,500rpm	146bhp @ 7,000rpm
Max torque @ 5,000rpm	99lb ft	124lb ft	125lb ft	124lb ft
Max speed	119mph	127mph	118mph	129mph
0–62mph (100kph)	9.7sec	8.5sec	11.0sec	8.4sec
Fuel consumption (mpg)				
Urban	26.1	24.8	23.7	21.7
Extra urban	42.8	39.8	39.2	37.7
Combined	34.9	32.5	31.7	29.8
CO$_2$ (g/km)	196	210	229	215

Weight	1,035kg (2,282lb)	1,065kg (2,348lb)	1,080kg (2,381lb)	1,100kg (2,425lb)
Gear ratios				
1st	3.136	3.136	2.45	3.76
2nd	1.888	1.888	1.45	2.269
3rd	1.33	1.33	1.00	1.645
4th	1.00	1.00	0.73	1.257
5th	0.814	0.814	-	1.00
6th	-	-	-	0.843
rev	3.758	3.758	2.222	3.564
Final drive	4.1	4.1	4.1	3.636

Wheels
1.6 and 1.8i — 185/60 R14 82V with 5.5JJ steel wheels
1.8i Sport — 205/45 R16 83V with 6.5JJ alloy wheels
Space-saver spare wheel

Standard equipment
Bucket seats
Power steering
Driver and passenger airbags with passenger seat airbag deactivation
Seatbelt pre-tensioners
Power door locks
Electric windows
Anti-lock brakes with EBD (electronic brake-force distribution)
Alarm
Immobiliser

1.8i Sport
Adds:
Leather trim
Leather-wrap gear knob and Nardi steering wheel
16in alloy wheels and high-performance 205/45R16 tyres
Remote central locking with boot release
Power door mirrors
Electric aerial
Radio and single CD player

OCTOBER 2002
All MX-5s gain ISOFIX child seat mounting points in the passnger seat, a fuel empty light, electric heated mirrors and an electric aerial. A cloth soft-top (instead of vinyl) and 15in alloy wheels are offered as a package costing £650

1.8i Sport
Gains a chrome filler cap, cloth soft-top and Bilstein dampers as standard, a new option for this model is satellite-navigation

DECEMBER 2003
New aluminium centre console surrounds the stereo and air vent/air con controls
New design 16in alloy wheels for Sport
1.8 and 1.8i Sport gain new windblocker equipped with two speakers
Three new colours: Strato Blue, Radiant Ebony (a dark aubergine mica), Titanium Grey for 1.8i Sport only

US standard equipment
Base — Air-conditioning, power windows, dual airbags, power exterior mirrors

LS — As Base plus leather seats, cruise control and a premium audio system

2002

Added six-disc CD changer

2003

LS gained a cloth rather than vinyl top as standard

2005

Two new colours: Razor Blue and Nordic Green

2006
MK3

Engines	Inline, 4-cylinder, DOHC, mounted longitudinally	
Type	MZR 1.8	MZR 2.0
Displacement	1,798cc	1,999cc
Bore and stroke	83 x 83.1mm	87.5 x 83.1mm
Max power	126PS @ 6,500rpm	160PS @ 6,700rpm
Max torque	123lb ft @ 4,500rpm	139lb ft @ 5,000rpm
Compression ratio	10.8	10.8
Transmission	5-speed manual	5-speed/ Sport 6-speed manual

Gear ratios		
1st	3.136	3.136/3.709
2nd	1.888	1.888/2.190
3rd	1.330	1.330/1.536
4th	1.000	1.000/1.177
5th	0.814	0.814/1.000
6th	-	0.832
Rev	3.758	3.758/3.603
Final drive ratio	3.909	4.100/3.727

Steering	Rack and pinion, power assisted
Turns lock-to-lock	2.7
Turning circle	10.0m (32.75ft)
Brakes (front)	290mm (11.4in) ventilated disc
Brakes (rear)	280mm (11in) solid disc
Suspension (front)	Double wishbone, gas-filled monotube dampers, 21mm (0.82in) anti-roll bar
Suspension (rear)	Multilink, gas-filled monotube dampers, 11mm (0.43in) anti-roll bar (12mm (0.47in) with 6-speed gearbox)
Tyres	205/50R16 or 205/45R17
Wheel size	16in steel as standard. 16in alloys optional
Spare wheel	None provided. Can of repair foam supplied instead.

Dimensions (external)	
Length	3,995mm (157.3inches)
Width	1,720mm (67.7in)
Height soft-top/hard-top	1,245mm (49.0in)/1,255mm (49.4in)
Wheelbase	2,330mm (91.7in)
Track (front)	1,490mm (58.7in)
Track (rear)	1,495mm (58.9in)

Dimensions (internal)	
Front legroom	1,096mm (43.1in)
Headroom (top closed)	950mm (37.4in)
Shoulder room	1,352mm (53.2in)
Luggage volume	101 litres (3.57cu ft)

	1.8	2.0
Kerb weight	1,080kg (2,430lb)	1,095kg (2,464lb)
Weight Distribution	50/50 f/r unladen	

Performance		
Max speed	122mph	130mph
0–62mph (96.5kph)	9.4sec	7.9sec
Fuel consumption (combined, mpg)	38.7	36.7/34.5 Sport

UK range at launch

MX-5 1.8i

Standard equipment — Black vinyl roof
Black cloth upholstery
16in steel wheels
Anti-lock brakes (ABS) with Electronic Brake Distribution (EBD)
Dual front airbags with passenger deactivation switch
Side airbags optional
Black leather interior trim and black cloth roof optional

MX-5 2.0i

Standard equipment — Adds:
2.0-litre engine with variable air-intake system and electronic throttle
Dynamic Stability Control (DSC) with Traction Control System (TCS)
Limited-Slip Differential (LSD)
Side airbags

MX-5 2.0i Sport

Standard equipment — Adds:
6-speed manual transmission
17in 10-spoke alloy wheels
Bilstein dampers
Strut brace
Heated leather seats
Front fog lamps
Bose sound system
Black leather trim with black cloth roof standard for Sport in most colours, but Saddle Tan leather trim and tan cloth roof standard with Galaxy Grey mica paint

Options (all models) — Option Pack comprising premium cloth soft-top, stainless steel scuff plates, leather steering wheel with audio controls, leather gear knob, leather handbrake lever with silver release knob, 16in alloy wheels, two additional speakers and front tunnel storage net, Climate control air-conditioning, Premium Bose audio system with 6-CD autochanger, seven speakers, digital amplifier, switching automatically between top up and top down (standard on Sport), heated leather seats, metallic paint

Colours (exterior) — Brilliant Black
True Red
Sunlight Silver metallic
Copper Red mica
Galaxy Grey mica
Highland Green mica
Stormy Blue mica

Colours (interior & roof) — Black Saddle Tan with Galaxy Grey (Sport)

MK3 for US market

Engine	2.0-litre (122.0cu in)
Power (manual trans.)	SAE 170bhp @ 6,700rpm
Power (automatic trans.)	SAE 166bhp @ 6,700rpm
Torque	140lb ft @ 5,000rpm
Transmission	5-speed manual, 6-speed manual and automatic options

Kerb weight	
MX-5 and Touring	2,474lb
Sport and Grand Touring	2,498lb

US Range at launch

Price range	$20,435–$26,700
Trim levels	Entry-level Club Spec, Base, higher-end Touring, Sport and Grand Touring.

All were powered by a new 2.0-litre four-cylinder engine that produced 170hp (up 28hp from the previous year's standard engine).

The Club Spec, Base and Touring packages came with a five-speed manual transmission, Sport and Grand Touring packages had a six-speed manual. A six-speed automatic transmission was available as an option on the Touring, Sport, and Grand Touring.

Standard features included power windows, dual front and side airbags, tilt steering wheel, CD player and anti-lock brakes. All but the Club Spec model came with air-conditioning and a leather-wrapped steering wheel. The Touring, Sport, and Grand Touring packages added power door locks and steering-wheel-mounted controls, while the Grand Touring added leather seats, among other options.

2007

Price range	$20,435–$24,500

SV, Sport, Touring, and Grand Touring trim packages
Power hard-top available on the Sport, Touring and Grand Touring packages (all three packages are also available with the soft-top).

Power is provided by a 166hp, 2.0-litre, four-cylinder with variable valve timing. A five-speed manual transmission is standard on the SV and Sport packages, while the Touring and Grand Touring versions get a six-speed manual. A six-speed automatic is optional with some packages. Also available is a Sport AT six-speed shifter, which can be controlled with either the shift knob or shift panels behind the steering wheel.

Standard features: power windows, dual front and side airbags, power exterior mirrors, a glass rear window, anti-lock brakes, and a CD player. The Sport package adds air-conditioning, while the Touring package adds power door locks, and the Grand Touring package adds leather seats, among other features.

2008

Price range	$20,585–$26,590

Base SV offers a basic standard features package, while the second-tier Sport adds a leather-wrapped steering wheel. The two upper trim levels, Touring and Grand Touring, add some upmarket features: cruise control, keyless entry and a CD changer on the Touring, and the Grand Touring adds leather upholstery, heated seats and a Bose audio system.

The Sport, Touring, and Grand Touring trims are all available as hard-top coupé.

All four Miata trims have a 2.0-litre, four-cylinder engine that delivers 166hp and 140lb ft of torque. The SV and Sport models use a five-speed manual transmission, while the Touring and Grand Touring upgrade to a six-speed unit. A six-speed automatic with paddle shifters is optional on all trims except the SV, but opting for the automatic drops power by 5hp.

2009 MK3.5 (MK3 Upgrade)

Engines	MZR 4-cyl-in-line DOHC 16-valve, mounted longitudinally	
Type	1.8i	2.0i
Displacement	1,798cc	1,999cc
Bore × stroke	83 × 83.1mm	87.5 × 83.1mm
Compression ratio	10.8	10.8
Max power	26PS @ 6,500rpm	160PS @7,000rpm (6,700 Powershift)
Max torque	123lb ft/167Nm @ 4,500rpm	139lb ft/188Nm @ 5,000rpm
CO_2 (g/km)	167, 177 (SE)	181 (2.0i Sport Tech) 188 (2.0i PowerShift)
Induction system	Electronic fuel injection	
Fuel tank	11gal/50 litres	
Fuel	Unleaded	
Transmission	5-speed manual	5-speed manual, Sport 6-sp manual PowerShift 6-sp auto with paddle shift

Gear ratios as for Mk3

Fuel economy (urban/extra urban/combined)	
1.8 SE 5spd	29.7/51.4/40.3mpg
2.0 SE 5sp	27.9/48.7/38.2mpg
2.0 6sp Sport Tech	26.9/47.9/37.2mpg
PowerShift (auto)	25.9/46.3/35.8mpg

Wheels	Alloy 16 × 6.5J	Alloy 17 × 7J
Tyres	Yokohama Advan 205/50R 16	Bridgestone 205/45R 17

Dimensions (external)	Soft-top	Retractable Coupé
Length (mm)	4,020	4,020
Width (mm)	1,720	1,720
Height (mm)	1,245	1,255
Wheelbase (mm)	2,330	2,330
Track front (mm)	1,490	1,490
Track rear (mm)	1,495	1,495

Dimensions (internal)		
Headroom (mm)	950	950
Shoulder room (mm)	1,352	1,352
Legroom (mm)	1,096	1,096

Luggage volume	150 litres
Turning circle	9.40m

	1.8	2.0 SE	2.0 Sport Tech	2.0 Power Shift
Kerb weight (kg/lb)	1,150/2,535	1,155/2,546	1,165/2,568	1,175/2,590
Performance	1.8	2.0 SE	2.0 Sport Tech	2.0 Power Shift
Max speed(mph) (Km/h)	120 194	132 212	132 213	119 192
0–100km/h (sec)	9.9	7.6	7.6	8.5

Colours at launch

True Red
Brilliant Black
Aluminium metallic (new)
Metropolitan Grey mica (new)
Sunflower Yellow (new for UK, not available in Europe)
Copper Red mica
Stormy Blue mica
Marble White (soft-top only)

Standard soft-top is black, Non-Recaro seats black, leather seats black or Dune beige
Leather and perforated Alcantara Recaro seats two-tone black plus one other colour

UK Standard equipment

Premium cloth soft-top
Driver and passenger airbags and passenger airbag deactivation
ABS (Anti-lock Braking System)
Thatcham Category 1 alarm and immobiliser
Body-coloured bumpers and body coloured mirror housings
Electric/heated door mirrors
Power steering
Electric front windows
Radio/Single CD audio system, 4 speakers and MP3 compatibility
Auxiliary input jack for MP3-player connection
External temperature guage
Remote central locking with dead locks, folding jack-knife key
Aero board cabin airflow defuser
Tinted glass
Height-adjustable steering wheel and driver's seat

2.0i Sport Tech and **2.0i PowerShift**

Adds:
6-speed manual transmission
Front fog lights
Front suspension strut bar
Bilstein shock absorbers*
Limited Slip Differential (LSD)*
Heated leather seats
Bluetooth connectivity
Premium Bose audio system with 6-CD autochanger and seven speakers
Climate control

*Not available on 2.0i PowerShift

Optional equipment

Metallic paint (£385 at launch)

US range at launch

Available as 2.0-litre only, hard-top coupé available on all trim levels except SV

Length	157.3in
Width	67.7in
Height	49in
Turning circle	30.8ft
Front headroom	37.4in
Front shoulder room	53.2in
Front hip room	50.6in
Front leg room	43.1in
Curb weight	2,447lb
Fuel economy	22mpg City, 28mpg Highway (EPA estimates)
Fuel tank	12.7gal

Standard Equipment
SV

ABS
Airbags with deactivation switch
Cloth upholstery
Power windows
Power mirrors
AM/FM in-dash single CD, 6 speakers, speed-sensitive volume control

Sport

Adds:
Auxiliary MP3 audio input
One touch power window
Speed-proportional power steering
Tilt-adjustable steering wheel
Remote trunk release
Air-conditioning
Leather-wrapped steering wheel
Height-adjustable driver's seat
Electronic brake-force distribution

Touring

Adds:
Cruise control
Two one-touch power windows
Leather trim on shift knob
Front integrated headrests
Front floor mats
Electro-chromatic rear-view mirror
Audio and cruise controls on steering wheel
Remote window operation

Grand Touring

Adds:
Climate control
Leather upholstery
Multi-level heating seats

APPENDIX C
GREAT WEBSITES

Mazda

www.mazda.com Mazda worldwide's official site

www.mazda.com.au Mazda Australia's official site

www.mazda.co.uk Mazda UK's official site

www.mazdausa.com Mazda USA's official site

CLUBS

www.MiataClubs.com Lots of links to useful sites for buyers and owners of MX-5/Miata (and Hondas).

http://people.freenet.de/clubsunracer Club Sunracer EV: this German site has a great list of links to other MX-5 club sites.

Miata Owners' Club does not exist any more. You can find a regional US club through www.miata.net.

www.MX5.com.au MX-5 Owners' Club Australia: Offers links to all the different state chapters.

www.mx5oc.co.uk MX-5 Owners' Club UK: Excellent site offering masses of information, advice and links. Eunos owners should check out the link to Les's Roadster Pages.

www.mx5club.org.nz MX-5 Owners' Club New Zealand: Lots of pics of reports of what the club has been up to, plus Q&A section.

www.MX-5-3rdgenerationlimited.com Paul Bateman's site dedicated to the Third Generation Limited. Like Facebook for Third Gen Ltd owners. Pics and stories from all over the world. Also lots of detailed information about other UK limited editions.

http://open-inc.co.jp/rcoj Roadster Club of Japan: Not strictly a great website for westerners because it's mainly in Japanese. Nice pictures, though. e-mail: rcoj@open-inc.co.jp

GENERAL

www.brainstormtuning.com Brainstorm - slogan: Modificate everything!

www.bulletcars.com Website of Bullet Australia is packed with photos of V8 conversions, race cars and lists of cars for sale.

www.flyinmiata.com What the performance-crazy boys at Flyin' Miata are up to; the current racing car, plus details of parts for sale.

www.miata.net The essential address for the MX-5/Miata community, with all the news. 'Ask Bob!' allows you to put questions direct to Bob Hall. Lots of forums and useful sections including Miata. net/ garage, plus links to enthusiasts' clubs all over the world and hundreds of individual websites. Why not add your own?

www.miata.net/ring A ring of websites – keep going and you come back to the Home Page. Register and request information.

www.mx5-mazda.co.uk Bourne Road Garage site has useful details and photos of all UK special editions.

www.monstermiata.com 'Mad engineering where too much horsepower is Not enough!' lot of pics, graphics and crazy ideas.

http://ox.mx5oc.co.uk/guide_eunos.htm Details of every Eunos and Mazda Roadster up to 2003.

www.ravenwingperformance.net Raven Wing Performance (US) Galleries of car photos, cool links and tech tips.

www.w-tune.com Mazda's online store in Japan, the Web Tune Factory (In Japanese). Buyers can spec up their car, then go to a dealer to sign the paperwork.

www.eunos.com/keith/wheels The Wheel Machine: Keith Tanner's site lets you see how different wheels would look on your car.

www.monstermiata.com Martin Wilson's site includes photos, figures and details of V8 conversion kit.

http://en.wikipedia.org/wiki/List_of_Mazda_MX-5_colors_and_special_editions Does what it says on the URL, colours worldwide with photos.

Sport

UK MOTORSPORT

www.doristars.com Drifting at its smokin' best

www.ma5daracing.com One-make echampionship

www.max5racing.com One-make championship

www.merlotmotorsport.blogspot.com Follow the progress of Project Merlot

www.good-win-racing.com Good Win Racing

US MOTOSPORT

www.grand-am.com/koni Grand Am Koni Sports Car Challenge (or www.konisportscarchallenge.com)

www.miataracing.net Site dedicated to SCCA Miata racing in the USA

www.mx-5cup.com MX-5 Cup website

www.proracing.com National Auto Sports Association

www.scca.com Sports Car Club of America (SCCA)

www.world-challenge.com SCCA Pro Racing Speed World Challenge

www.Specmiata.com Spec Miata site

JAPANESE MOTORSPORT (IN JAPANESE)

www.jaf.or.jp/e/index.htm JAF Japan Automobile Federation (with English translation)

www.jnr-a.com JNR-A (Japan NR-A Race Association)

http://partyrace.nr-a.com Information about the Party Race

APPENDIX D
PARTS, ACCESSORIES AND SERVICE

The following details were believed correct at the time of going to press. However, as these are subject to change, particularly area dialling codes, no guarantee can be given for their continuing accuracy. See www.miata.net/directories/vendors.html for even more companies.

ADDCO MANUFACTURING CO. INTERNATIONAL 1596 Linville Falls Hwy, Linville NC 28646 Tel. +1 800 621 8916 Fax +1 828 733 1562 Website: www.addco.net E-mail: sales@addco.net Performance handling parts, sway bars and suspension kits.

APEX AUTOMOTIVE ENGINEERING 61 Lacombe St #5, Marlborough, MA 01752 Tel. +1 508 229-0090 Website www. apexautoeng.com E-mail: apex@miata.net Repairs and performance.

AUTOLINK (UK) Ltd Unit 1, Lycroft Farm Industries, Park Lane, Upper Swanmore, Southampton, Hants SO32 2QQ Tel 01489 877770 or 07973 138194 Fax: 01489 877900 Email: admin@autolinkuk.co.uk Websites: www.autolinkuk.co.uk, for parts: www. boundville.co.uk Eunos roadster specialist.

AUTOPOWER INDUSTRIES 3424 Pickett St, San Diego, CA 92110 USA Tel + 1 619 297 3300 Fax + 1 619 297 9765 www. autopowerindustries.com Roll bars, restraint systems etc for racing.

AUTOSUPERMART.COM 28 Overlook Farms, Killingworth, CT 06419 Tel. +1 888 68 MR CAR Accessories.

AUTOTRIM SYSTEMS Wesle Street, Leicester LE4 5QG UK Tel. +44 (0) 116 266 4112 Fax +44 (0) 116 265 0652 Hoods, leather seats, upholstery repairs and hard-top covers.

AUTOTHORITY 5312 Eisenhower Ave Alexandria VA 22304 USA Tel. +1 703 323 6000 Showroom or +1 703 323 0919 or Chantilly VA Tel +1 703 212 0900 Website www.autothority.com ECU upgrades and performance products.

BBS Locations in Germany, USA, Italy, France and China. BBS of America Inc. 5320 BBS

Drive, Braselton, GA 30517 Tel. +1 877 832 8209 E-mail: sales@bbs-usa.com Tel. +1 703 323 6000 Showroom www.bbs.com Specialist wheel manufacturer.

BELL ENGINEERING GROUP, INC (BEGI) 203 Kestrel Drive, Spring Branch TX 78070 Tel. +1 830 438 2890 Fax +1 830 438 8361 www.bellengineering.net Turbos/intercoolers, superchargers and other performance products.

BILSTEIN OF AMERICA INC 14102 Stowe Drive, Poway, San Diego CA 92064 Tel. +1 858 386 5900 Website www.bilstein.com Shock absorbers.

BORLA PERFORMANCE INDUSTRIES 701 Arcturus Ave Oxnard, CA 93033 Tel. +1 805 986 8600 Fax +1 805 986 8999 www.borla. com Aftermarket exhausts.

BOURNE ROAD GARAGE LIMITED, Bourne Road, Crayford, Kent DA1 4BU UK Tel. +44 (0) 1322 521595 www.mx5-mazda.co.uk Mazda dealer and MX-5 specialist offering cars, parts and accessories.

BOUNDVILLE.CO.UK parts see Autolink above.

BRAINSTORM TUNING Panagias Korifinis and Thessalonikis Gonia, Mudania, Halkidiki Greece 63200 Tel. +30 237 330 0393 Website: www.brainstormtuning.com email: contact@brainstormtuning.com Wild performance mods. Sadly, no UK dealer (yet).

BRAINSTORM PRODUCTS 12568 W Washington Blvd, Los Angeles CA 90066 Tel. +1 310 313 0088 Website http:// brainstormtuning.com Email from site or contact@brainstormtunong.com Visual mods such as BSP low-profile twin headlamps, chin spoiler, moulded armrest, sport grille, aluminium dash inserts, performance exhausts, uprated suspension.

BRIDGESTONE TIRES 1 Bridgestone Place, Nashville, TN 37214 Tel. +1 615-391-0088 www.bridgestone-eu.com www. bridgestoneamericas.com

BRODIE BRITTAIN RACING (BBR) Unit 1, Oxford Road, Brackley, Northants NN13 5DY

UK Tel. +44 (0) 1280 702 389 Fax +44 (0) 1280 705 339 Turbocharging; creators of the original MX-5 BBR Turbo.

BR PERFORMANCE 403-E Miller Road, Greenville, SC 29607 Tel. +1 864 288 4449 Fax +1 520 447 6261 E-mail: br@ brperformance.net www.brperformance Forced induction and performance products.

BULLET CARS 10 Octal Street, Yatala QLD 4207 Australia Tel. +61 7 3382 0018 Fax. +61 7 3382 0019 E-mail: tom@bulletcars.com High-performamce parts. Website: www. bulletcars.com

CABRIO WORLD 396 Littleton Ave, Newark, NJ 07103 Tel. +1 973 642 4058 Fax. +1 603 309 7761 E-mail: info@cabrioworld. com Hoods, fasteners and products to protect soft-tops.

CARHOOD WAREHOUSE LTD Chessington, Surrey Tel. +44 (0) 20 8391 5324 Website: www.carhood.co.uk E-mail: Info@autohoods.co.uk Replacement soft-tops.

CARTECH 18975 Marbach Ln, Suite #812 San Antonio TX 78266 USA Tel. +1 210 333 1642 Fax. +1 210 333 1749 www.cartech.net Turbo specialists.

CLASSIC ADDITIONS Upper Farm Barns, Rorrington, Chirbury, Montgomery, Shropshire SY15 6BX UK Tel. +44 (0) 1938 561717 Website www.classicadditions.co.uk Email: sales@classicadditions.co.uk Wind deflectors and car covers.

COX & BUCKLES WORKSHOP Elm Grove, Wimbledon, London SW19 UK Tel. +44 (0) 20 8944 7100 Website www.cox-and-buckles-workshop.co.uk Servicing, mechanical work or repairs by ex-Moss mechanics.

CRAZY RED ITALIAN 8161-B Belvedere Ave Sacramento, CA 95826 Tel. toll-free (US only) 888 412 7299 Int. tel. +1 916-456-2277 E-mail: crazyred@miata.net www.crazyred.com Air horns for MX-5/Miata.

CULCHETH CAR SPARES 457a Warrington Road, Culcheth, Cheshire WA3 5SJ Tel: 01925 762279 Offers well priced new and used parts.

DANDY CARS 330–332 Eastern Avenue, Ilford, Essex IG4 5AA Tel.+44 (0) 845 450 4589 Website www.dandycars.com Email: david@dandycars.com Sales, parts and accessories, hoods, servicing.

DAYTONA INT. TRADING CO. Tel. +81 538-35-6111 Fax +81 538-37-0809 Aftermarket supplier in Japan.

DDM Works, 99 South Harris Road, Piedmont, SC 29673 USA Tel +1 864-907-6004 Email sales@ddmworks.com, tech support dave@ddmworks.com Website www.ddmworks.com Performance specialists for Miata, Mini, Solstice and Sky.

DISCOUNT TIRE DIRECT 7333 E. Helms Drive, Suite No. 7 Scottsdale, AZ 85260 Tel. +1 800 589 6789 Fax +1 602-443-5621 www.discounttiredirect.com Wheels, tyres, suspension parts. Interactive graphic allows you to try out wheels and tyres.

DONUTZ 1 Beech Lees, Farsley, Pudsey, West Yorkshire LS28 5JY UK www.donutz. co.uk UK-based company, sells solely from the net; visual mods for body and cabin, plus dual headlamps, performance exhausts and suspension kits.

DUETTO MOTORS LLC 21601 Vanowen Street Suite 109, Canoga Park, CA 91303 Tel. +1 818 999 0969 Fax. +1 831 536 1656 Website www.duettomotors.com Email from website Tops and aftermarket accessories.

DUNLOP TYRE COMPANY PO Box 1109 Buffalo, NY 14240-1109 Tel. +1 800-828-7428 Fax. +1 716-639-5200 www.dunloptires.com

ENTHUZA CAR Kennesaw GA, USA Tel. +1 404 310 3302 Fax. +1 678 921 0220 Website www.enthuzacar.com Email from website. MX-5/Miata exhaust specialist.

EREBUNI CORP 158 Roebling St, Brooklyn NY 11211 Tel. +1 718 387 0800 Fax. +1 718 486 7957 E-mail: info@erebunicorp.com Website: www.erebunicorp.com Suppliers of wings, spoilers and full body kits.

EURASIAN PARTS SELECT Tecumseh CA USA Tel. +1 800 824 8814 and +1 909 308 1745 Fax. +1 909 308 1751 Synthetic oil and maintenance items.

EURO-SPEC 2000 Ltd Unit 401 Henley Park Industrial Estate, Normandy, Guildford GU3 2AF Tel/Fax: 01483 234 879 email: sales@euro-spec2000.co.uk Website: www. euro-spec2000.co.uk Specialist in Japanese performance cars, has been working on MX5s since 1990. Servicing, repairs and tuning.

EVERYTHINGMX5, Rear of 213 North Street, Romford, Essex RM1 4QA UK Tel. +44 (0) 1708 754882 or (0) 7773 229362 Email: info@everythingmx5.com Website www.everythingmx5.com Servicing and second-hand parts.

FINISH LINE AT ROSENTHAL MAZDA 750N Glebe Road, Arlington VA 22203 USA Tel. 800 347 3493 Int. tel. +1 703 875 2757 E-mail:mazdaparts@finishlineperformance. com Parts and accessories.

FITTIPALDI MOTORING ACCESSORIES 1425 NW 82nd Avenue, Miami, FL 33126 Tel. +1 305-592-8177 www.4autostuff.net/wheels/ fittipaldi Wheels.

FLYIN' MIATA 331 South 13th Street, Grand Junction, CO 81501 Tel. +1 800 FLY MX5S or +1 800 359 6957, tech 970 464 5600 Fax. +1 970-242-9199 Website: www.flyinmiata.com E-mail: info@dlralt.com Turbocharging, and designs own suspension kits; exhausts, larger brake kits, fully programmable replacement engine computers, performance accessories, Dynojet dyno tuning.

GOOD-WIN-RACING 927 Wilbur Ave. No. 3, San Diego, CA 92109 Tel.+1 858 775 2810 www.good-win-racing.com Performance specialist. Run by enthusiasts who race their own cars.

GRASSROOTS MOTORSPORTS 555 W Granada, Suite B9, Ormond Beach, FL 32174 Tel. +1 386 239 0523 Fax. +1 386 239 0573 Toll-free 1 888 676 9747 E-mail: GRMPer@ aol.com www.grmotorsports.com Magazine for racers, website has a list of links to racing club sites.

HARD DOG FABRICATION 5391 Bethania Rd, PO Box 50, Bethania, N.C. 27010 USA Tel. 800-688-9652 US orders Tel.+1 336-922-3018 International orders and tech line Fax. +1 336-924-8293 www.bethania-garage.com Roll bars, fire extinguishers, harnesses.

HKS 13401 S Main St, Los Angeles CA 90061 Tel.+1 310 491 3300 Website: www.hksusa. com US branch of Japanese performance parts specialist.

HOLLEY Website: www.holley.com Performance products and nitrous oxide kits Buy online or see list of suppliers.

HOODS GALORE UK Beckney Lodge, Lower Road, Hockley, Essex SS5 5LD Tel: +44 (0) 17202 562077, Fax: 01702 205313, Email: enquiry@hoodsgaloreuk.co.uk Website: www.hoodsgalore.co.uk Specialists in hoods and upholstery.

HOT HOODS 17 Heathfield Park Drive, Goodmayes, Romford, Essex RM6 4FB Tel.+44 (0) 7957 273 270 Mail order line 07949 763657 Websites www.hothoods. co.uk or www.hothoodsMX5.com Email: enquiries@hothoods.co.uk Replacement hoods.

HYPERSPEED, INC. 5403 West Crenshaw Street, Tampa, FL 33634 Tel. +1 813 685 7342 Fax. +1 813 888 9893 Spoilers, body kits and aerodynamic components.

IL MOTORSPORT Innungstr 1, 50354 Hürth-Gleuel, Germany Tel. +49 (0) 2233/977349 and 78471 Fax. +49 (0) 2233/977348 www. ilmotorsport.de (English or German) Tuning, accessories or replacement parts.

JACKSON RACING SUPERCHARGER 440 Rutherford St, Golita CA93117 Tel. 888-888-4079 (toll free USA) or+1 805-681-3410 Fax. +1 805-692-2523 www.jacksonracing. com E-mail: jacksonracing@mossmotors.com Performance parts and supercharging kit. (See also Moss.)

JI-PERFORMANCE 186 Avalon House, Wellhall Road, Hamilton, South Lanarkshire ML3 9XP Website www.JI-performance.com High-performace parts.

K&N ENGINEERING PO Box 1329, 1455 Citrus St, Riverside, CA 92502 Tel. +1 800 858 3333 or +1 951 826 4000 Email tech@ knfilters.com www.knfilters.com Aftermarket air systems.

K&N FILTERS (EUROPE) LTD John Street, Warrington, Cheshire WA2 7UB Tel. +44 (0) 1925-636950 Fax. +1 (0) 1925-418948 email uk.sales@knfilters.com www.knfilters. com Aftermarket air systems.

KG WORKS Sugeta-Cho 2737 Kanagawa-Ku, Yokohama-City Kanagawa-Pref, Japan Tel. +81 (0) 45-471-2841 Fax.+81 (0) 45-472-9013 www.kgworks.co.jp E-mail: info@kgworks. co.jp Wild visual mods, including a Ferrari-style gear lever gate.

KNOBMEISTER Quality Images, 3595 Gray Circle, Elbert CO 80106-9652 USA Tel. +1 303 730 6060 Fax +1 303 730 6425 Email: joe@knobmeister.com Website: www. knobmeister.com Knobs, badges, licence plate surrounds and fun accessories.

KRAFTWERKS PERFORMANCE GROUP 2050 5th Street, Norco, CA 92860 USA Tel: +1 951 808 9888 Fax: +1 951 808 9889 Email: sales@kraftwerksusa.com Website www.jacksonracing.com and click link. Supercharging specialist.

LARINI SYSTEMS Tel.+44 (0) 870 777 9060 www.larinisystems.com Stainless steel exhausts and manifolds.

LUSSO CAR CARE PRODUCTS 63 Oak Street, Norwood, NJ 07648 Tel. +1 800 851 2737 Fax +1 201 784 8848 E-mail:sales@lusso.com Website: www.lusso.com Car care products.

MAZDA AUTO RECYCLING 3450 Recycle Road Rancho Cordova, CA 95742 Tel. +1 916 635 5900 Toll free +1 877 280 3100 Email: info@mazdarecycling.com Website: www.mazdarecycling.com Claims to be the world's largest Mazda recycler. Website's photos of trashed MX-5s are heart-breaking, but compelling all the same.

MAZDA UK Tel. +44 (0) 8458 50 56 05 www.mazda.co.uk Official parts and accessories, or spec-up your dream MX-5.

MAZDASPEED MOTORSPORTS DEVELOPMENT 1421 Reynolds AveIrvine CA 92614 USA Tel: 1-800 435 2508 (US only) Intl tel: +1 949 222 2652 Fax. +1 949 222 2650

Mazda's Motorsports division offers factory-engineered vehicles, performance parts and accessories for anyone who's racing or building a Mazda for racing. Parts are strictly for racing and this is a membership programme: parts are not sold to the general public.

MAZMANIA Kell Green Hall Farm, Kell Green Lane, Marthall Knutsford WA16 7SL Tel +44 (0) 78121 52250 Website www.mazmania.co.uk Email info@mazmania.co.uk MX-5 hoods and interiors.

MAZMART, INC. 4917 New Peachtree Road, Atlanta, GA 303413122 USA Tel. +1 800-221-5156 Local tel.+1 770-455-4848 Fax +1 770-451-1999 E-mail: info@mazmart.com www.mazmart.com Used parts, late-model MX-5s dismantled.

MEGUIARS online shop for US and UK. Website www.meguiars.co.uk or www.meguiars.com. Car waxes to leather cleaners, cleaner for plastic windows.

MIGHTY PRODUCTS 6376 Foster Street, Palm Beach Gardens, FL 33418 Tel. +1 800-76-Miata and +1 407 744 7238 Aftermarket.

MM MARKETING/MMMIATA 222 Franklin St, Fayetteville, NC Tel. +1 800 MM Miata (1 800 666 4282) E-mail: info@mmmiata.com www.mmmiata.com Miata parts and accessories.

MODERN PERFORMANCE Website: www.modernperformance.com Tel. 713 270 8520; toll free (USA) 877 247 6366 Performance, lighting and appearance accessories.

MOMO USA 2100 N.W. 93rd Avenue, Miami, FL 33172 Tel. 305 593 0493 and 305 593 1937 www.momousa.com Steering wheels, racing seats, race wear, sills, mats and other cool stuff from Italian specialist.

MONSTERMIATA 382 Enterprise St, Suite 108, San Marcos, CA 92078 Tel: +1 760 510 9682 Email: Martin V8@juno.com Website www.monstermiata.com Performance parts including V8 Miata kits.

MOSS EUROPE Tel. +44 (0) 20 8867 2020 (London) +44 1274 539 999, Bristol +44 (0) 117 923 2523, Manchester +44 (0) 161 480 6402 Catalogues +44(0) 20 800 281 182 Email: sales@moss-europe.co.uk, bristol@moss-europe.co.uk, bradford@moss-europe.co.uk, manchester@moss-europe.co.uk Website: www.mossmx5.co.uk Massive range of parts and accessories including steering wheels, dual headlamp conversion, replacement hoods, wheels and tyres, interior styling items and performance and handling parts.

MOSS MOTORS (USA) 440 Rutherford St, Goleta CA 93117 Tel. toll free 800 642 8295 International +1 805 681 3400 Fax. +1 805 692 2525 www.miatamania.com email from website.

MROAD 1779 Wells Branch Pkwy No. 110B PMB 330 Austin, TX 78728 Tel. +1 512-695-7432 Fax. +1 603-697-6336 E-mail: info@mroad.com www.mroad.com Body stripes, tops, roll bars, exhausts.

MX5CITY Sheffield Rd, Conisbrough, Doncaster DN12 2BY Tel.+44 (0) 845 2300 856 Fax. +44 (0) 845 2300 857 Email sales@mx5city.com Website www.mx5city.com Sales of used MX-5s, servicing, repair, accessories and performance parts.

MX5 HEAVEN Unit 4, Charminster Farm estate, Wanchard Lane, Charminster, Dorchester, Dorset DT2 9RP Tel +44 (0) 1305 268149 Mob +44 (0) 7788 411810 Website www.mx5heaven.co.uk Email info@mx5heaven.co.uk New and used parts, service and sales.

MX5MAD Tel.+44 (0) 845 345 2727 Website www.mx5mad.com Email info@mx5mad.com Performance parts including Good-Win Racing and Racing Beat products, turbo and boost kits, visual mods.

MX5mods.com www.mx5mods.com Performance and visual mods, tech tips shared, gallery of customers' cars.

MX5 Owners' Club Shop www.mx5.c.uk/store clothing, luggage, gifts and accessories.

MX5PARTS.CO.UK 1 Orion Court, Rodney Road, Portsmouth, Hampshire PO4 8ST UK Tel.+44 (0) 845 345 2384 Fax. +44 (0) 2392 644 600 Website www.mx5parts.co.uk E-mail sales@mx5parts.co.uk Offers 'necessities and accessories' for all MX-5 and Eunos Roadsters from Scimitar International Ltd ordered online.

OZ RACING Email: Website www.ozracing.com for local dealers in Italy, Germany and Japan. Performance alloy wheels.

OZ RACING UK AND IRELAND, Toshe Trading Ltd, Enkalon Industrial Estate, Randalstown Road, Antrim, Co. Antrim Northern Ireland BT41 4LD Tel. UK 0871 200 3784, Rep of Ireland 048 9446 5151 Tel. Global Tel. +44 (0)28 94465151Email: sales@performancealloys.comWebsite: www.ozracing.co.uk Performance alloy wheels, suspension and brakes.

PERFORMANCE5 PO Box 418, Pinner, Middlesex HA5 9AA Tel. +44 (0) 845 230 4505 Email: info@performance5.com Website www.performance5.com Performance specialist, offers work and parts including BR Performance superchargers, Flyin' Miata turbos, Hard Dog roll bars and the Racing Beat range in the UK.

PIPERCROSS SHOP Unit 11 Twigden Barns, Brixworth Road, Creaton, Northampton NN6 8NN Tel: 0845 430 3400, +44 1604 500 111 email sales@thepipercrossshop.co.uk Website: www.thepipercrossshop.co.uk

PBC (PERFORMANCE BUYERS CLUB) 14500-C Lee Road, Chantilly, VA 21051 Tel. +1 866 678 8289 Intl. +1 703 818 9840 Fax +1 703 818 9559 E-mail: info@performancebuyers.com Website www.performancebuyers.com Sells parts for the Miata, RX-7 and RX-8.

POWERSTOP BRAKES Range Road, Witney, Oxfordshire OX29 0YB Tel +44 (0) 1993 707230 Website www.powerstop.co.uk Email info@powerstop.co.uk MX-5 brakes.

PRESTIGE CAR HOODS UK Tel. +44 (0) 151 643 9555 UK Fax. +44 (0) 151 643 9634 US Tel. +1 800 659 2649 US Fax. +1 212 208 6801 Website www.prestigecarhoods.com Soft-tops, carpet sets and interior trim.

RACING BEAT 1291 Hancock Street, Anaheim, CA 92807 Tel. +1 714-779-8677 Fax +1 714-779-2902 Website: www.racingbeat.com Performance-boosting parts including exhaust systems, high-flow intake manifolds, suspension packages, style bars.

RAVEN WING PERFORMANCE 19079 Grovewood Dr, Corona, CA 92881 USA Tel. toll free (US only) 877 581 FAST (3278) Tech. support +1 951 817 5644 http://ravenwingperformance.net Performance products, suspension mods, wheels and tyres, tops and tonneau covers. Tech tips. Check out the gallery of staff and customers' cars, or send some in.

RED LINE SYNTHETIC OIL CORPORATION 6100 Egret Court, Benicia, CA 94510 Tel. (707) 745-6100 or (800) 624-7958 Website www.redlineoil.com

ROADSTERBAG Suitcases UK AeroStylez Rene Schmitz, Lehnengasse 23, 50354 Hürth, Germany Tel: 00 49 (0) 2233/613 553 Email: info@roadsterbag.info Website: www.roadsterbag.co.uk Luggage sets to fit MX-5.

ROBBINS AUTO TOP COMPANY 321 Todd Court, Oxnard, CA 93030 USA Tel/fax. +1 480 753 9377 Fax. +1 805 604 3201 Website www.robbinsautotopco.com Soft-tops and tonneaus.

ROBERT'S AUTOSPORTS 12814 South 40th Place Phoenix, AZ 85044 Tel. and Fax. +1 480 753 9377 www.robertsautosports.com Aftermarket accessories.

RONAL USA 15692 Computer Lane, Huntington Beach, CA 92649-1608 Tel. +1 800-899-1212 and +1 714-891-4853 Fax +1 714-897-5611 www.ronalusa.com Alloy wheels.

RSPEED 1011 South Marietta Parkway, Suite 4, Marietta, GA 30060 Tel. 888-551-0025 and 678-290-7504 Fax 678-290-7535 E-mail: questions@rspeed.net Website: www.rspeed.net Aftermarket parts from Germany and IL Motorsport.

SAM GOODWIN Unit 2, Kelsey Close, Attleborough Industrial Estate, Nuneaton, Warwickshire CV11 6RS Tel./Fax. +44 (0) 24 7635 3909 Website www.samgoodwin.com Email sam@samgoodwin.com Servicing, repairs and accessory fitment for MX-5s and Eunos Roadsters.

SCCA (SPORTS CAR CLUB OF AMERICA) PO Box 19400 Topeka, KS 66619-0400 Tel. toll free (USA only) 800-770-2055 or +1 303-694-7222 Fax. +1 303-694-7391 Website www.scca.org

SCIMITAR INTERNATIONAL see MX5Parts.co.uk above.

SELECT IMPORTS Broadmere Garage, Ipswich Rd, Grundisburgh Woodbridge Suffolk IP13 6TJ Tel. +44 (0) 1473 738 958 www.select-imports.org, http://www.aboutus.org/Select-Imports.org Import and sales of Eunos Roadster in the UK.

SFT MX5 PARTS 991 Wolverhampton Rd, Oldbury, West Midlands B69 4RJ UK Tel. +44 (0) 121 544 5555 Fax. +44 (0) 121 544 4340 www.davidmanners.co.uk Parts and accessories. MX-5 Owners' Club members receive discount rates.

SPORTS & CLASSIC SOLUTIONS Green End, Great Barford, Bedford MK44 3HD Tel. +44 (0) 1234 871499 Fax. +44 (0) 1234 871599 E-mail: Sales@sandcs.com Borla exhausts, ceramic headers, front and rear roll bars, Hard Dog roll-over bars.

SUPERFLEX LTD Hornsmead, Knowle Lane, Wookey, Wells, Somerset BA5 1LD UK Tel. +44 (0) 1749 678152 Fax. +44 (0) 1749 671404 Email sales@chriswitor.com www.superflex.co.uk Polyurethane suspension bushes.

TEAM MIATA 1521 Ridgewood Dr. Martinez, CA 94553 Tel. +1 925 370 6485 Fax. +1 925 370 8532 Email MX5@teammiata.com Website: www.teammiata.com Performance parts and accessories.

TEAM VOODOO P.O. Box 501612 San Diego, CA 92150-1612 Tel. +1 858-486-4711 www.teamvoodoo.com Polished metal gear knobs, air valve caps. Sold in the UK by Donutz.

TIRE RACK 771 West Chippewa Avenue, South Bend, IN 46614-3729 Tel 888 541 1777 (USA) or +1 574 287 2345 Fax. +1 574 236 7707 www.tirerack.com Aftermarket tyres and wheels.

TODA RACING AKH Trading, 130 McCormick Ave, Suite 107, Costa Mesa CA 92626 Tel. +1 714 327 0181 Fax. +1 714 327 0184 Email toda@todaracing.com www.todaracing.com Performance parts, accessories and clothing.

TRUSSVILLE, MAZDA 1503 Gadsden Hwy. Birmingham, AL 35235 Tel. 800-633-8285 Intl. tel. +1 205-836-8671 Fax +1 205-886-0195 Dealership, used cars and accessories.

WEAPONSPEED 480 Collins Ave #C, Colma, CA 94015 Tel. +1 650-992-9669 Website: www.weaponspeed.com Email: sales@erzperformance.com High Performance parts.

WESTCO BATTERY 1645 Sinclair street, Anaheim, Ca 92806 Tel. 800 372 9253 Intl. tel. +1 714 937 1033 Fax +1 714 938 5307 www.westcobattery.com Miata battery specialist.

WHEEL ALIGNMENT PLUS 174 Terrace Avenue Port Chester, NY 10573 Tel. +1 914 939 7888 Website www.wheelalignmentplus.com

WICKED WHEELS The UK's largest mobile alloy wheel refurbishment company www.wickedwheels.co.uk

WOLF ACCESSORIES LIMITED Omega House Sarbir Industrial Park, Cambridge Road, Harlow, Essex, CM20 2EU UK Tel. +44 (0) 1279 411014 Fax. +44 (0) 1279 450352 E-mail: sales@wolfmiata.com

WOOLIES TRIM Whitley Way, Market Deeping, Peterborough PE6 8AR Tel 01778 347347, offers leather restoration kit recommended by club members in the UK.

ZUN SPORT Tel +44 (0) 870 442 1865 Website www.zunsport.co.uk Email info@zunsport.co.uk Stainless-steel grilles.

MX-5 INSURANCE (UK)

A-Plan Insurance Group 84 Queensway, Bletchley, Milton Keynes MK2 2RU Tel +44 (0)1908 271 771 Fax +44 (0)1908 271 776

Footman James Tel +44 (0)845 223 6129 Website www.footmanjames.co.uk

Index

Acknowledgements

This book would not have been possible without the help and support of so many people. It was a joy talking to all those involved with bringing the MX-5 into the world. Not only were their stories fascinating and sometimes very funny, but they are all still brimming over with enthusiasm for their creation.

Thanks must go first to Steve Kubo who got up at the crack of dawn in Japan to talk to me at 'Cinderella Coach time' in the UK, and who then painstakingly translated Mr Hirai's fishbone chart (pages 22 and 24).

I owe a debt of gratitude to Toshihiko Hirai for allowing me to publish his private notes. I would also like to say thank you to Bob Hall, Mark Jordan, Norman Garrett III, Tom Matano. Takao Kijima and Peter Birtwhistle for all their time and for some great stories. I enjoyed talking to all of you.

The MX-5 is certainly unusual in having an owners' club before it was even launched, and again, I could not have written this book without the help of the clubs worldwide. I've spent many hours reading about road trips, barbies and parties, looking at photos of beautiful cars and of people in some very strange outfits. In particular, however, I'd like to thank all those club members who gave up their time to talk about MX-5s, to come on photo shoots, or who entrusted me with their precious photos and brochures. These include, in the UK, Tracey Sparling, editor of the award-winning owners' club magazine, *Soft-top Hard-top*, Clive and Maureen Southern, Charlotte and Doug Nadin, Andrew Fearon, Andrew Priest, Sue Duncan, John and Vanessa Batup, Colin and Hilary Frewer and Mike Hayward, Tim Robinson and Paul and Jayne Grogan. In Japan, Tak Yamamoto of ROCK's in Japan and Junko Meschievitz, my friend in Ann Arbor, Michigan who acted as Japanese to English translator, Mike Hicks and Roger Tretheway in the US, and Howard Fox in New Zealand.

In particular I'd like to thank Allan Legg, Chairman of the UK Club when the first edition was written, and his wife Joy, who came out with James Mann and I to take photos, even though they were about to become grandparents. The good news, arriving just as we had a cup of tea, put the cherry on the top of a very successful day.

This edition owes a huge debt of gratitude to Paul Bateman, founder of the 3rd Generation Limited Register, who came up with the insane idea of gathering every UK limited edition for the series of photoshoots at Beaulieu (see Chapter Seven). He not only gathered one of each but two, so each car had a reserve, plus he persuaded a local dealer to bring along a face-lifted car for everyone to see in the metal for the first time. On the day 176 cars turned up, just for the fun of it and everyone enjoyed a great day out.

So thanks to everyone who came, including: Mk1s Gary Plumb (Merlot), Sue Lupton (Dakar), Derek Webb (Monza),

Kristian Daines (Harvard), Chris O'Dwyer (Classic), Nigel Carver (Berkeley), Nick Parker (Gleneagles), Philip Jones (SE 1st Release, this car also has a BBR Turbo kit), Marina Krisko (SE second Release), James Fowler (California), Gareth Chew (Monaco), Darren Paice (Limited Edition), Sue Duncan (Le Mans). Mk2s: Steve Wittingslow (Icon), Richard Mitchener (Isola), Karen Partridge (California), Philip Wittenberg (Jasper Conran), Chris Roche (SE), Ian Forrester (10th Anniversary), Ian McDowall (Sport) Mk2.5s Sandra Reeves (Nevada), Graham Brooks (Angels), John Pegg (Indiana), Donna Oberhard (Euphonic), Richard Owen (Arctic), Terence Manders (Icon), Brian McMillan (Phoenix), Colin Martin (Arizona), Sean Stanley (Trilogy), Graham Lines (Montana); Mk3s: Angela Reed (Niseko soft top), Jenny Ward (Icon), Chris Hackett (Z-Sport), Paul Bateman (3rd Generation Limited) Emily Browning (Niseko Coupé).

A huge thanks, too, to Lord Montagu, Judith Maddox and all the staff at Beaulieu for allowing us to take over the place!

I'd also like to thank Norman Garrett III, Andrew Stott of Autolink, Richard Ducommun of Maztek, Keith Tanner of Flyin' Miata, and Dominic Bovington and Iain McMillan of Moss Europe for their help with the technical chapters. Richard's gorgeous supercharged MX-5 can be seen on page 146, and I can testify that the acceleration forces it generates are like a brick to the head.

For the stunning pictures and information in the motorsport chapters, many thanks to the ever-enthusiastic Deac Case, Communications Manager of Mazdaspeed in the US, thanks go to Luca Pregliasco of Astra Racing in Italy, Jeff Bloxham, Alan Muir, Richard Foster, Jonathan McCormack, Danielle D. Engstrom (National Solo Communications Director for the SCCA) in the States, Darren Hodgson of DH Photo in Australia and Patrick Watts, winner of the UK one-marque championship.

For the specially commissioned photos throughout the book, I'd like to thank photographers James Mann, Dougie Firth, Simon Farnhell and Simon McInerney. Finding the rest of the archive photos was quite a job, and I'm eternally grateful to Denni Frater and Samantha Williams of Mazda UK, Jeremy Barnes, Danica Laub and Eric Booth of Mazda North America and Barbara Beach, ex-publisher of *Miata Magazine*; Craig von Essen, Hideki Taira, Asuza Kunigo, Ken Haruki, Yukari Hara, Yayoi Miyo and Furukawa Midori of Mazda Japan, Mark Fryer of MCL, Sue Loy and Nigel Fryatt, Mick Walsh, editor of *Classic & Sports Car*, Nigel Swan, then picture editor of *What Car?*, and the ever-friendly and helpful staff at LAT.

Last but not least, thanks to my long-suffering and much-neglected husband Richard for all the coffee and sympathy.

Liz Turner
October 2009